Teaching in Transition:
The Challenge of Mixed Ability Grouping

JOHN EVANS

Open University Press

Milton Keynes · Philadelphia

Open ~~Co~~ ~~ge C~~ose
12 ~~Co~~ ~~ge C~~ose
Stony Stratford
Milton Keynes MK11 1EY, England
and
242 Cherry Street
Philadelphia, PA 19106, USA

First Published 1985

British Library Cataloguing in Publication Data

Evans, John
    Teaching in transition: the challenge of
    mixed ability grouping.
    1. Education, Secondary—Great Britain
    2. Nongraded schools
    I. Title
    373.12'52   BL1029.N6

    ISBN 0–335–15041–1

Library of Congress Cataloging in Publication Data

Evans, John.
    Teaching in transition.

    Bibliography: p.
    Includes index.
    1. Individualized instruction—Case studies. 2. Group
work in education—Case studies. 3. Ability grouping in
education—Case studies. I. Title.
LB1031.E93   1985   371.3'94   85–2933
ISBN 0–335–15041–1

Text design by Clarke Williams
Typeset by Cambrian Typesetters, Frimley, Camberley, Surrey
Printed in Great Britain by M. & A. Thomson Litho,
East Kilbride, Glasgow, Scotland

For my Family

Contents

List of Tables, Models and Figures

Models

Figures

Acknowledgements

This study is the outcome of a joint research work. Although I accept full responsibility for this account it must be emphasized that the planning and carrying out of the research required the collaboration of the research group – Brian Davies, Peter Corbishley and Cathy Kenrick. I feel a deep sense of gratitude to them all. However, I am particularly indebted to Brian Davies (Professor of Education at Chelsea Centre for Science and Mathematics Education), for his persistent encouragement, his patience, intellectual support and the many hours spent reading and correcting earlier drafts of this work. I could not have completed this study without his help. I am also grateful to Tony Edwards (Professor of Education at Newcastle University) and Martyn Hammersley (Open University) for their encouraging, critical but constructive comments on earlier drafts of this work. Sadly, the limits of my ability, time and space have not allowed me to accommodate all of their suggestions.

I should also like to thank the teachers and pupils of Sageton School for granting me permission to spend time in their classrooms and for giving me their co-operation and help throughout the period of research. My hope is, that in some small way, this book will help others better understand and appreciate how difficult and challenging are the tasks of teaching and learning in comprehensive schools such as Sageton.

I am also grateful for the financial support provided by the Social Science Research Council, and deeply indebted to my wife, Janet, for her advice and encouragement at every stage of the project.

Preface

In recent years, many secondary schools have taken the decision to abandon selective methods of grouping children for teaching purposes, especially in the early years. Instead they have adopted the practice now commonly known as mixed ability grouping. However, very little research has been undertaken which treats seriously the questions of what this innovation means for the curricular and classroom activities of teachers and the educational opportunities of secondary school children. In this study of Sageton School, a large, single-site, co-educational, urban comprehensive, an attempt is made to address these questions directly. Attention is focused on the problems and possibilities which teachers experienced when trying to make the transition in their thinking and action from mixed ability grouping to mixed ability teaching. As such, the study relies heavily upon the perspectives and opinions of Sageton teachers. However, this is also a study of the Comprehensive experience of secondary school children, caught up in an innovation over which they had little direct control, but which had important implications for their developing conceptions of teachers and of being taught, and for their responses and attitudes towards schooling.

Unlike many books on mixed ability teaching then, this one does not set out to describe or prescribe how mixed ability teaching 'ought to be'. On the contrary, it attempts to provide, as honestly as possible, a description and analysis of what teaching in mixed ability grouping was actually like, for teachers and pupils working in conditions which were often very far from ideal. The descriptions of classroom life presented are thus not intended as examples of any accomplished, complete or finished curricular practices, rather they are evidence only of teaching in transition, of the genuine struggles of teachers to provide a curriculum which is both meaningful and accessible to the majority of their pupils.

Chapter 1 locates the Sageton study against a broader background of debate in educational and political circles – debate about the nature and purpose of comprehensive schooling in general, and mixed ability grouping in particular; and it also introduces some of the theoretical and methodological aspects of the Sageton study. Chapter 2 sets the institutional and organizational context of Sageton School and of mixed ability innovation there. The conflict, disaffection – even alienation – amongst many teachers, created in part by this innovation is, it is argued here, the product of a complex interplay between intra-school structural reorganization and the extra-school pressures for certain types and levels of order, control and examination success to which Sageton and other secondary schools are increasingly subject. Chapters 3–7 are the substance of the book. They provide detailed descriptions and analyses of 'subject' teaching and learning in mixed ability classrooms. Languages, Mathematics, Science, Integrated Studies and English teaching each characterize and represent a different classroom response to mixed ability grouping at Sageton. Thus, Chapters 3–7, respectively, are studies of whole class method, individualized, 'group based', individuated, and 'mixed' modes of curriculum organization and transmission. We shall explore the significance of each mode for classroom teaching and learning, both for teachers and pupils.

Above all else, the Sageton study is an attempt to generate and explore a variety of perspectives, in order to capture the interacting dynamic of a school and its innovation. Hopefully this account reflects the concerns of pupils, teachers and, where possible, parents as well as those of researchers. The variety of concepts and methods used in the study, powerful and necessary as they were to confront the complexity of school life, precludes any simple notion of objectivity. No methodological technique can encapsulate classroom practice, mood or interaction 'just as it was'. The originating classroom situations have gone. Traces remain of raw information, not all of which can or need to become part of our description. We will leave you to judge whether we present a spurious or reasonably evidenced pattern of the working of classrooms. We invite an open and additive reading of our material in a field in which almost everything remains to be done.

one

Preaching and Practising Mixed Ability Innovation:

The Background to the Sageton Study

The development and expansion of comprehensive schools in post-war Britain has been an uneven and problematic but important change in the organization of schooling. The system has, as a result, moved some way towards providing a school type which is more equally accessible to all pupils irrespective of their ability, sex and social background. However, the nature of the Comprehensive debate has shifted somewhat in recent years. The focus of attention has been drawn to what goes on *inside* comprehensive schools and, in particular, to the various ways of grouping pupils for teaching, and to what and how they shall be taught.

In many respects, debate about the ways in which pupils are grouped within schools has simply mirrored the wider debate about the organization of schooling. Patterns of ability grouping, like types of school provision, are imagined to mirror particular forms of society and somehow to prepare pupils for that society. A change in the focus of debate has not signified a change in the form of debate. In the more extreme and mostly ill-informed noise amongst politicians (see Boyson, 1981) and in much of the educational literature, mixing abilities is often crudely associated with the activity of 'levelling down', with the ideology of egalitarianism and socialism. By contrast, selective grouping is associated with élitism, conservativism and the needs of capitalism (Bowles and Gintis, 1977). When subjected either to the rigours of philosophical analysis (Bailey and Bridges, 1983) or historical and cross-cultural comparison (Corbishley, 1977), the sheer nonsense of such claims is more than apparent. However, educational literature and research on comprehensive schools and mixed ability grouping has done very little to contribute towards a more informed debate about the nature and purpose of these innovations. In much of the educational literature (Pedley, 1978; Daunt, 1975; Kelly, 1975, 1978; Wragg, 1976; Elliot, 1976; Davies, 1975) mixed ability grouping is seen mainly as a logical extension of comprehensive schooling, the organizational means of realizing fundamental egalitarian principles. Kelly (1978), for example, in characteristic missionary manner invites us to accept the argument that:

> The introduction of Comprehensive education requires not only common schools but also common classes. For the principle of both is that every pupil should be given access to education in the full sense of the word and offered as many educational advantages as he or she is capable of profiting from. The move to mixed ability classes then must be seen as a major contribution toward the move away from the stratification of knowledge with its resultant social division and towards a greater measure of equality of educational opportunity for all (pp. 43–4).

Other books (Wragg, 1976; Davies, 1976; Kelly, 1975) host a series of descriptions which tend to prescribe both why and how mixed ability teaching ideally ought to be. These accounts are, as Sands and Kerry (1982, p. 12) point out, 'interesting and valuable, though the advice given is not always generalisable'. The merits and de-merits of the egalitarian values and the principles contained in much of this literature are not, however, at issue in this book. Indeed, as a teacher at Sageton I had taught in mixed ability grouping and like many teachers elsewhere (see DES, 1978; ILEA Inspectorate, 1976) would enthusiastically support the kind of egalitarian sentiment contained in the above statement. The contention of this book is simply that much of the pro- and pre-scripture debate provides very little evidence of what mixed ability innovation actually is. How does mixed ability 'teaching' match up to the kinds of images of practice contained in this literature? Research on ability grouping, with very few exceptions (Lundgren, 1972, 1977; Ball, 1981), has not provided answers to this kind of question.

Research on ability grouping in schools has tended to reflect the concerns and aspirations of politicians and higher educators rather than those of teachers.[1]* It has tended to start not with a focus on teaching but by

> aiming at a simple answer to the question of which is better, organisation A or organisation B? The reasons for preferring A or B have already been discussed in the didactical or political context before the research even begins (Lundgren, 1977, p. 17).

*Superscript numerals refer to numbered notes at the end of this book.

The Banbury study (see Newbold, 1977; Postlethwaite and Denton, 1978) might be cited as a typical example. The *effects* of mixed ability grouping are demonstrated by showing correlations to exist between various inputs (pupil ability, social class) and learning outcomes. But in research of this kind, the complexities of the teaching process and the material and organizational circumstances in which they are located are largely ignored. Despite the not inconsiderable research and investigation which has been expended on this issue, the findings produced have been generally inconsistent, often quite contradictory and the accummulated body of knowledge quite minimal (see Corbishley, 1977). Indeed, because much 'mixed ability' research has failed to provide details on the organizational context and classroom, curricular and teaching activities of teachers, it is impossible to discover *why* different outcomes are produced in different schools by what (on the surface) seem to be the same organizational practice. We learn nothing of what it is to be involved in the process of mixed ability innovation.[2]

By contrast with much of the research on ability grouping, recent sociological and social psychological research has concentrated its attentions on what goes on inside schools and classrooms (see Hammersley, 1980; Delamont, 1976; Woods, 1980a,b for overviews). This research has identified some important features of classroom life in secondary schools, a good deal of it highly germane to understanding Sageton. With some regularity, research in Britain and in the USA has documented that the method of whole class teaching dominates secondary school classrooms. 'Verbal encounters' wrote Edwards and Furlong in 1977,

> are still the main features of transmitting knowledge and they are encounters of a very specific kind. For older children especially, the main characteristics of classroom talk are not only that there is so much of it, but that so much of what is said is both public and highly centralised (p. 11).

It would also seem that even within homogeneous teaching groups, teachers tend to conceive of pupils as being above, at or below average and to pitch their lesson at a *steering group of pupils* (the just below average) (Dahllof, 1971; Lundgren, 1972, 1977). Research also suggests that teachers and pupils can largely agree upon and work in terms of a classroom hierarchy of displayed pupil abilities (Nash, 1973); that there is a tendency for teachers to act towards pupils in terms of perceived social class; and that some pupils seem to reject the middle class values and orientations of schools and teachers (Lacey, 1970; Hargreaves, 1967; Willis, 1977; Corrigan, 1979; Ball, 1981). However, while much of this research has usefully focused upon the perspectives and actions of teachers and/or pupils, it has had very little to say about how the social and educational behaviours of children relate to the curriculum content, the subject methods of teachers, or the organizational contexts. Indeed it is somewhat ironic that so great has been the emphasis in British sociology of education upon the hidden curriculum and the effects of social class that the actual or 'overt' curriculum of schooling has itself seemed quite indistinguishable, even hidden. Only recently has any real attempt been made to correct this imbalance, with studies which focus upon both curriculum content and organizational context (see Hammersley and Hargreaves, 1983); and the research of Woods (1979), Turner (1983), Salmon and Claire (1984) and MacPherson (1983), has begun to indicate that the behaviours of children towards teachers and schooling are far more varied and complex than has regularly been suggested in the sociological literature. Pupil behaviour in classrooms cannot always be explained with reference only to their (or their teachers) class or cultural backgrounds. It is crucially connected to a pupil's interpretations and understandings of teachers, teaching, the relevance of subjects and the influences of peers (see Salmon and Claire, 1984; MacPherson, 1983). Nevertheless, even though this research is both interesting and highly revealing, it has little to say about the complex process of teaching, the curriculum or the broader school organizational context.

My preliminary investigations of teaching at Sageton (Evans, 1977, 1982) had suggested that teaching in the mixed ability innovation there, as elsewhere (see Reid *et al.*, 1981), is a much more varied and complex phenomenon than is often suggested by recent classroom research. Faced with the practice of mixed ability grouping, the propensity of teachers for conventional teaching methods has undoubtedly been weakened (cf. ILEA Inspectorate, 1976, p. 15). At Sageton a variety of ways of organizing and transmitting curriculum material (what we call *modes of transmission*), were in evidence. In response to mixed ability grouping, some teachers continued with the practice of *whole class teaching*; some, as in Science teaching, '*group based*' their curriculum; others *individuated*, all pupils having the same set of work sheets for a common period of time, as in Integrated Studies; or they *individualized*, which means that pupils may be working from work sheets or cards on different topics and at their own pace, as in Mathematics; while still others, mostly English teachers, '*mixed*' these modes of transmission. The Sageton study makes apparent that mixed ability teaching is a more complex and varied phenomenon than is often suggested. And that in deciding on what mode to use, teachers or a department are affected by a range of factors including subject curriculum content, the number of timetabled periods, the state of school discipline, the abilities of pupils to be taught, and teachers' own articulated and unexpressed ways of teaching and handling relations with their pupils.

The Sageton Study

The Sageton research formed part of a larger study of mixed ability grouping sponsored by the SSRC in two stages as *A Preliminary Study of Unstreaming in London Secondary Schools* and *Teacher Strategies and Pupil Identities in Mixed Ability Curricula* (HR 4998/1). The first stage of the project involved a mapping of grouping practices in Greater London secondary schools (see Davies, 1977; Davies and Evans, 1984). What stood out from this research was that mixed ability grouping in London secondary schools was essentially a first year phenomenon and that any organizational change was often motivated by concerns very far removed from those attributed to innovators by educationalists and politicians alike. A great many secondary school Heads or their nominees focused on the inadequacies of primary school test procedures or the need to shake staff into new habits (Davies and Evans, 1984) as the reason for adopting mixed ability grouping. However, the highest common factor, wrote Davies in 1977, was the 'desire to get away from the worst features of streaming which included demoralised, demotivated, unteachable middle school groups, bad for themselves, their teachers and other children' (p. 27). The work of Reid *et al.* (1981) has since endorsed the same sort of motivations.

However, this picture of mixed ability change, as painted *ex post facto* by senior staff, revealed little of the relationships between the concerns of senior decision makers and the interest, pressures and classroom practices of individual departments or teachers.

Thus we set out to examine in further detail the relationships between organizational change and the curricular activities of teachers and the learning opportunities of children. Sageton was one of two case-study schools. It represented (in contrast to School V; see Corbishley and Evans, 1980; Corbishley *et al.*, 1981; Davies and Evans, 1984) a school in which problems of pupil order and classroom control were the initial focus for mixed ability innovation. As explored in Chapter 2, streaming had produced difficult-to-manage 'sink' groups and mixed ability grouping was looked to as the means to dispense with them.

The fieldwork for the study was carried out at Sageton in the 1977–8 school year. Sageton was 'lived in' throughout the year in an attempt to recognize and understand the problems and dilemmas experienced by teachers and pupils in mixed ability innovation. My earlier experience of teaching Physical Education at Sageton, during the 1975–6 school year, had the advantage of already providing a teacher's eye view of classrooms, and of the issues and attitudes prevailing within the school setting. I had also carried out a limited piece of research into teaching (Evans, 1977) at the school while studying full-time for a higher degree, during the 1976–7 school year. This had helped in making the sometimes difficult transition from teacher to researcher (Burgess, 1980).

Access to the working lives and perspectives of either teachers or pupils cannot be achieved by simply proclaiming anonymity and confidentiality. In this respect my earlier incursion into research at Sageton had provided an invaluable opportunity to re-define my identity for both teachers and pupils as a more neutral participant in the school. The same process helped to divorce myself from the interest groups and associations which readily flourish in staffroom life (cf. Ball, 1984) and to shake off the trappings of teacher authority and status. The degree to which I succeeded in this endeavour may be indicated in the excitement with which pupils generally approached and sought out interviews. I was frequently asked in one form or another 'are you the bloke that lets us have a say about teachers?' (second year pupil). The thoughtful and elaborate insights gained from them merely emphasized how limited were the opportunities routinely presented by the institution for pupils to air and express their views.

Inside the school, our strategy was to examine the process of mixed ability teaching in the first three years of schooling. At the same time we assumed that classrooms could not be studied and understood without reference to the history of subject departments within the overall organization of the school. The project began the school year by concentrating attention on first year classes in term one, second year classes in term two, and third year classes in term three, also returning in the third term to first year pupils. This use of time reflected the incidence of mixed ability grouping in years 1–3 (see Table 1). It also assumed that focusing on initial encounters with first year pupils could provide valuable insights into how these structured the interactions and identities observed in subsequent years.

While focusing on classrooms, we also moved repeatedly from them into the various other areas of activity and decision making, both within subjects at department and faculty levels, and at the broader school organization level, at senior management meetings and so forth.

During the year a great many lessons were observed (see Table 2), mainly in the broad academic curriculum (Mathematics, Science, English, Humanities and Languages). Classroom observations were

Table 1 The incidence of mixed ability grouping[a] found in years 1–3

Year	Maths	Science	Humanities	English	Languages
1	MA	MA	MA	MA	MA–S
2	MA	MA	MA	MA	S
3	S	S	S	MA	S

MA, mixed ability; S, setting.

[a] The Remedial department in the school extracted pupils across the range of subjects from years 1–5. Both the Mathematics and Humanities departments also operated their own remedial withdrawal policy.

Table 2 Number of lessons observed in each of the subject areas in years 1–3

Year	Maths	Science	Integrated Studies	Languages	English
1	19	16	17	8	20
2	7	7	11	4	8
3	5	9	16[a]	8	7
Total	31	32	44	20	35

[a] Periods of History/Geography/RE and Multicultural Education (see Chapter 6 for elaboration).

very largely concentrated on one particular form from each of the first and second years who were followed through their timetable. Setting in the third year precluded the opportunity for class following and a more fragmented pattern of observation was necessary. In this account we concentrate mainly upon Form 1p (see Table 3).

It was not assumed that any of these classes would form a representative sample of all teaching groups in their respective years, although classes which were top or bottom heavy in ability as defined by available school tests of reading ability, or which were taught by a predominance of 'new' (probationary) or senior teachers, were avoided.

Inside the classroom, observations focused initially on the teachers' use of time. Our interest predisposed us to focus on how teachers distributed their attention across the ability range (for which we drew on pupil records, teacher ratings and standardized test scores[3]). At the same time we also focused on how pupils responded to the situation presented to them by teachers. We assessed pupil involvement in *work*

3 Composition of case study – Form 1p

Pupil	Ethnicity	Fathers occupation[b]	NFER total	Reading age
Mark	WI/British	Scientist	A	12.0
Naren[a]	Asian	Self-employed (shopkeeper)	C	9.4
Abdul[a]	Asian	DK	C	8.9
Michael	WI/British	DK	—	11.10
John	British	NF	C	Above Top.
Hugh	European	DK	C	10.10
Jerry	WI	DK	—	7.11
Ryan	WI	Carpenter	—	8.7
Rene	WI	Carpenter	D	8.2
Peter	WI	Driver	C	Above Top.
David	British	DK	—	—
Paul	British	Self-employed (shopkeeper)	C	10.3
Jenny	British	NF	C	12.10
Mary	WI	Road worker	E	11.4
Heather	British	Factory worker	C	9.11
Liona	WI	DK	D	8.2
Caroline	WI	Mechanic	—	8.7
Odette	WI	Unemployed	D	9.0
Maureen	WI	Lorry driver	E	9.11
Lynne	British	Porter	—	10.5

Footnotes

Form 1p contained one other Asian pupil who spent most of her time in a separate
LEA unit and is consequently left out of any analyses.
[a] Pupils not born in Britain.
[b] Fathers occupation as reported by pupil.
WI, West Indian; NF, no father; DK, not given or not available.

and *interest activity*. The latter term is used to encompass a wide range
of non-task related behaviours. We also noted with whom, and about
what, teachers talked. Much of the data collected at this level was
impressionistic (based on paper and pencil note-taking) observation
and description of classrooms, and this led to a need for more exact
information, not merely as a means of further illustrating or revealing
processes, but also as some check of the impressionistic data.

Therefore, we attempted a more systematic study of the classroom
and, armed with stopwatch, pen and paper, focused upon teacher talk
and teacher–pupil interaction. Our initial, lengthy and elaborate
description of classroom events allowed us to construct broad but basic
descriptive categories. Teacher talk was categorized as either *regulative*

or *instructional* in content and either *public* or *immediate* in form. 'Public' refers to communication between a teacher and an individual pupil, group, or the class as a whole, undertaken (usually from the front of class position) in everyone's earshot. 'Immediate' refers to the 'face to face' communication between a teacher and an individual pupil or group, undertaken more privately and quietly at the teacher's or pupil's desk. Using a variety of shorthand symbols (e.g. TA, Teacher attends; P, public), it was possible to capture much of the more obvious interaction between pupils and teachers. However, it must be acknowledged that the term systematic is used here in the knowledge that when compared with what is generally taken to constitute systematic study,[4] our measures are extremely crude indeed and are more appropriately compared with the exploratory mapping techniques devised for informal classrooms by Walker and Adelman (1975). This method of data collection was intended only as a supplement to the wealth of ethnographic and observational data which had already been generated. And it must be stressed that the quantitative descriptions of interactions and events presented in subsequent chapters are intended only as general pictures of classroom patterns, as props for the more descriptive and revealing data reported in the text.

Whether systematic or impressionistic, all observations tend to involve the substitution of fieldworker perceptions for those of the teacher. The tendency to overlook the teachers' own construction of what they were doing and trying to achieve was therefore consciously resisted.[5] A great deal of accompanying teacher and pupil talk about lessons was collected during and shortly after lessons, along with a range of material from informal interviews and questionnaires. All of these have been utilized in conjunction with data from general reasoning tests for all pupil, variable amounts of pupil information from school files, general school documentation and observer reports on a wide range of informal and formal school meetings.

So categories such as 'work', 'interest', ability, teacher 'talk' as well as sex, age and some notion of social class formed part of the common sense of the Sageton research and were directly useful in classifying and ordering information. Terms like 'piloting' and 'steering group' were drawn from previous analyses (particularly Lundgren, 1972, 1977). As mentioned earlier, the latter corresponds to the teacher's common-sense need to pitch lessons at a particular level. Talk in the whole-class method tends to be steered by the teacher in a question and answer format requiring overwhelmingly 'closed' (predictable and unelaborate) answers from pupils. The Swedish research found that teachers using this mode tended to have a particular repertoire of questions for pupils of average ability and were (largely unconsciously) using this group to determine whether it was time to transfer to new curriculum content. Pupils who fell below the ability of the steering group routinely failed to enter into the process of teaching and learning.

The concept of the steering group links teacher talk, the range of pupils in the classroom, the amount of time given to a topic (within a lesson, over a year, and for even longer periods of schooling) with the structure of the curriculum. Our interest in this concept is clearly reflected in subsequent chapters. The organizational analyses of teaching provided by Lundgren caught our imagination during the course of the Sageton study. However, in some senses, we feel that the body of the analyses presented in the subject chapters may revolve rather too rigidly around notions like 'steering group' and the 'counter' steering group (representing the discovery of children beneath its level who would in ordinary 'whole class' teaching have fallen below the teacher's working horizon and behind the pace of instruction, but whose difficulties are less easily overlooked in more individual instructional forms). However, in any empirical study, particular data are generated and particular concepts are used to elucidate their meaning. What is important, is to see the sometimes cloudy and cautious analyses presented here as a means – a step – to asking better classroom questions, and not as a conceptual writ to be defended at all costs.

The concept of frame used in this study addresses even more general issues in recent empirical and theoretical work in the sociology of education concerning the relationships between action and social and organizational structure (see, for example, the work of Bernstein, 1971; A. Hargreaves, 1980; Hammersley, 1980b). As mentioned earlier the Sageton study embodied a strong reaction against studies of classroom life which pay little attention to the connections between individual teacher and pupil intentions and action, and to the organizational contexts in which they are found. The concept of *frame* was then used in the research, to identify and examine specific educational factors and to connect them with various levels and contexts of decision making at Sageton. (How the concept is differently used in the work of Bernstein (1971), Lundgren (1972, 1977) and Douglas (1966, 1973), need not be detailed here (see Evans, 1982).) Our usage (which owes much to Lundgren, with digressions into Bernstein), provided the study with a flexible way of indicating how specific factors of classroom life and the outside are interrelated. The descriptions which follow show how different combinations of educational factors become differently framed, and how they are *both* constructed by *and* for teachers and pupils.[6] At the school organiz- ational level three major aspects of framing are delineated (see

Corbishley *et al.*, 1982). The first is the *curriculum* which defines for teachers and pupils the organization and content of what is to be taught. The second is the *timetable* which puts groups of pupils together with teaching staff and resources within designated curriculum areas. It is this which generates planned diversity in the context of order. It decides the social and physical space of pupils, subjects and teachers. At Sageton, for example, we find that the total teaching time available per week was 23 hours 20 minutes (see Table 4). But, as quite often occurs, this is not evenly distributed amongst subject disciplines. This necessarily acts as a limit upon the action of teachers.

Table 4 **The distribution of timetabled time amongst the various subject areas**

70-minute periods per week	Maths	Science	Social Sciences	Languages	English	PE	Technology/ Home Economics	Music	Art
Year 1	3	2	3	2	4	2	2	1	1
Year 2	3	2	3	2	4	2	2	1	1
Year 3	3	3	3	3	3	1	1	1	1

The third factor, *schooling*, is a more complex phenomenon and in our view is not synonomous with *all* that goes on in schools. The view taken in this study is that to be *schooled* normally entails having the cognitive and emotional attributes prerequisite to learning in large classes. Within them, as we see, different modes of transmission make different demands and requirements of children. Whether there are processes, skills or attitudes which are constantly required by pupils to facilitate access to curriculum content (whatever their measured ability) was of primary interest to the Sageton study. Indeed the data presented in subsequent chapters suggest that we need to make much more complex our ideas of what it is to be 'able' or otherwise in school.

Decisions taken in the broader school organization concerning the timetable, curriculum and 'schooling' can thus be seen as frames forming limits or possibilities for the actions of teacher and pupils. Model 1 may help to clarify this conceptual scheme. We can thus look at the classroom as a context of transmission which is constituted by the interrelation of related frame factors – *what* is made available to pupils (content frame), *how* it is made available (transmission frame), *when* it is made available (pacing frame) and the relationships between teacher and pupil (disciplinary or schooling frame) along with those of resource (physical and human). These factors constructed by and for teachers and pupils define the parameters for teacher–pupil inter-

Model 1: Organizational frame factors and teaching process

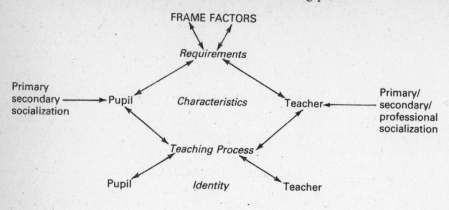

actions. As frame factors they define what is required of pupils and teachers by way of skills, understandings and social competences if a successful performance as a pupil or teacher within the classroom is to be achieved. At the intersection of these factors with the characteristics with which teachers and pupils are predisposed, occurs a process and a structure of communication in which pupil–teacher identity is constructed. Teachers and pupils enter into the context with attitudes, interests, expectations and abilities which form the basis for action and interpretation of the problems and possibilities which schooling presents. Pupils arrive with expectations of what constitutes a proper lesson, a good teacher, real learning. As recent work has indicated they are likely to deploy strategies to negotiate an acceptable existence. Cultural influences may be a prominent feature of strategies. These may be established in the broader context of peer groups' subcultural–class relationships (Willis, 1977), in professional training which may build upon and sediment personal experiences of schooling (Mardle and Walker, 1980), or within the school itself (Hammersley, 1980a). According to the characteristics teachers and pupils have, frames may be differently experienced as limits, constraints or possibilities.

The descriptions of classroom life presented in Chapters 3–7 will make much more concrete this somewhat abstract conceptualization of teaching and schooling. However, we begin this account of mixed ability innovation at Sageton by exploring the historical and current contexts of decision-making in the school, which will inform our later discussion of particular classroom interactions.

two

Sageton School:
History, Structure and Decision Making

In 1977, Sageton, like many schools, was in the business of maintaining its pupil intake. Its problems were exacerbated both by the school's poor local reputation and the national context of falling rolls. Teachers and Head were clearly aware of the need to establish a certain public image and good public relationships if the upheaval of a merger or, worse still, school closure, was to be avoided. The major contention in this chapter is that the Head experienced these 'external' constraints in a qualitatively different way to classroom teachers, and that differences in the perspectives of Head and teachers are central to understanding the internal decision making process in schools such as Sageton, and to understanding 'the nature and extent of the participation that teachers have been demanding in the running of schools in the last few years' (Hunter, 1979, p. 124).

Sageton was formed in 1956 as a mixed, four-form entry high school, having space problems but enjoying, in Mr Alsan's (the Headmaster at that time) terms, 'good academic standards and good discipline' as well as good community standing.[1] In 1967 Sageton officially became a 13–18 comprehensive and began to witness a decline in the academic, and a rapid change in the ethnic, compositions of its intake. By 1971, the problem of controlling its 'less intelligent pupils' (Mr Alsan) along with that of dealing with a large number of pupils 'with serious language problems' (Mr Alsan) became growing concerns. In the community, Sageton's reputation as a disciplined academic institution was eroded, exacerbating further the problems of a low academic intake as parents of 'academic' pupils became reluctant to send them to Sageton. In 1971 Sageton found itself in a critical situation. Striving to resolve its own internal problems, it was at the same time expected to organize and administer an impending massive organizational change. In September 1971 two local junior high schools were closed to provide Sageton with an all-through age range of pupils. As one teacher put it, virtually 'overnight' Sageton became an all through 11–18, 1500 strong comprehensive, the largest in the authority. Conflict between staff and pupils ensued as 'four different groups of people each with different histories, traditions, attitudes and age ranges were thrown together': the staff and pupils of the two schools which were closed, those already at Sageton and the complete newcomers (both first year pupils and new staff). To make matters worse, buildings were unfinished and the period of the three-day week and pre-Houghton teacher anxieties exacerbated this historical legacy. Teacher turnover in this period and the next few years was huge – 40% per annum at worst. At the same time, pupils came increasingly from a variety of ethnic backgrounds, with special growth in the numbers of West Indian and East African Asian children. Little preparation was made for them.[2] Mr Alsan's policy was a contemporaneously normal one to assimilate these pupils into existing curricula and preferred 'middle class values' (Head) rather than accommodate them by any reform of practice.[3]

Mixed ability innovation began in January 1974. In the face of successive 'depressed entries' and increasing problems of pupil disorder, the Academic Board narrowly adopted mixed ability and a four-period day for September 1974, the Head being persuaded that these measures (the latter in cutting down movement) would reduce the school's serious problems of pupil order and control (see Table 5).

Pastorally, as with many schools in the early stages of becoming comprehensive, the initial problem was that of size. In response, Mr Alsan organized a series of mini schools for the lower, middle and upper age groups. The model of pastoral care remained that of the smallish secondary or grammar school where it has been directly the province of the Deputy and Head. The new Heads of Schools simply took on these traditional powers which included those over curriculum. They dealt as appropriate with admissions, reports, liaison with parents and they could administer corporal punishment. From the perspective of one of the three School Heads,

> We were allowed to be Headmasters. He used to come into our office, thank us, saying what a wonderful job we were doing.

Form tutors were asked to regard themselves as having a special concern for both the pastoral care and learning of members of their forms. They were clear about the responsibilities of their job – 'we knew exactly who our leader was.' At the same time the academic structure remained relatively unchanged and unsophisticated. Teaching arrangements were, as stated by the Head, 'the principal concern of the Heads of Department' who formed 'one of the principal channels of communication in the school'. The academic structure was thus

Table 5 The chronology of innovation and change

1956	High School period: Sageton opens as small four-four entry (120 pupils) high school. Problems of space and control. Owing to effects of 'bulge' had to accommodate six-form entry. Late 1950s and mid-1960s, period of stability; good reputation with community as a school with 'good academic standards and good discipline' (Mr Alsan).
1967	'Secondary School' period: 'officially' became a comprehensive catering for the age range 13–18. Increasingly witnessing change in the academic and (quite dramatic change) in the ethnic background of its clientele.
1971	Depressed entry period: striving to resolve internal problems at the same time expected to organize and administer impending massive organizational change. September 1971 – re-organized from senior high school of 600 pupils, 13–18 age range, to an 'all through' high school for the 11–18 age range with 1500 pupils.
Jan. 1974	'Academic Board' meet to discuss proposed change in pupil grouping policy (banding). A decision to implement mixed ability grouping (and four-period day) is narrowly accepted.
Sept. 1974	Mixed ability grouping in the first year, all subjects.
Sept. 1975	Headmaster retires. Mr Fillmore appointed. Concerned to 'change the identity of Sageton'.
1977	Eight-form entry (198 intake), mixed ability except setting in Modern Languages after year 1, term 1 and in Maths, Science and Humanities from beginning year 3.

centralized but unsophisticated. Heads of Department represented a direct line of communication between the interests of their departments and those of senior management (Model 2 may clarify this structure).

The Heads of Department together with the Heads of the three Schools, the Second Mistress, Deputy Heads and Headmaster of the school meet at least once a term to discuss the general running of the school and of the teaching aspects in particular. They constitute an academic board (Policy document).

A fully formed pastoral system, retaining balance with the academic, had apparently been formed. Heads, Deputies and Second Mistresses are represented vertically, as in the 'staff guide' (Model 2) because, although it is possible to identify the beginnings of a pastoral academic split, each Deputy was expected to oversee both the pastoral and academic interests of their pupils, but with one of the Deputies taking special responsibility for the general discipline of the boys, and the Second Mistress that of the girls.

Model 2   Senior academic and pastoral structure, 1974.

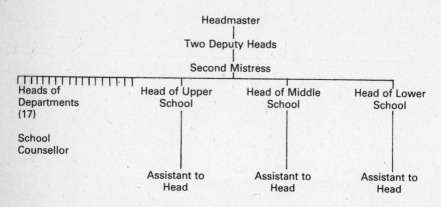

In 1975 a new Headmaster, Mr Fillmore, arrived, acutely aware of the need 'to change the identity of Sageton' and above all to improve the parent's image of the school in order to move toward a more balanced intake. In 1977 its 198 pupil intake was divided into eight forms within a year system, which served not only the pastoral units but the mixed ability teaching groups for all first year chidlren in all subjects (save French, which set after term 1); 34% of the 1977 entry had a reading age of below nine years.

Further changes were made in both pastoral and academic structures (see Model 3). A year system was adopted and assistants appointed. Sageton underwent, as it were, a second phase of reorganization. The tone with which pastoral care and the organization of learning was now approached became far more liberal. Nevertheless, the system of pastoral care, even with the addition of a school counsellor, proved incapable of establishing disciplinary control. Parental fears remained concerning the size and the social and ability composition of the school. The measured ability intake of the school's supposedly comprehensive intake, though now improving, was still worse than when the school opened as a secondary modern.[4] The post of school counsellor was phased out and plans laid to organize in a more complex way, with less dependence on such semi-autonomous professionals. Changes also took place in the academic structure which

Model 3 Sageton's organizational structure under Mr Fillmore (1975–).

Notes: (1) 100% = 19.40 hours. Timetable = 23.20 hours.   (2) Figures after the plus sign refer to teaching for pastoral rather than academic purposes.

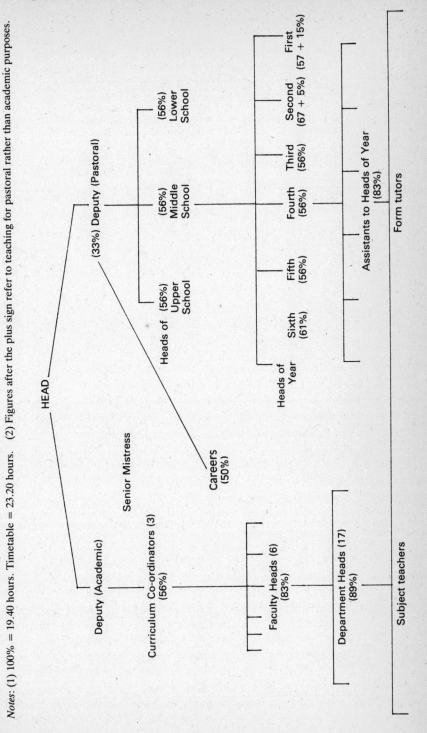

HEAD

Deputy (Academic)

Senior Mistress

Curriculum Co-ordinators (3)
(56%)

Careers
(50%)

(33%) Deputy (Pastoral)

Heads of Year

Heads of
Upper
School
(56%)

Middle
School
(56%)

Lower
School
(56%)

Sixth
(61%)

Fifth
(56%)

Fourth
(56%)

Third
(56%)

Second
(67 + 5%)

First
(57 + 15%)

Assistants to Heads of Year
(83%)

Form tutors

Faculty Heads (6)
(83%)

Department Heads (17)
(89%)

Subject teachers

became considerably more complex. An elaborate subject organization was funnelled into six faculties, each with an appointed head with a range of responsibilities, central to which was the encouragement 'of curriculum study and development in the faculty and its evaluation' (staff guide), and two (later three) senior teachers were appointed as curriculum co-ordinators. No comparable reference to curriculum is found in the literature issued by the previous Headmaster.

As an eight-form entry school Sageton had a teacher–pupil ratio of one to 15. Excluding form tutors, 17% of the staff were involved in pastoral care. The normal teaching load was 19.40 hours. Allowance points were published, 28% of the points going to the pastoral side.[5] In terms of teaching loads, the Heads of Schools together with those of each year formed a second-tier management group along with the three curriculum co-ordinators, with Faculty Heads and Deputies forming a third tier.

The overall impression to be gained from Model 3 is, then, of an organizational structure which is both well defined and somewhat hierarchical and specialized. Theoretically (as defined in a policy document) each system was linked at base and senior management levels, and in role definition at each level.[6] Tutors were also subject teachers, while pastoral Heads of Schools formed part of the management group which met once a week and were *ex-officio* members of the Board of Studies, the body formally responsible for curriculum matters. Senior academic staff, however, could not attend pastoral meetings. But as one Head of School put it, agreeing with a colleague that they were faced with the 'pastoral need' of pupils from an area of 'economic and social disadvantage',

> although I'm officially responsible for pastoral and academic progress of the children, really and truly I feel the pastoral side is the one I should look after. We've got a very strong faculty system, many people who are paid high salaries to look after that side. And I feel I don't want to interfere too much. All I ever do is at management, I can make the odd comment . . . but I don't lay down the law.

The role of the three Heads of Schools was no longer perceived as equivalent to that of a headmaster but only as the Head of a specialized subdivision within the school.[7] Responsibility for curriculum planning was considered the primary domain of suitably specialized and well paid others. What we can see, however, is that the fulfilment of these specialized role responsibilities was, within the conditions in which they operated, problematic for the teachers concerned.[8]

The evolution of an elaborate pastoral and academic organizational structure has generally been viewed as a concomitant of comprehensive reorganization. In effect, however, such elaboration decentralized and complicated the development and co-ordination of policy, academic and pastoral. The task of curriculum organization and development had been distributed among further layers of responsibility and more sub-units. While effectively removing from the Head any direct influence of Departmental Heads as a group, this change also made more difficult his endeavours to influence the actions of individual teachers. The initiation of, for example, Faculty Head meetings and later in the term, Heads of Year meetings with the Head can be seen as measures intended to resolve this unintended consequence of organizational changes. Before taking this point further we will outline the formal organizational bodies constructed by the Head for policy formation, administration and communication (see Model 4).

The mechanisms for policy formation, administration and communication were indeed complex. A policy document drew attention to seven types of meeting chaired by the Headmaster or Deputies which were timetabled to convene at set intervals. The remainder were the responsibility of Heads of Schools, or Years, or Faculty and Departmental Heads instructed to hold meetings at 'regular intervals'. The precise role and responsibility of each of the above meetings, however, remained somewhat ambiguous. A staff guide merely referred to 'staff meetings and weekly bulletins' as 'our formal lines of communication'. Thereafter seven types of meeting were simply formally named and timetabled. Their status, however, could be discerned from the regularity with which they were held, along with their membership. Hence meetings 1–3 can be seen to have formed a first tier of 'communication' and the most important form of representation for the full spectrum of staff interests. As the name indicates, (1) dealt with curriculum matters and consisted of Faculty Heads, curriculum co-ordinators, *ex-officio* pastoral Heads of Schools and Deputy Heads; (2) the senior management body was constituted by the most senior academic staff, i.e. curriculum co-ordinators, pastoral Heads of Schools, Deputies and Headmaster, along with a representative from the Staff Association, a body elected to represent the interest of the staff; and (3) the pastoral committee which consisted of pastoral Heads of Schools and Heads of Years (1–6).

These highly representative procedures established by the Headmaster were repeatedly enshrined in a supporting rhetoric which stressed open government and easy access.[9] The Head's attitude was popularly held to be summed up in his phrase 'my door is always open to any member of staff who wants to see me'. Repeated appeals were made to staff to 'use agendas' for the effective representation of interests and demands. However, despite the construction of these elaborate mechanisms for participation and representation, there persisted much evidence of a widespread disaffection and disenchant-

Model 4 Formal structure of policy making, administration and communication, Sageton, 1975– :

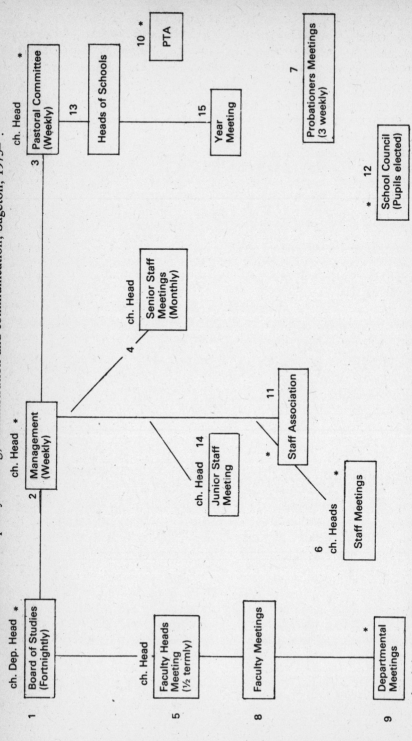

ch., chairperson; PTA, Parents Teachers Association. * Also existed under previous Head when 2 and 3 were combined to form 'chief assistants meeting'; the Board of Studies was then the Academic Board, and the Staff Association, the Staff Council.

ment with the opportunities presented for involvement in policy formation and decision making. For example, following a management meeting, one pastoral Head of School commented on a decision relating to the reallocation of available room space:

> The number of meetings we have to attend here is just ridiculous. How many of these items could he have dealt with on his desk? There was no decision made. I'm sure he's becoming incapable of making a decision. He keeps putting it off. I don't think we can let him move S, that ought to go around the table. I'm sure everybody would want her to stay in that room. He says management is important, so *we* ought to take a decision on it, but we won't. It's all decided in his room. If he says something like that . . . I'm sure that's what he'll do . . . .

At another meeting a more junior member of staff remarked:

> It's a problem of the quality of meeting not the quantity. We could triple the meetings and not make things better. We are talking about a waste of ideas. There's a frustration at not being allowed to speak. People feel abandoned . . . .

and

> decisions made in committees are always reversed by the Head . . . .

Objections such as these, made informally, represented attacks on the way in which decisions were arrived at. A feeling was being expressed that such occasions had a great deal more to do with the dissemination of policies predetermined by the Head (and a small group of selected followers) than providing genuine opportunity for all staff to influence its formation. Consequently such meetings, indeed meetings in general, tended to be considered both irrelevant and a further intrusion into already limited time. This feeling was greatly exacerbated later in the school year with the creation of a further body, a Policy Forming Group, concerned essentially with curriculum matters and constituted by teachers selected solely by the Head rather than upon principles of representation or general staff selection. For many staff, this development laid bare the façade of democracy which the plethora of meetings were felt to represent. As one teacher commented:

> It's a façade. I didn't feel this at the beginning but its obvious now that this P.F.G. has been formed. I've very strong feelings about what the Head is doing. There's never been a time when people feel so unhappy and unsafe as at present.

Against the background of previous responsibilities and status imputed to the role of senior teachers (pastoral and academic Heads), such occasions thus represented a repeated source of frustration and for thinly veiled antagonism. The different perspectives held by Head and staff and the power distribution made such exercises largely irrelevant to many staff (cf. Hunter, 1979, p. 125).

The creation of such a further layer of responsibility affording an highly specialized occasion for 'policy discussion' did not provide unlimited opportunity for pastoral or academic Heads to fulfil their appointed responsibilities. Faculty Heads tended to see the Board of Studies meetings merely as a 'talk shop' with little reference to their immediate curricular concerns, a feeling indicated in the above statement evinced by the creation of a new Policy Forming Group[10]. The reasons for this perceived control by the Head over the content and outcome of meetings are to be traced with reference to the broader framework of expectations and demands within which the school operated and, in particular, to his powerful need to implement certain policies in the academic and non-academic spheres.

On arrival at the school Mr Fillmore defined his problem as attracting a 'better clientele' to 'ease the burden placed upon teachers who are confronted with a preponderance of low ability children'. In his view, given parental choice and falling rolls, Sageton was firmly entrenched in a 'market economy situation'. He recognized that parents and primary school Heads judged the school less on the merits of thorough but long-term curricular reform than upon such public symbols of educational excellence as order, the wearing of uniform, respectful children, and good public examination results. Moreover teachers and Head, as elsewhere, were increasingly aware of closer scrutiny from extra-school sources, highlighted by government spokesmen, official reports and media. Outside political and economic pressures apparently pointed to the need to increase the accountability of teachers and exacerbated those already felt in schools such as Sageton. Concerns such as these were highlighted in a report by the Head presented at a Governors Meeting. It began

> Now that social control has been established, more and more time may be spent on assessing our approach to the formal education offered by the school. Flexibility of approach has become the key concept. Mixed Ability grouping of all pupils in the first three years is the basic approach but faculty Heads may "set" within their faculty if such is the wish of the large majority of the members of any one faculty . . . .

It went on to announce the creation of a 'Co-ordinator of assessment procedures and pupil development' (CAPPD):

> what the DES requires nationally from their newly created APU surely all schools require for their individuals. Its purpose, to establish a monitoring system so that eventually all "under" and "over" achievers will be spotted . . . .

and to emphasize the qualities of all its teaching staff:

> any pupil for example studying (subject) A, at Sageton at the present would come under the inspirational guidance of Mr. P. (lists academic qualification) ably supported by Ms. L. (qual) and Mr. V. (qual). The "A" results this year will make my point.

The official image, here presented to governors, is of a school secure in its social order, well able via its grouping practices, newly formed CAPPD position, and professional expertise to make an academic provision which is both responsive and caring of all its pupils' learning requirements. Indeed, as presented, the mention of mixed ability grouping (which had been initiated largely under a rhetoric of sink stream avoidance, control and motivation improvement), juxtaposed with the introduction of a CAPPD, is a neat justification of the Head's message that Sageton caters for *all* pupils. This was intended to allay Governors' fears that, despite mixed ability groupings, both the able and disadvantaged would receive less than full recognition. Overall, this document represented a forceful public defence of the school but at the same time drawing to the attention of significant others the nature of the constraints within which the school had to operate. In particular, attention was drawn to the following factors:

> We are finding the answer to most questions but the solution to one question still eludes us, viz., how to convince the public at large that we are a purposeful, happy, caring and achieving institution. One week before half-term there was an open meeting for all parents of transfer pupils and our impressive facilities and dedicated teachers excited and well satisfied all visiting parents and children. It was all the more disappointing to note that there were only two parents from our nearest Primary Schools. I believe it to be the responsibility of my Primary colleagues to urge the parents of their transfer pupils to visit all the High Schools within reasonable distance.

The Head defined parental and primary school teacher expectations, along with the principle of selection via parental choice, as significant constraints upon Sageton's development. These constraints compelled teachers at Sageton, as elsewhere, to work within a framework of pupil ability which made the task of teaching and the realization of the Head's valued educational goals extremely problematic.[11]

> Sageton . . . academically has done fairly well this past year (*vide* Public Examinations). How well would it not do with its gifted staff and pleasing facilities if its intake were distributed standardly across the ability range?

The message is clearly that of how much better could Sageton care for all its pupils who might expect to further benefit in the event of the school being allowed a real ability balance.

However, the picture of school life at Sageton which the above statements portray was not quite representative of the normal day to day experience of the great majority of pupils and teachers. Other statements reveal glimpses of a tension between a picture of how Sageton life ought to be (i.e. as represented to Governors) and how, upon a pragmatic appraisal of the opportunities presented by certain limiting factors, which teachers are compelled to operate within, life at Sageton was. Drawing attention to a decision taken by the Faculty of Social Sciences to introduce setting in year three, the Head remarked:

> Philosophically I am opposed to such a step but must accept the very real arguments that mixed ability grouping if continued too long in imperfect conditions may have a deleterious effect on the brightest of pupils. Pragmatism wins, though I remain convinced that when the time comes for extra investment in ancillary services such as the School Library and in the associated Media Resource Centre (a sore need as I see it) then there will be a quick end to selection before the fourth year in any subject . . . .

However, other than this brief mention of selective practices, little attention is given to the extent of setting within years one to three, of the problems of control experienced by teachers, of the lack of informal consensus verging upon disharmony within the school. Indeed even the Head's policy, as suggested, of appointing the 'more able' teacher as defined by academic qualification did little to facilitate the availability of expertise for teaching within mixed ability grouping. For the most part those teachers having followed a degree course expressed as great a concern for the failure of their professional training to equip them with a knowledge of mixed ability *teaching* as their 'teacher trained' counterparts.

The honesty and the genuineness of the intentions behind such policies are not however at issue. We are suggesting, simply, that the position of the Head is an unenviable one. The weight of broader economic, political and social pressures mediated through parents, LEA personnel and the press, create constraints which inevitably distort any straightforwardly held pastoral or academic ideals. They have an immediacy which is forcibly experienced by Heads. Many teachers, however, readily and sometimes critically perceived both the Head's devotion to changing the public image of the school and his choosing to establish his own control rather than give a lead to curriculum change. Within the constraints which he experienced the Head invoked a variety of strategies of control. These consisted mainly of control over the internal decision making process (facilitated by the definition of the role of meetings as 'consultative' rather than as sharing in the decision making procedures), in the construction of meetings as channels for downward communication which better facilitated the dissemination of his concerns for order and 'standards', and in his determination of the content of discussion at such meetings. Although he repeatedly appealed for the better use of agendas, having created a situation in which members felt their interests to be of little real significance, such appeals were met with little enthusiasm. At a Board of Studies meeting, for example, the tone for all future meetings was established early in the year. Reference was quickly made to the tested reading abilities[12] of the new pupil intake and to the school's poor achievement in public examination. There followed a brief 'discussion' of

Why are such poor results repeatedly achieved?

From Faculty Heads, a number of explanations are offered:

A lot of it's due to mixed ability. The transition to mixed ability caused a great deal of instability. There wasn't any planning. It was just too rapid a change. We weren't prepared (Mr Bird).

Another stressed the absence of professional expertise amongst the staff:

mixed ability maths teaching needs good teachers and teachers who are good at mathematics. There's a terrific absence of teachers with both qualities in the maths department . . . (Mr Peters).

Another focuses on the 'inability to construct project work suitable for the reading ability of our pupils' (Mrs Owen).

In Mr Fillmore's perspective, however, senior academic staff are left in little doubt as to the nature of the problem, where it lay and how it might quickly be corrected.

I think we must put blame on ourselves, Faculty Department Heads. There's a lack of concern. There's a real lack of concern for homework, punctuality, approach. There's a lack of pressure. I think we've got to achieve a more professional attitude amongst the teachers.

Despite the very real constraints referred to by the Faculty Heads within which teachers worked, to some, the Head appeared not to be concerned with their own analyses of their problems. It is however hardly likely that he did not recognize these factors named by Faculty Heads as relevant to the problem. One must assume that they were passed over by the Head because he felt he had little capability to effect dramatic alteration in their circumstances. Consequently, the Head did not launch detailed analyses of existing curriculum and pedagogical problems but instead regularly appealed for senior staff to exercise more rigorous vigilance and control over the professional responsibilitiess of themselves and others. Hence, in subsequent meetings, discussion focused predominantly *not* on the analysis of curriculum matters or the expressed concerns of faculty and department members, but on the introduction of new forms of assessment, e.g. the creation of the new CAPPD and discussion of its nature and form, its existence having been already determined by the Head; the extension of internal examinations; and the structure of a newly constructed timetable for future introduction.[13] All these measures can be seen as specifically designed to locate and develop existing pupil talent while leaving untouched/unchanged the more precarious and long-term questions of curriculum or pedagogical reform. There was little discussion of the problems of mixed ability teaching. Indeed, the situation in the school in this regard was not unlike that found by Gross *et al.* (1971) and Ball (1981). Teachers received little help within or outside their classrooms as they attempted to implement curriculum innovation and there was little communication between teachers and administrators about the problems to which the teachers were exposed during this period. At senior management levels curriculum matters were confined to decisions which provided an organizational framework in which curricular innovation could better be implemented. For example, an in-service course was provided for the whole of the English Department. Having effected this opportunity, however, little further attention was paid by senior management to such problems as time for further planning and preparation, of putting into practice the ideas which had been stimulated in the 'educationist context'. Faculty areas were reorganized to effect better opportunity for interaction and co-operation between themselves. A media resources centre was planned and established. However, within this framework of organizational change (initiated by the Head) there remained little analysis of existing problems of teaching mixed ability groups. In the statements and policies mentioned above, Mr Fillmore attempted to bring pressure on senior academic staff to effect greater control over their dominions. In turn, the nature of their competency was being defined in terms of the extra school pressures and demands which the Head routinely experienced, that is to say, according to their capacity to effect conditions (better assessment procedures, 'professional attitudes') conducive to the provision of immediate evidence of the school's academic achievements and social control.

A similar emphasis on *pupil* control is found in the content of discussion at pastoral meetings. Heads of School interpreted their role in a way consonant with that expressed publicly by the Head in documents presented to parents, staff or governors. The approach was liberal and all embracing. In practice, however, they considered their responsibilities constrained by the dominant expectations of the Head.

> I would love to do more pastoral work but I can't. The Head would love to see me standing in the corridor every minute of the day. I'm a policeman that's all I am . . . .

The origins of this perspective can be located in the informal interactions between pastoral Heads and the Head, and are evidenced in the content of discussion at pastoral meetings. These tended to be dominated by discussion of measures intended to effect the better 'policing' of pupils,[14] including examination of the effectiveness of existing practices and the possibility of introducing new ones. A great deal of debate centred on the introduction of 'green slips' (documents used to survey levels of attendance and lateness), Headmaster's detentions, the introduction of a lower school sanctuary and ways of improving corridor supervision and of pupil suspension. Again, the tenor of the Head's perspective is to stress the responsibility of senior staff to effect the working of such policies amongst the teachers for whom they are responsible:

> what action are you taking to ensure that we get larger returns? (of green slips). If staff don't do it . . . they can leave. I'll thump the table at the next staff meeting.

Pastoral care is seen as the means for creating the internal order and coherence which is commonly supposed to be behind a good public image. Given the contentious nature of many of the issues forwarded for discussion at each of these pastoral and academic meetings (for example, the introduction of 'green slips' entailed an increased level of administrative work demanded of pastoral Heads, thus impinging on 'pastoral time'), such occasions were repeatedly a source of antagonism and frustration. While the extension of the academic and pastoral systems under these conditions bore most heavily on School Heads and senior academic staff, a cycle of personal recrimination was also set-up which moved from senior staff, to tutors or subject teachers, back to senior staff or horizontally to pastoral or academic structures. Typically,

> I'd like to know if Heads of Department sit around worrying about home work . . . [and] . . . Heads of Departments are to blame, they're not doing their jobs. These people have to be pushed (Pastoral Heads of year).

For teachers this rhetoric was of little help or relevance in their particular school experience. The evolution of two separate and distinct internal structures had provided little opportunity for harmonizing and unifying the interests of each sector. Although 'integrated' in Board of Studies and management meetings, the frequency with which faculty or departmental interests concerning curriculum or pedagogy surfaced for discussion (a feature exacerbated by the absence of Faculty Heads at pastoral meetings) ensured that the routine demands and dilemmas of subject teachers rarely became matters for serious discussion and thus rarely entered the consciousness of senior pastoral staff.

Summary

Under the conditions in which Sageton functioned any mere change in structure could not, alone, have facilitated an improvement in the pastoral or academic conditions of care and learning experienced by pupils and teachers at the school. Analyses of the content and form of discussion at senior management meetings revealed that there persisted a dislocation between the nature of talk at this level and that evidenced at the individual teacher, department and faculty level. The content and organization of classroom method and related problems were left to be resolved within departments and faculties. A definite autonomy appeared to be granted to subject departments by senior management in the school and formalized in the organizational structure, a feature which may not have been an altogether intended outcome of organizational change. It extended to individual teachers and was symbolized in the tentativeness with which senior management entered through the classroom door. Enough has been said however, to suggest that such autonomy was of an extremely 'restricted' kind,[15] involving both low levels of participation in decision making and of opportunity to effect curriculum or pedagogical change or reappraisal. As Ball (1981, p. 186) similarly discovered at Beachside, teachers considered themselves to be under pressures from a variety of sources all of which engendered limitations on practice in classrooms. Amongst them was the 'culture of the school as a whole', which defined for the individual teacher 'acceptable practice' in terms of classroom style and control relationships. At Sageton, academic achievement, especially in terms of examination passes, along with an emphasis upon discipline and control, were given particular importance and value and had their origins in contexts far removed from the arena of classroom life. What emerged was a framework of expectations defining appropriate practices in the classrooms which were neither precisely specified nor without contradiction but within which teachers were routinely expected to construct and operate their management and instructional strategies. While, then, by virtue of change in organizational structure a definite autonomy was granted to subject departments and pastoral Heads, the academic and pastoral structures were marked by a senior management and in particular the Head-master's need for downward communication geared to establishing and maintaining the school's good standing in the community. Centralization of certain functions followed, particularly in relation to discipline (but also curriculum, as evidenced in the establishment of the Policy Formation Group) so as to implement appropriate policies. The upshot of this was an increase in administration and a formaliza-tion of certain duties. Its overall effect was to treat professionals as clerks (see Corbishley and Evans, 1980).

The ambiguities and irrationalities within Sageton, local contin-gencies apart, relate to this wider tension between a demand to implement centrally directed policies and a professional sense of autonomy and responsibility for decision making in key aspects of school life. Mr Fillmore sought greater control over the internal communicatory working of the school in order to achieve better dissemination of his immediate concerns about standards and disci-pline. Demands for further opportunities to participate in decisions which influenced school life and for a greater autonomy from the demands of the Head in order to realize prefered strategies or philosophies of pastoral care or learning, given pressures from the press, parents and local politicians, were those to which senior management felt unable to comply. The consequence was a context of teaching in which teachers in general felt there to be little possibility of dramatic or immediate amelioration in their school or classroom conditions of work. There was a sense of frustration, antagonism, even disunity amongst staff which exacerbated their immediate concerns to achieve an acceptable curriculum or pedagogy for Sageton pupils.

Teachers at Sageton had experienced organizational change at great pace and had been presented with little opportunity to prepare and plan for mixed ability grouping. They had little experience of any curriculum or pedagogic reforms of any sort. Staff were thrust into a form of organization by fiat rather than by their own choosing (see also Reid *et al.*, 1981). The mixed ability innovation at Sageton was undoubtedly aiming at a moratorium (Davies, 1977) and at producing a climate in which the supply of pupil abilities might become normally distributed by altering the intake. It was in this context that curriculum innovation took place, and it is against this background that the classroom and curricular practice of teachers needs to be seen.

three

Modern Languages:
Whole Class Curriculum

Our incursion into the history of organizational change at Sageton reveals an educational system inevitably orientated towards the twin goals of maximizing talent and securing orderly pupil behaviour. The picture which emerges, in this and subsequent chapters, is of teachers grappling a good deal of the time with seemingly intractable problems of discipline and control. Their expressed concerns relate to how to maintain order while at the same time establish and evolve a curriculum capable of resolving pupils' learning problems, often within the contexts of limited resources and support, and of conflicting expectations. The following description of whole class curriculum and teaching method/strategy in modern language represents one of the variety of curriculum responses to mixed ability innovation at Sageton. We discuss it first, not least because the 'whole class' mode is the most pervasive of secondary strategies and the baseline from which secondary pedagogical innovation usually begins, but also because it is the least complex starting-point as, at the time of the observations, little was happening *qua* innovation in this subject area. However, we must be clear about one disadvantage which this organization of the chapters entails. Our pupil grouping typology, derived by combining pupil ability and work orientation and within which we locate ideas like those of the steering and counter steering group, was evolved initially in the analyses of Maths and Science data, which in the research context was temporally *prior* to detailed work on French. Therefore, the analysis of French is 'informed' and directed by concepts which emerged from our observations of Maths and Science and which are explained more fully in Chapter 4.

Whole class teaching was used by teachers in other subject areas, but it was a most characteristic and pervasive feature of the modern language. Central to this account is the understanding that the processes of teaching and learning cannot be fully appreciated without reference to the history of a subject area within the overall organization of the school. The discussion begins, therefore, by describing first the background of curriculum change in the department and the materials currently used in the teaching. Attention is then focused on interaction between pupils and teachers and these we suggest are 'created' by a complex interplay between teachers and pupils, the organization and content of the curriculum, and the broader school organization and practices.

Departmental Background

Prior to mixed ability grouping at Sageton, teaching French had reflected a philosophy and method prevalent within language teaching. It had, as one teacher reflected, been taught selectively only to 'the able pupils in the top four groups of pupils in each year group'.[1] Mixed ability grouping represented an organizational change which Mr Thomas (then Head of Department) received reluctantly and coolly. On the one hand he recognized its potential for pupil control, 'I found myself in conflict, – socially and disciplinary wise I favour mixed ability teaching', and on the other hand, 'there does not seem to be the academic progress in the grouping that would be expected of these work sets'. Confronted with a broadened range of pupil abilities, this teacher's problems were far greater than those of mathematics or science, for whom, as we shall see, adoption of 'new' or adaptation of 'old' curriculum material were available strategies.[2] Hawkins, for example, notes retrospectively,

> In the early 60's only 25% of all eleven year olds began a modern language. By the middle 70's, 80%. No other subject in the country had to change in a decade from being a minority subject for 1 in 4 of secondary pupils to being a subject for the great majority. We were unprepared (1979, p. 71).[3]

At Sageton, subject to the same pressures, the French Department made few changes in syllabus. A mode III in French, however, was adopted, supported by 'largely self produced materials in years one to three' (Head of Department).

In 1976, a new Head of Department was appointed from within the Department, who had taught at Sageton since 1970. In this teacher's view the response to mixed ability grouping had been largely 'to leave things as they were'. In order to modernize existing practice he introduced 'a full course of Hawkins'[4] and began to 'experiment with practice within the 15–18 age range in an effort to discover how to make success in French more attainable for our students', an endeavour motivated by what he reported as an '80% drop-out rate at the end of the third year'. The linguistic content of courses in years 1–3 reflected the 'newer' emphasis in language teaching. Hence 'the language of ordinary conversation, that pupils master orally is given emphasis'.[5] In year 1, Hawkins Book 1 formed the basis for teaching supplemented with 'self produced' worksheets and material, and oral and aural work was emphasized. Upon setting, however, pupils continued to use Hawkins, but with the top two sets moving onto Book 2. The less able made greater use of Ellis and Pearce. This included 'sign language, speaking, it's designed for slower pupils. It is modular based'. In year three, top groups followed a course [7] 'more grammatically based, middle groups couldn't take it'. The latter continued with courses in which the orientation was 'aural and oral work which is practised in meaningful contexts' and 'survival situations'.

This variety of material, presented to pupils in years 1–3, reflected the Head of Department's view that 'no one course is suitable for Sageton pupils'. At the same time, however, there remained a great deal of dissatisfaction with existing texts and an opinion that suitable material had not yet been found. In this respect the response to mixed ability grouping was considered a

> gradual evolution . . . of content, based on our changing experiences and understanding of different ability groups (Head of Department).

As such, the existing courses, particularly Hawkins, the one most highly used, represented a number of constraints upon teachers and pupils alike. In the Head of Department's view its content was considered:

> clear and good in its early stages . . . arguably suitable for mixed ability groups, but later it becomes far too difficult for the slow and average pupils.

The scheme implied, therefore, a level of ability incommensurate with that thought to prevail amongst the majority of the pupil intake to Sageton.[8] Moreover, its contents were considered to represent to pupils a cultural discontinuity, hence a source of low motivation, with all that that implied for pupils' discipline and order:

> Much of Hawkins is irrelevant to the lower and average ability, they are more mature than the able pupils. They are fed up with school and family life, Hawkins is a middle class family. They're fed up with this (Head of Department).

This problem was held to be particularly acute at Sageton because, as the Head of Department noted,

80% of our pupils are immigrants, mostly second and third generation, they come from working class backgrounds. Their problems lie in their inability to use standard English. Many already speak a patois or foreign language at home. At school they are expected to conform to English culture and to use standard English as well as learn yet another foreign language.

Having made a curriculum response to mixed ability grouping, the outcome (as adjudged in pupil responses to the material) was felt to be unsatisfactory.

We've got mixed ability and we've tried to produce courses to cater . . . but so far we've missed the point . . . we've got courses for the good but not for the slower and below average pupils (Head of Department).

and

There's nothing much available for the average and below average pupils. Next year there will be more staff . . . hopefully (French Teacher).

As we see in the above statements, we find a department struggling to make the transition from mixed ability grouping to mixed ability teaching. It was, at the time of our study, locked in debate about the nature of curriculum practice and forms of pupil grouping. In this context the Head of Department recognized a discrepancy between teacher perspectives and the content and method of teaching in mixed ability groups.

There isn't consensus in the department about mixed ability teaching or about teaching French. Most people remember their own experience of being taught French which was very formal. This is the biggest set-back to change. We need far more in-service courses.

Some support for this view was found in the questionnaire responses of the teachers concerned. Although the majority were teacher trained, only one of the seven modern language teachers on whom we have data (from the departmental total of nine) indicates that this initial training provided any insight into mixed ability teaching, and that by virtue of being 'primary' trained. The majority had experience as pupils of being taught in selective groupings (and had previously taught groups of this nature) or else were having their first teaching experience at Sageton. For the most part, then, teachers entered into the context of mixed ability grouping with a perceptual frame in which, as the Head of Department suggests, the conception of teaching was 'formal'.[9] In this situation (unlike that seen in Maths, Science or Integrated Studies) lacking a pedagogy which was pre-defined for them or a curriculum thought wholly suitable, they were in the position of having to work things out for themselves.

To this end the teachers themselves focused on what they saw as restricting opportunities to effect a syllabus and pedagogy suitable to mixed ability grouping.

> We have a department of nine (staff), five of these are involved pastorally.

> They're not really interested in French. One of them now does careers, but keeps the very slow 3rd year French group. Ms. Farr moved to another school, as a result her timetable and Mr. Donne's are amalgamated for a new post, two-thirds French and one-third English. They didn't appoint a specialist, the advisor wasn't involved. The person 'knows' French having lived in Lille, but he has to be trained to become a specialist (Head of Department).

This comment is associated with wider LEA and national problems of staffing in particular subjects. The problem was exacerbated within the school because of a heavy involvement of staff in other areas of responsibility. This accounts for the view of the Head of Department that teaching is 'restricted' because such dual responsibilities and interests are resolved in favour of pastoral rather than subject teaching. The sociology of education has, until recently,[10] paid little attention to the way in which teachers (rather than pupils) are imputed an identity as a good or successful teacher, by their peers. In this situation, we see that opportunities to achieve such an identity can be structured by factors (a particular history of subject teaching, and time made available by the organization) over which teachers have little control. The teachers themselves, for example, noted that   .

> There's not enough time as a pastoral head to prepare work. I would use these meetings (Departmental) to prepare work. I know all the theory . . . there's just no time to put it into practice (Mrs Little).

and

> I don't have the time to prepare materials suitable for mixed ability classes . . . I can't do it justice (Mr Haley).

The upshot of this conflict of professional interests was a subtle, but definite, element of mutual recrimination. Pastoral staff felt that scarce time was not being used in the best way, while the Head of Department felt that there was a lack of teaching interest from pastoral staff.

It is against this background of departmental concerns about curriculum, pedagogy, staffing and time that the debate about mixed ability grouping within Modern Languages has to be considered. In contrast to each of the departments subsequently considered, the majority of modern language teachers at Sageton, as elsewhere (cf.

Reid *et al.*, 1981; Ball, 1981), expressed a view which held that their teaching was extremely difficult, if not impossible, within mixed ability grouping. For example, one teacher stated:

> in general, mixed ability is OK, like in Maths kids can do individual work. You can tell a kid to get on with something. In French, without him knowing something . . . you can't do that. I hate kids getting stuck in one group and not having the chance . . . but I've got mixed feelings about mixed ability in French.

and another

> I think you've got to set them because you have to deal with such different abilities . . . It's cumulative you see . . . you build on what they are learning. For some it will take a couple of weeks . . . for others you can move on quickly.

It is possible to locate this opposition, in the same manner as Ball (1981, p. 178), in the 'subject sub-culture' tradition of language teaching. Subject subculture in Ball's view refers broadly to 'the professional self image of the members (teachers) as subject specialists' and particularly views of teaching current within the subject. In modern languages the view is taken that the 'deep structure' of the subject makes it very difficult or impossible to teach it to mixed ability groups without a radical reduction in the level of academic work normally expected of the 'brighter' pupil.[11] However, this is not sufficient explanation of the incidence of setting within Modern Languages, and the opposition of teachers to mixed ability teaching at Sageton. While the majority of staff expressed their opposition, 'they were all moaning that mixed ability is not working, you can't teach the whole ability range', the Head of Department remained firmly committed to the idea/possibility of mixed ability teaching in Modern Languages: 'I was more convinced than the others that it could work'. She recognized, however, that the conditions to achieve this end were not currently being met.

> I would group according to ability after year 1 if personnel are not trained or confident in teaching mixed ability. If my members of the department were confident . . . with . . . more team teaching in mixed ability situations, then we could have mixed ability teaching up to and including the third year.

Setting, thus conceived, was an organizational coping strategy,[12] the means of accommodating the professional limitations of existing staff within the pressures for standards and success to which the Language Department, like all others, was increasingly subject.

> We haven't enough teachers for German in the second year, so we need to set earlier. It's important that the top group think of themselves as a

top group. There'll be plenty of flexibility. If only I can get one group of
pupils successful at German, getting results, then I can argue for more
teachers. The Head isn't for German in the second year. It's important
to locate the more able. The earlier the better (Head of Department).

Against this background, a further encroachment on mixed ability
grouping was made in 1977, setting taking place at the end of the first
term in year 1. Mixed ability was thus retained only for a short period
for diagnostic purposes. With senior teachers in the broader school
context increasingly expressing mixed feelings about teaching modern
languages to Sageton pupils, *setting* was, therefore, instrumental to the
department's endeavours to secure not only a means of defending its
very existence (locating and producing at least one group of 'able'
pupils) but also a base from which to argue for its further expansion.[13]
A practice which was opposed in principle by the Head of Department
was pragmatically adopted because of its recognized, potential
outcomes. As A. Hargreaves (1978, p. 82) suggests:

constraints not only determine possible educational policy as a set of
mere pragmatic responses with which the practitioners need not
necessarily agree with in principle, but that they also lead to a broader
shaping of educational goals and desirable definitions of teaching itself,
is the essence of coping strategies and their institutionalisation.

It is possible to view even the oppositional views of teachers to
mixed ability grouping as somewhat less directly contingent upon
professional socialization into subject subcultural philosophies than as
produced or at least mediated by immediate, material conditions of
practice. In this view professional socialization provides the accompanying rhetoric[14] (or interpretative frame) with which to *explain*
rather than cause problems and dilemmas routinely experienced in the
course of teaching.[15]

That such constraints obstruct the development of favoured teaching
approaches (mixed ability grouping, team teaching) and elicit a
consciously adaptive response (setting), at least on the part of the
Head of Department, has been illustrated. As we will see, however, as
far as this strategy leaves untouched conditions of practice, it does
little to reduce problems of instruction and control experienced by
teachers with most of the pupils. As this comment of a teacher of third
year middle group pupils indicated:

at present in the second and third year, pupils in the lower groups are
bored to death. They're very difficult to teach. They could be doing
something else, more useful, English or Maths. It shouldn't be
compulsory. The lower ability groups should ideally be taught in small
groups. If they weren't such a problem to control, then you'd teach
them French through discussion and talk.

The resulting 'unintended consequence' of setting as a second level[16] coping strategy to the problems described, was a further 'shaping of educational goals'.[17] In the opinion of the teacher above, language teaching should further be restricted to those who voluntarily want to learn.

Teacher Strategies in Whole Class Method

Unlike most of the subjects subsequently discussed, language teaching was not characterized by a formally, precisely defined curriculum or pedagogical mode of transmission. Within a broad framework of expectations (subject subculturally defined) *vis-à-vis* content, e.g. the emphasis upon oral-aural work and methodology, and the use of language laboratories, teachers were left to their own devices as to how to teach. Given the perceptual frame of the teachers concerned, their opposition to mixed ability, the particular subject subculture identified with it and the limits of time, little variation in teacher approach was observed, *whether in set or mixed ability classrooms*. As elsewhere, lessons observed were 'of a traditional book based, teacher-centred variety'.[18] In contrast to Integrated Studies, Science and Mathematics teaching at Sageton, where worksheets predominated, language teaching used teacher *talk* as the primary instructional mode.[19] Thus in language classrooms listening, rather than literacy, was critical to the successful operation of this method of teaching.[20] Lessons typically followed a rigid question-and-answer pattern, 'the teacher supplying a model statement and persuading the children to grasp the principle by repeating similar statements.'[21] Talk was public and highly centralized: for much of the time whatever the teacher said demanded the attention of all.[22] Teachers had to work to organize the class so that they were the hub, the focal point of attention and interaction.[23] Unlike in individualized and group based instruction, traditional social relationships and teacher authority were repeatedly and *publicly* announced, in the act of speaking.[24] Each of the lesson-proper phases described below took place against a background of positional, structural meanings in which the teacher's authority was explicitly announced in settling phases of the lesson and less occasionally during the lesson proper, e.g. in public, regulative messages. For example, in the classroom of Mrs Wilks with the pupils of 1p . . .

right . . . I've arrived . . . stop talking . . . or there'll be a detention.

Stop talking, completely and utterly.

We won't start until you're all silent . . . are you listening?

Pupils were left in no doubt as to the asymmetry of classroom relationships. Pupil behaviours were confined within far narrower parameters of acceptability than in group based and individualized instruction. The boundaries between interest and work behaviour were rigorously defined. All this was reinforced by such teacher tactics as 'lining up', standing on teacher entry, and registration.

That teachers experienced difficulties in establishing and maintaining a frame of control appropriate to whole class method became increasingly obvious to them and myself as the first term progressed. This can be explained largely by reference to the limited opportunities for successful learning which class teaching presented to some of the pupils. In lessons observed, the pace of work was totally dominated by teacher in oral interchange with a minority of pupils in each form. The French that tended to be 'learned' within the lesson was confined to and displayed only by a competent minority.[25] In class teaching, as the teacher set a common pace in the act of exposition, it was extremely difficult to gauge just how much of what was being said was currently being or already understood by the pupils, or how much new knowledge was being acquired. In contrast to worksheet based instruction, particularly of the individualized, group-based type, where learning problems become surface features of interaction, in whole class method such problems became apparent only occasionally, and in contexts removed from the immediate environment. One teacher of first year pupils remarked:

> You can only tell what they're like when they've done written work or have a test . . . you can't tell in the class.

As Edwards and Furlong (1978, p. 108) have similarly stated of whole class method, finding the answer to this question is a haphazard business indeed.

> A few pupils answer questions and this can give the impression that everyone understands. It is not until the teacher looks at the pupils' written work that he discovers how much of his cherished exposition was over the heads of many of the class.

Examples from the work of two teachers with first year classes, in French mixed ability grouping, highlight and represent some of these general features. Both are language teachers with many years of experience teaching at Sageton and elsewhere. Ordinarily, in these examples, the lessons' opening and closing sequences are omitted.

Each count referred to in Tables 6 and 7, as in subsequent tables, refers to a *complete verbal interaction* as judged by the fieldworker and not to a speech utterance of a specific length. Each count is thus a categorization of a piece of teacher action which could carry a number

Table 6 Differences in the incidence of teacher talk during a 30 minute period of class teaching in two first year mixed ability Modern Language lessons

Teacher/Class		Public regulative	Public instructional[a]
Mrs Preece	1s	4	30
Mrs Wilks	1p	3	15

[a] Interactions (in this instance a question/answer sequence) between teacher and individual pupils in everyone's earshot during the phase of whole class teaching.

of messages. The Sageton research was concerned primarily but not solely with the regulative and instructional meanings carried in the course of classroom communication. The former category (in a very similar way to that found in Lundgren, 1977) refers to talk orientated towards the *behavioural control* of pupils; while the latter contained a variety of the *instructional* (involving the transmission of content, or meeting demands for help with content) the *administrative* (task related talk, e.g. instruction on procedures, use of equipment, etc.) and the *evaluative* (involving questions which are either closely tied to the content of a topic or theme or those which facilitated a more 'open' response).

However, interpretations of what a piece of teacher talk was intended to achieve or mean, or how it was 'received' by pupils, and as to when an interaction had begun or ended, could not always simply be 'read off' from the content of what was being said, or when the talking had started or stopped. The significance of an interaction could only be 'known' with further reference to the perspectives and actions of teachers and pupils and our developing understanding of the context in which they were located. For example (and as will become increasingly apparent in subsequent chapters), teacher talk which could appear as instructional in *content* (and for the sake of consistency was always coded as such) was very often regulative in *function*. The numerical snapshots contained in the tables thus need to be considered very cautiously. The relative paucity of regulative talk which some display not only belie how routinely problematic were the behaviours of many pupils for Sageton teachers but also distort the pattern and flow of classroom events.

Table 7 reveals a basic structure of communication. The notion of structure does not refer to linguistic structure but, in a similar way to Lundgren (1977, p. 146), *to the pattern of 'who communicates with whom about what in what situation'*.

The structural features of classroom talk in whole class method are

Table 7 Distribution of Mrs Wilk's talk during the above
(Table 6) 30 minute period of class teaching with the pupils of
1p.

Pupil	Ethnicity	Phase 1 11 min.	Phase 2 19 min.	Teacher rating[a]	NFER total
Mark	WI/British	Absent		BB	A
Naren	Asian	(X)		BB	C
Abdul	Asian	XX		AA	C
Michael	WI/British		X	AB	—
John	British	X	!	CB	C
Hugh	European		X	AA	C
Jerry	WI	X		CC	—
Ryan	WI			CC	—
Rene	WI			CC	D
Peter	WI	Absent		CC	C
David	British			CC	—
Paul	British			CB	C
Jenny	British			BB	C
Mary	WI		XX	AA	E
Heather	British	X	!X	BB	C
Liona	WI			CC	D
Caroline	WI	(X)X		CC	—
Odette	WI			BB	D
Maureen	WI			AB	E
Lynne	British		XX!	BA	—

X = public instructional talk; in this case a question/answer sequence between teacher and an individual pupil in which the latter gives a correct reply, or (X) an incorrect or no reply.

! = a public regulative interaction between the teacher and an individual pupil.

[a] Teacher ratings refer to a 5-point, A-E scale of 'effort' (left side letter) and 'attainment' used by teachers to assess pupils, in this case for Autumn term school reports.

fairly well established. The teacher dominates the teaching, usually from the front of class position and the roles of the teacher and pupils are relatively fixed. The teacher explains content, asks questions, pupils answer and the teacher's role is that of structuring, soliciting, and instructing (Bellack *et al.*, 1966; Lundgren, 1972). Individual help which occurs when the teachers talk privately to a pupil, perhaps leaning over the desk giving individual guidance at, what we call, the immediate face to face level, is not a salient phenomenon (cf. Lundgren, 1972).

In the example of class teaching referred to in Table 7, we found 18 of the pupils of Form 1p awaiting Mrs Wilks' arrival. She arrived somewhat late, having been detained dealing with pastoral matters, and asked the pupils to stand and waited for silence. One pupil was asked to distribute paper and the lesson proper began. This proceeded through a series of recognizable phases, the first lasting 11 minutes which involved a re-introduction of content previously covered.

Mrs Wilks   I'm going to ask you what you said about your friend . . . I'll begin with Abdul. How did you say 'Here is my friend?'

Abdul replied correctly, the teacher repeated and the class repeated.

Mrs Wilks   Caroline . . . 'She lives in London' . . . [waits] . . . you're too slow . . . I'll give you nought.

Jerry provided a correct reply and the teacher asks Caroline to repeat.

The lesson continued with both John and Heather giving correct replies. Naren was next to be asked but he pleaded, 'I wasn't here at the last lesson', and the question was put to Abdul who again replied correctly. The correct replies of five pupils on six occasions were taken as evidence that basic structures and vocabulary were known sufficiently well by the class for the lesson to progress. Abdul who supplied the opening and closing reply of this phase along with John are the only pupils in this class later to be found in the top set.

The second lesson phase (which continued for 36 minutes) involved the pupils drawing in their exercise books 'a picture of yourselves' and 'personal items'. After only three minutes, however, the teacher asked 'has anybody finished?' Four pupils, Michael, Mary, Hugh and Lynne indicated that they had. 'Right, who can tell me, how do I say . . . "here is my?" ' Lynne provided a correct reply. Already the teacher had generated a learning dilemma for many pupils. Theirs was a choice between either listening to the teacher, or attempting to finish the initial task. Many chose the former, carefully containing their actions to avoid the teacher's surveillance. Apparently recognizing that not all were listening, the teacher repeated the statement and turned to the blackboard:

Mrs Wilks   OK, I'll put it on the blackboard.

The teacher then introduced and explained new content (*le*, *la*, *mon*, *ma*, etc.), publicly rebuking Lynne, John and Heather.

Mrs Wilks   You can't afford not to listen.

A series of sentences were provided – 'here is my chair, etc.' – and written on the blackboard. The pupils copied them into their exercise books.

There was further progression:

Mrs Wilks	Now think about what you are going to say about your friend. How do I say 'he has a pen? . . . a chair?' It's the same word for the number . . .

The teacher elaborated, examples were placed on the blackboard. She turned to the pupils:

Mrs Wilks	OK . . . Heather, how do I say 'she has a book?'
Heather	[replied correctly . . . and is rewarded with]
Mrs Wilks	Well done you're working beautifully.

Mary was asked, gave a correct reply, pupils repeated and were instructed to finish off their drawing and blackboard work.

There was then, a great deal of teacher talk, and only a small number of pupils were needed to tell the teacher that instruction was adequate. Moreover, the pace was defined by the 'able' pupil. Both Mary and Heather in the teacher's perspective are defined as 'promising pupils . . . pleasant to teach . . .' and these along with other pupils defined as able, account for the majority of interactions throughout the lesson. Thus the teacher strategy progressed, aided by the able child and supported by a generous use of the blackboard as a supplementary form of instruction. Only in later phases of the lesson and on a subsequent occasion was the instructional adequacy of whole class method called into question. In a latter phase of the lesson proper, for example, Rene was asked:

Mrs Wilks	How would you say . . . 'here is my chair?'
Rene	. . . voici (mon) . . .
Mrs Wilks	Try again.
Rene	I can't.
Mrs Wilks	[annoyed] . . . I'll put you in detention if you don't listen . . . [provides answer . . . asks to repeat]

Involved for the first time during the lesson, Rene was able to correctly recall content introduced during an earlier phase ('here is') but not that of later lesson developments (gender, 'my' or vocabulary, 'chair'). Somewhere along the line, either because he has failed to pay attention, or because of the teacher's instruction, he has not understood. Upon an assumption that all pupils are listening when the teacher is talking and that talk is an adequate instructional mode, Rene's learning problems were reduced to a feature of his behavioural nonconformity. Genuine learning problems were thus overlooked. For Rene, as for other pupils, especially Jerry, Ryan, Liona, Peter, David, Paul and Caroline, defined as 'less able' or just 'average' by Mrs

Wilks, and who tended to experience similar problems largely due to the pacing of the instruction, such learning problems became acute. As time went on during the year, and more and more overt 'content' was added, given its cumulative nature, French tended to become more and more incomprehensible.[26] It is well worth stressing that these pupils at the beginning of the year had approached language lessons with the same kind of enthusiasm and intrigue displayed by their more 'able' counterparts. Frustration was increasingly expressed, particularly by Jerry, Ryan, Rene and Liona, in difficult forms of behaviour. As suggested in the teacher's ratings of effort, her attention was increasingly drawn towards these pupils, whose identity was subject to further closure in a partly self-fulfilling process.

In a follow up lesson, for example, the lesson proper began with Mrs Wilks again adopting a strategy of eliciting pupil responses to questions, rather than waiting for replies to be volunteered. Attention was initially drawn to the actions of a small number of pupils, slow to settle, to whom, with obvious control intent, opening questions were addressed:

Mrs Wilks	I'm going to ask Mark . . . then . . . Jerry . . . and you Ryan . . . Mark, you're going to say . . . OK . . . 'This is my?' . . . [holds up pen]
Mark	[no reply]
Mrs Wilks	Right . . . just say what it is.
Mark	[replies correctly]
Mrs Wilks	Good . . . can you say something else. 'Here is? . . . My? . . .' Perhaps you've forgotten . . . or you haven't listened.
Mrs Wilks	[to Jerry] . . . 'I have a ruler?'
Jerry	[no reply]
Mrs Wilks	Say '*here* is my ruler' . . . Say anything you can! . . . there's no doubt about you, you don't listen . . . Come and sit at the end . . . here . . .

Clearly the nature of teacher talk was neither arbitrary nor indiscriminate. The message addressed to Mark, who is given the benefit of the teacher's doubt, is far less harsh or damaging to identity[27] than that received by Jerry, whose failure to respond correctly merely confirmed an identity already established in the teacher's perspective. Interpreting behaviour in this way provided little, if any, opportunity for such pupils to re-negotiate their deviant or less able identity. While (as we see in Chapter 4) an individualized learning context tended to bring *immediate* help from the teacher for Jerry, Ryan, Rene and Liona, in whole class method the response was a public admonition with no further exploration of the pupils' problems.

Mrs Wilks' actions doubtlessly would fall far short of those recommended in the wider subculture of language teaching and indeed of the teacher's own desires. Buckby, (1979, p. 79), for example, argues that

> The golden rule for the teacher – one which has far reaching implications . . . is to treat each pupil with respect, as a person and as an individual. One important consequence of this is never to force anyone to speak when he has not volunteered to do so. Provided that the discussion or activity is interesting and within their linguistic grasp most pupils will want to participate.

The proviso is an important one. With neither the time nor the ability to prepare work suitable for mixed ability teaching . . .

> There's just no time . . . I personally am not a good enough teacher to do this. I find that even the brightest need the teacher's time and the slowest can't do anything much (Mrs Wilks).

. . . opportunities to effect more ideal patterns of teaching are limited by their counterpart and emergent problems of control. Emphasizing the instructional rather than the disciplinary functions of teaching, Buckby's comments severely underplay the significance of certain instructional techniques (such as addressing questions to pupils who have not volunteered an answer) as readily available, immediately functional, *controlling* strategies.

Mrs Preece's actions do however display characteristics frequently advocated in broader language teacher circles, the kind of quick fire question technique advocated, for example, by Varnava (1975, p. 26). With commendable idealism he argues:

> In oral work, correct responses can be transformed from one pupil to another, the same question put in turn to the weaker pupil and finally the whole class.

The occasion described in Table 8 displays greater involvement of pupils than in Mrs Wilks's lesson.

In Mrs Preece's lesson referred to in Table 8, there are 27 interactions with 14 pupils in the 17 minute question–answer sequence. The following 13 minutes were used for independent pupil work (from worksheets) and featured few pupil–teacher interactions. However, even a cursory glance at the pattern of interaction reveals that the lesson was no less problematic for the 'less able pupils'. The pace of the work was dominated by the teacher in oral interchange with abler pupils, a feature which would seem to be in apparent contradiction to this teacher's view that

Table 8 Distribution of Mrs Preece's talk during a 30 minute phase of the lesson proper with the pupils of Form 1s.

Pupils	Distribution of teacher talk during		Autumn term teacher ratings[a]
	Phase 1 (17 min)	Phase 2 (13 min)	
1	XXX		CB
2	XX(X)X		BA
3	XX!		BB
4	XXX		BB
5	XX		AA
6	XX		BB
7	X		DD
8	(X)XX	X	BB
9	XX		BB
10	X!		DD
11	X		CC
12	(X)	X	BB
13	X		BB
14	X		BB
15	!	!	CC
16			CC
17			CC
18		X	CC

X = public instructional talk; in this case a question/answer sequence between teacher and an individual pupil in which the latter gives a correct reply, or (X) an incorrect or no reply.

! = a public regulative interaction between the teacher and an individual pupil.

[a] Teacher ratings refer to a 5-point, A–E scale of 'effort' (left side letter) and 'attainment' used by teachers to assess pupils, in this case for Autumn term school reports.

the top pupils can't be catered for in modern languages mixed ability, you can't let them do it individually . . . they've got to know how to start.

The picture to emerge from our data is that of a curriculum and pedagogical mode of presentation which produces a steering group phenomenon. As the class progressed *en masse* at a pace defined by the teacher and/or abler children, many pupils (particularly Jerry, Rene, Ryan and Liona in Form 1p) found it difficult to enter into the learning process. Their problems were expressed in difficult behaviours, but these tended to be dealt with rather summarily. Consequently, in the teacher's view, they achieved negative identities as social types: they are 'unable to listen', 'can't listen and watch carefully', 'don't understand', 'doesn't try to remember', they are 'not attentive enough'. Deficiencies were imputed to the pupils themselves, or else located in previous school experience:

> the memory . . . it's of prime importance. It just isn't there . . . there's no drilling in primary schools, they emphasise understanding not drilling (Mrs Wilks).

Other teachers saw the problem in home background.

> It's that they all have problems, with families, all of them are such a problem.

A difficult home background, the failure of primary schools to provide a supportive pedagogical style, or simply deficiencies in the pupils themselves were interpreted as contingencies creating the inability to 'pay enough attention'. Quite clearly, the constructs/ criteria used to define pupils as social types do not transcend the social setting in which they are used. They take on their specific sense from the setting, the pedagogical mode of operation. Hence, whereas in individualized instruction the perceived deficiency is lack of 'independence', here it is 'recall', memory and attention.

Teachers, in the pupils' perspectives, were similarly defined. In their view it is teacher instructional inability:

> say you get stuck, she just carries on as if nothing happened, with what she was saying . . . It's hard when you have to do a test and say you weren't there last week, you don't know how to do it . . . you still have to do it (Ryan, Form 1p).

and

> they don't teach you in the first place . . . what's the point of teaching you if you don't know how to put it in a sentence . . . that's dull. They ask you the question . . . but they don't teach you the French (Jerry, Form 1p).

> Even though you're slow, the teachers should give you attention . . . to those he knows are not so good. If they think they can solve the problem . . . they should leave them (pupil 18, 1s).

> You know . . . when you're in the class . . . and then the teacher asks . . . you haven't been listening properly . . . and the teacher . . . asks you a question . . . and you take 30 seconds to answer and they start sniggering, and that makes you all tensed up more . . . so you don't really answer it . . . you say you don't know (pupil 16, Form 1s).

A moment of inattention, a missed lesson, or poor pacing of instruction within a cumulative subject content, clearly mean for some pupils that opportunities to achieve success are immediately frustrated.

It is perhaps for these reasons that French, of all subjects, was experienced as the least enjoyable, at least for the pupils of Form 1p. Only two of the pupils, Abdul and John (both of whom later found in the top set), found the subject enjoyable, whereas a third or more of the pupils express enjoyment of all other subjects.

Frame Factors, teaching process and pupil identity

The pattern of first year teaching in modern languages is perhaps now evident from the brief excerpts presented above. Class teaching tended to involve few pupils, and to create a spurious appearance that the class as a whole was successfully progressing through and comprehending subject content. In fact, the lessons tended to be characterized by 'copy cat' replies and conformity to teacher's rules of attention.

Many of the pupils were engaged in what Lundgren has elsewhere referred to as collective *piloting*, the 'strategy whereby a teacher avoids problems by simplifying them so that students are able to solve them by answering a simple chain of questions' [1977, p. 200]. It creates the illusion that learning is occurring. Collective piloting occurs when the teacher works in front of the whole class. For those pupils who lack the prerequisites necessary for learning in large groups, in limited time, collective teaching tends inevitably to become mere collective piloting. In these circumstances, some pupils learn only that they have received instruction but they still have not understood. They *meta-learn*, learn about their own 'learning', in this case about their ability to comprehend instruction in modern languages. As Ryan remarked:

> Sometimes she tells us something and we don't understand and we ask her . . . she doesn't tell us.

while Caroline found that

> She talks but doesn't take any notice of us.

As time went on, however, given the cumulative nature of the subject teaching, some pupils were unable to take part altogether. Teachers had to choose between recovering content which pupils failed to understand or to progress to new content. Discipline problems emerged as the process became more and more meaningless for some pupils. It is perhaps for this reason that Mrs Preece felt that not enough time was given to the able pupils and that setting was considered a necessary solution.

With reference to the analyses of language teaching it is now

Model 5:   *Frame factors and learning requirements.*

FRAME FACTORS

Requirements

(i)	Can the pupil handle content?	+	–
(ii)	Can the pupil handle the mode of transmission?	+	–
(iii)	Can the pupil work within the time made available?	+	–
(iv)	Can the pupil work within the form of teacher control (e.g. dependently or independently)?	+	–
(v)	Can the pupil endure routine and boredom?	+	–
(vi)	Does the pupil have a social milieu outside the school supportive of these characteristics?	+	–

Learning   Piloting

Meta-learning

---

possible to provide further specification to Model 1. In order to learn successfully in this context, pupils must be able to meet the requirements given by a complex interaction of frame factors (Model 5). They must be able to cope with a content which is often abstract and, as suggested earlier, culturally discontinuous or disruptive,[28] and too difficult (factor i). They meet this content in specific pedagogic modes (in this case whole class method, with strong emphasis on 'closed' question and answer) and time frames, experienced mainly as pacing. Moreover, to manage successfully the learning, they must willingly enter into the teachers frame of control, 'pay attention' to teacher talks, which is the primary mode of transmission (factors iv and ii). This willingness or ability may itself be related to previous school experience, and perhaps the social milieu outside the school, as well as immediate interpretations of the adequacy of subject content and teacher (factor vi). They must do all this within the limits of time imposed by teacher, or the pace as defined by able pupils (factor iii). Moreover, an inability to meet certain requirements, e.g. (i) and (ii), may of course contribute to a pupils willingness or otherwise to meet other requirements such as those of (iv). Those pupils least able to cope with these requirements were the greatest victims of routine and boredom (factor v).

Confronted with groups of increasingly 'difficult pupils' teachers tended to narrow rather than explore the range of curricular options to be offered:

> I don't do games with them because there's too much bother. They get out of hand. I doubt whether they'd be able to do that anyway (third year middle group teacher).

and (as stated earlier, p. 36)

If they weren't such a problem to control, then you teach them French through discussion and talk (third year middle group teacher).

Second level decisions about the selection of appropriate curriculum thus became inseparable from questions of and concerns for social control.

They all said they hated French. I said what would you like to do given that you have to do it till the end of the year? It's totally impossible to do language work with them so they just do background French . . . so does Mr . . . they write about French food, or they do crosswords. They know nothing, they can't say 'I am'. If they don't want to know, they'll just sit there (third year top middle teacher).

Only by invoking the kind of 'negotiation strategy' outlined by Woods (1977), 'if you play ball with me and I'll play ball with you', is the teacher able to survive in a context which neither party considers is particularly productive. The teacher offered, in exchange for good order, an escape from real work. 'Background French' provided an available and acceptable (having the appearance of doing French) means of social control.[29]

The fate of the pupils of Form 1p further evidences the relationship between frame factors (time, curriculum, control and transmission) and pupil identity. Eight pupils wound up in the bottom two of the five language sets. Amongst them were Jerry, Ryan, Rene and Liona. These pupils were defined by Mrs Wilks in conversation, and formal ratings (confirmed in the cases where we have NFER test scores) as amongst the least able and most 'difficult' children in the class. Paul, Caroline and Odette were defined as 'not very able but about average for Sageton'. Together these pupils seem effectively to fall outside the curriculum, content and pedagogical mode of transmission. Their needs could not be met in the available time. Judging by later teacher ratings of ability and effort and research observation, the policy of setting did not significantly alter their initial identity created in the mixed ability classroom. Set 3 contained Peter and David, also perceived as 'average' pupils by Mrs Wilks, but somewhat less difficult than Jerry, Ryan, Rene and Liona; Set 2 contained Hugh, Heather, Mary, Maureen and Lynne. For the last two pupils this was a significant improvement in their position as defined in Maths, Science and English. This could be explained with reference to the mode of transmission, whole class method, which for Maureen was far less problematic, given her reading age of eight years nine months, than that of other subjects. This, along with her obvious level of interest in and commitment to the subject, meant she was able to sustain the attention required by the teaching method. Lynne's success can also be attributed to the frame of teacher control which characterized and underpinned class teaching. Against a background of 'strict' control far fewer opportunities arose for peer group interest activity than in group based or individualized instruction. The boundaries between work and 'interest' were rigidly defined. This seemed to curb Lynne's outside interests which she carried into other subjects (often in interaction with Heather). This would also partly explain the success of John and his allocation to Set 1: control was imposed on his peer group activity with Hugh and Paul. He, along with Hugh and Mary (a quite difficult but 'able' girl in the eyes of many teachers), were more positively appraised behaviourally in French than in other subjects where they were generally considered as 'able' but 'underachieving' pupils.

Given a well-defined frame of teacher authority and the levels of attention required by the mode of transmission, we could expect success for Mark, Naren, Abdul, Michael and Jenny. These pupils generally portrayed to the researcher and the teacher all the attributes of what we called 'total workers'. They usually appeared completely committed to the task in hand and rarely displayed anything like 'difficult' or uninterested behaviours. Their attributes were thoroughly congenial to whole class method. It is hardly surprising, therefore, that they were all, except Naren, placed in the top two sets. Abdul was the most successful and was placed in Set 1.

Abdul's success, along with Maureen's, lends support to the view sometimes expressed, that Modern Languages provide the non-reader, or in this case the poor reader, a means in oral work of participating 'unhampered in their involvement and progress' (Varnava, 1975, p. 28). The 'success' of Maureen, with an NFER score of E also lends caution to the view that it is 'undesirable to teach languages to the slow learner'.[30] However, the continued failure of other pupils with similar reading ages in the same class (Jerry, Ryan, Rene and Liona) stresses that success in modern languages is also related to the effective interactional skills, especially 'attention'. This being the case, the position of Naren, placed in the bottom set 5, is of some interest. This pupil's opportunities to succeed in languages were structured by the cumulative nature of the content, and by school policy on remedial withdrawal (whereby some pupils were extracted from their mainstream lessons, by the Remedial Department, for 'special English' lessons), which for Naren occurred during some language lessons. Even though, when present, he displayed behaviours appropriate to the context, his learning problems became increasingly acute as the term progressed and remained so after setting had occurred:

I can't go up to the top group. On Fridays I go to special English. That's why I'm in the bottom group. I'm trying hard to get in the middle group.

Failure to achieve the success he desired was imputed to teacher-instructional deficiencies:

> She doesn't start straight away. If the class before was dirty, it takes five minutes to clear and we have to wait. That's no good, we are wasting time and missing out on the lesson and we don't understand. We're still in the bottom group. I don't like that.

These comments reach out to a wider school context and to a policy of remedial education over which neither he nor the teacher had any control.

Setting offered some teachers relief from their problems of instruction and control. The 'successful' pupil, 'predisposed' by behavioural characteristics and 'ability', made the whole class mode of teaching less problematic with top sets. Mrs Preece's comments suggest that

> It's marvellous . . . now they really are being stretched . . . I'd put them in for 'A' level tomorrow . . . setting . . . it's excellent. I'd do it earlier . . . but you need some time to see what they're like . . . you can't go to Junior School reports.

For the most part, however, teachers of middle sets experienced (and were observed to experience) considerable teaching problems:

> It's assimilation, they can do exercises and retain it, but the middle groups can't retain . . . there's no serious attitude. The top group will take work home, the middle group can't do that. There's a responsible attitude in the top group, they'll worry about learning. The middle group are very slow, they can't remember, they are careless (teacher of middle group).

Setting provided a means by which the department could respond to experienced pressure for success. In middle and lower groups, teaching merely acted as a further upward 'sieve' to pupils able/willing to display appropriate predispositions, behaviours and 'abilities'. Teaching continued to display all the features already described and so was generally conducted between teacher and a small number of able/willing pupils. Without significant changes in curriculum or pedagogy the majority of pupils continued to experience limited learning opportunities, and the teachers continued to experience problems of control. Significantly, however, small-scale departmental experiments with new curriculum options for third year bottom groups subsequently led to marked change in opinion about the nature of pupil ability.

> They aren't really a slow group, it's just that something's gone wrong somewhere that's put them off, they don't want to work. But the other slow group . . . in the third year I share with Mr Selwyn are doing work

from this new York Examination. They are working . . . they can see a point to it . . . this other group could have done just as well (Mrs Preece).

Model 5 implies that the process of identity construction has a dynamic and transient quality. Changes in curriculum and pedagogical frames such as the third year experiment signify concomitant changes in prerequisite 'abilities', hence varying opportunities for pupils and teachers to construct and reconstruct their identities. As we have seen, however, such opportunities were rare in the Modern Languages teaching practised during this period at Sageton.

four

Mathematics:
Individualized Curriculum

The response of the Mathematics Department to mixed grouping provided a stark contrast to that of Modern Languages. Recent research on mixed ability grouping (Ball, 1981; Reid *et al.*, 1981) has suggested that Mathematics teachers, like Modern Languages teachers, express a reluctance for mixed ability teaching on the grounds that Mathematics has a 'logical (knowledge) structure through which pupils must proceed in a pre-scribed way' (Reid *et al.*, 1981, p. 130). At Beachside, Mathematics teachers felt that the 'deep structure' of their subjects made it very difficult or impossible to teach the subject to mixed ability groups without a radical reduction in the level of academic work normally expected of the brighter pupil (Ball, 1981, p. 179). At Sageton, however, as we see below, a similar conception of mathematical content or knowledge held by the Head of Department, forms the basis for quite a contrary view:

> Non streaming is a word I would use. Any group in Maths is a mixed ability group and has to be treated as such. I'd rather attempt not to group in any way.

For this reason individualized schemes were seen as a wholly appropriate method, irrespective of grouping. This points up the need for caution in making any straightforward analytical derivation of pedagogical practice from expressed ideologies or subcultural views (see also Bailey and Bridges, 1983, p. 50). However, as we will see, factors other than the Departmental Head's view on the nature of mathematical knowledge underpinned the choice and adoption of an individualized scheme.

Departmental Background

Mr Phillips (Head of Department at the time of the study) was appointed Head of Maths in 1969, two years prior to the school becoming comprehensive. He found

> a syllabus that didn't come to anything: it was not imaginative, arithmetical, using various sets of books. Pupils were streamed.

In order to modernize existing practice he adopted a new scheme. Three years after comprehensive reorganization, with the introduction of mixed ability grouping, the syllabus was again changed, this time to SMP (the School Mathematics Project). This decision arose from a complex of factors. While Mr Phillips was sympathetic to planned mixed ability teaching he was not supportive of the change to mixed ability grouping as proposed by the Academic Board:

> I resisted it, we weren't prepared . . . I abstained on the vote, the whole department had just left the previous summer.

The last comment reaches out to wider LEA and national decisions on resources and staffing, particularly in what would now be called 'inner-city' schools. Not only was 1974 the year of mixed-ability change, it was also the immediate pre-Houghton period.[1] So

> In the summer of 1974, I spent time looking through SMP . . . staff were employed during the summer; I was only one short. I presented them with a complete system.

SMP had several advantages. It seemed suitable for a range of abilities both in terms of content and mode of presentation, and so it seemed to deal with the 'mixed ability problem'. Because it provided a pedagogy and a content which was predefined for teachers, it also effected greater control over teachers. It was an attempt, in the face of severe teacher shortage (partly the result of badly planned LEA changes), to establish order and continuity of teaching method and content.

> I never liked the (old) books. It left too much to the teacher . . . There was a great deal of tension because of staff problems – problems because staff were given the choice to come here or some other school. Many of the staff only had junior school experience (Mr Phillips).

At the same time, however, Mr Phillips recognized the discrepancy between the content and organizational style of the workcards and the teachers' perspectives and abilities.

> One of the problems is . . . you need to be more highly specialised to get the best from the situation. It needs taught organisational skills which many teachers don't have.

And again

> their knowledge of maths is how they've been taught in school. They
> have fixed ideologies about how maths should be, which contrasts the
> maths we have. There's conceptual barriers to break down. They saw
> silent pupils, the blackboard and class teaching.

At the time of study the Maths Department consisted of nine
teaching staff, with another four teachers 'helping out' in the subject
for a few lessons a week. In one sense, then, the introduction of the
workcard scheme clearly represented a planned means of *control* over
these teachers.

Obviously, this did arise partly from the limits of teacher supply,
and from the difficulties involved in mounting qualitatively effective
short-run responses to changed circumstances. Nevertheless, it also
offers some surface support for the views of Apple (1980) and Buswell
(1980), for example, who suggest that such curricular packages echo
late corporate capitalist modes of production, represent aspects of 'de-
skilling', and contain new forms of control over both teachers and
pupils (Buswell, 1980, p. 294). The evidence which follows will
indicate (particularly with reference to SMP maths and Integrated
Studies) that teachers are to some extent 'de-skilled' in relation to
their previous command of whole class teaching expertise. It also adds
weight to the notion that a good deal of curricular and pedagogical
change in the last four decades has been orientated towards making
classroom practices more 'teacher proof' and hence, in part, more
'controlled'. However, we will also suggest that the 'new' modes of
presentation in Maths and other subject areas require far more of
teachers than simply the acquisition of new skills of management and
control. We will also, at least tacitly, |expose the romanticism of the
view (cf Apple 1980) that teachers had significant craft skill to be
robbed of in the first place, and perhaps emphasize that much of the
de-skilling thesis is unsatisfactory, because it lacks analyses of the
mechanisms by which wider (extra-school) social and economic
changes are translated into pressures and practices within schools.

The SMP Scheme

In 1974 the Mathematics Department adopted the SMP workcard[2]
scheme for use in years 1–3. The scheme had two main sections, each
corresponding to a year's work for a pupil going on to do 'O' level.
Immediately, it *implied* a particular pacing of work if the scheme is to
be completed. Nevertheless, the scheme could be used for three rather
than two years for the remainder of pupils who also fall in the top 80–
85% of the ability range. Pupils in the bottom 15% of the range would
find difficulties with completing the scheme at all.

A pupil could enter a section of any of ten topic points. There were 28 topics in both sections so the range of starting points was comparatively broad. Most of the topics were subdivided into units which offered material at different levels of competence/ability. The first section contained 38 such units with five possible levels of difficulty, the second 46 with six levels. There was some overlapping of levels between sections 1 and 2. The schem, however, combined choice of topic, discreteness from other topics, and an inbuilt hierarchy of difficulty. It represented therefore, a considerable restructuring of the straightforward linear and sequential view of mathematical curricula. A first year pupil could, for example, do all ten starting points in turn as none assumed a lead onto another. Additionally there were preliminary materials (mainly arithmetical) to section 1 and supplements to both 1 and 2. The individualized character of the scheme lay in the fact that each pupil worked on a separate set of cards on a unit not necessarily being done by any other pupil. Within the broader time assumptions built into it, the scheme was self-pacing. The content of the cards was not geared to the specific needs or interests of any particular pupil or group as might occur with more individuated work prepared, more often than not, by Sageton teachers themselves. The decision to use this scheme has to be a departmental one because of the resources involved. Individual teachers can deviate,[3] say, from the normal pedagogic assumption entailed in the card format by sticking to elements of whole class method, or from its content by the use of 'private' materials, though this, on our evidence, tended to require some seniority as the basis on which to evade the departmental policy.

Providing teachers with a predefined curriculum content *and* the mode of its transmission, the scheme imposed strong constraints on the teacher's pedagogical role. Each unit on the scheme contained different numbers of individual cards. Some of these may be marked with an asterisk, signifying the need to have work looked over. Each unit also contained a checkcard for the pupil's own self-monitoring, and a test-card, the results of which have to be marked by the teacher. The teacher therefore must direct and re-direct each individual pupil's work demands. The monitoring built into the system created recurring work demands from the whole range of pupils. As stated in the SMP's (1973)[4] *Teachers Notes* 'the teacher sees children often but briefly'. In whole class presentation a teacher need not question or talk to all pupils, nor do pupils have to answer teacher's questions, because answers are frequently volunteered by others. In SMP, however, if a pupil *did not* contact a teacher at least occasionally this was a positive sign of non-work. Furthermore, as the expectation that pupil will contact the teacher is built into the scheme, different ranges of pupil (in terms of work or ability) could create very different demands on how the teacher allocated time between them.

Changes occured too in the social and disciplinary relationships of teacher and pupils. The traditional social relationships of teacher to the whole class as a social unit were broken up. The teacher's role became more differentiated. The curriculum content of the scheme required the provision of different types of paper and equipment which had to be administered by the teacher at least minimally by making sure that there were adequate supplies. Removed from the front of class position so characteristic of whole class method, teachers could feel that they have ceased to 'teach' and become managers instead. Statements to the whole class tended to retain only their disciplinary character. Didactic pedagogical talk moved from the *public arena* into the *immediate*[5] one-to-one situation.

The scheme was designed for pupils to work singly or in groups and the variety of cards and ancillary equipment generated talk about who has got what. Further discussion may or may not be encouraged by the teacher depending on their point of view. In the teachers' perspective a distinction must often be made between conversation about work and 'interest' talk. Interest behaviour[6] is common to all classrooms, but in certain classroom organizations (e.g. in open classrooms) such behaviours can become increasingly problematic for teachers (see Kohl, 1970; Denscombe, 1980b). Its increasing incidence and apparency has implications for the construction of teacher competence, and thus identity. Individualized schemes such as SMP, where pupils sit in pairs, singly or in groups, builds in self-pacing by the pupil. A pupil's level of involvement, attitude, motivation and ability to work independently of teacher attention now become surface features of classroom life and thus more crucial to classroom management. The degree of legitimacy pupils afford to teacher's attempts to define their interest-behaviour reveals features of classroom life which can be overriden in whole class presentation. As teacher talk ceases to be mainly to the whole class, so the surface content of teacher talk is more clearly separated to the opposite ends of the control–content spectrum. The difference between public and immediate talk therefore tends to overlap with the separation between pupil interest and work activity which is also promoted in individualized instruction. Public talk becomes largely regulative and immediate talk, instructional. A change in the mode of transmission from whole class to individualized, thus shifts the balance between key features of the classroom. Peer group friendships (cf. Walker and Adelman, 1976), the relationships between pupils, and reading abilities (cf. Edwards and Furlong, 1978), which in whole class curriculum stand on the edge of the teacher's awareness, now become central.

Teacher Strategies in Individualized Curriculum

Mathematics teachers at Sageton themselves focused on problems of pupil control as their major concern.[7] Only one of the teachers observed found the new scheme problematical, and he did not use the scheme as the Head of Department recommended. He preferred to adopt whole class teaching and when using SMP included 'opening' and 'ending' phases of tables to 'cover basics'. This teacher was also a senior member of the pastoral staff and so could 'resist' the scheme. He noted of (SMP):

> It doesn't allow the teacher to have the appearance of authority. A lot of movement, a lot of chatting.

The remaining teachers, while sometimes critical of various aspects of SMP content and method and/or mixed ability grouping, endeavoured to follow the modes of working into which Mr Phillips, by co-teaching, socialized them. The order imposed by the scheme and the power vested in the position of Head of Department served to contain but not suppress intradepartmental opposition. This, in turn, led to teacher emphasis on establishing procedural competence among first year pupils, as can be seen from Table 9.

Again we would stress that each count from which these percentages were constructed refers to a complete interaction as judged by the fieldworker and not to a speech utterance of a specifiable length. Each is a categorization of a piece of teacher action which potentially carries

Table 9 Contrasts in the talk of five Mathematics teachers over seven periods of 40 minutes excluding beginnings and endings)

Teacher/class		First year class		Second/third year classes	
		Public regulative	Immediate instructional	Public regulative	Immediate instructional
Mr Phillips 1s	(R)	15	44		
Ms Tripp 1p, 3p	(R)	19	42	5	40 (3)
Mr Rees 1q, 2q	(R)	22	43	7	41 (2)
Mr Kelly 2r	(D)			6	18 (2)
Mr Burrell 3s	(R/D)			6	38 (3)
Totals		56	129	24	137

(R), going round the room – 'doing the rounds'; (D), at the desk; (2), second year class; (3), third year class.

a number of messages. We were concerned primarily, but not solely, with the disciplinary (regulative) and instructional message issued by teachers, distributed and received amongst pupils. In individualized instruction with worksheets mediating between the teacher and pupil, the centralization of talk is rare and tends to be required during the brief 'opening' or 'closing' phases of the lesson. In the main body of the lesson proper teachers tend to interact at an immediate and private level, interspersed by public regulative messages. Individual help, with the teacher talking to a pupil at the desk or moving round to lean over the pupil's desk, becomes typical. The normal practice in Sageton Maths lessons with first year pupils was for teachers to move around the room. The differences between teachers, recorded in Table 9, represent different strategies for achieving order. Mr Kelly saw individual pupils at his desk and, along with Mr Burrell, preferred this position because it provided a vantage point from which to oversee pupil behaviour and symbolically announced teacher status. These strategies reflected concerns for control contingent upon the individualized scheme. As Mr Kelly put it:

> you can't get the class together over three years. First three years don't allow the teacher to establish himself. It's very chatty in the first three years and remains like that in 4th and 5th years.

The major differences revealed in Table 9 in the amount of public regulation received by older and younger pupils inverts the expectation that older pupils would receive more regulation for their greater indiscipline.[8] Overall some 30% of teacher talk in the first year is public and regulative. However, this amount is halved in succeeding years. Only Mr Kelly, teaching from his desk, in the second year registers the high level (25%).

The teachers concerned explained this in terms of pupil ill-preparedness for work with the SMP package. Ms Tripp, for example, felt that

> Pupils are used to more formal environments. The cards allow for so much more noise and movement, they've been spoon fed, they are too insecure to get on on their own. They need constant supervision. They need security of knowing that their work is correct

while Mr Rees located pupils' inability to work with the cards to home background:

> When I started here I was amazed at the standard of ability. Everybody is so slow. I don't really know why. They've got problems at home, that is the main problem. Those that turn up on Open Day are those on box 2. A lot of pupils tell their parents they don't get homework, they get the wrong idea.

A difficult home background, the failure of parents to support and hence motivate their children (exacerbated by the pupils' own misrepresentations) were interpreted as contingencies creating the inability to 'concentrate for more than a few minutes'. Teachers, then, especially in the first year, constantly encouraged pupils to have that autonomy which they hoped would reduce the demands made on their own time and presence in the classroom, to be 'a bit more self reliant. It's not the primary school now. There's no need to ask me every time you do a question . . .' (Mr Phillips).[9] Or, 'think when you put up your hands. Do you really need the question answered?' (Ms Tripp). As the term progressed, however, such exhortations were transformed from the public arena to the immediate level.

Mr Phillips	Well how do you do these questions?
Pupil	I don't know.
Mr Phillips	Well you try and look through the pack and I'm sure you'll find how to do it then.

The emphasis on public communication in the first year at Sageton was, then, the product of teachers identifying pupils as ill-prepared to work in the pattern required by the scheme. The higher incidence of public regulative talk can be explained by reference to the perceived disjuncture between pupil behaviours and the conception of pupil learning embodied in the scheme. Teaching procedures before content was the teachers' foremost aim.

Individualized Instruction and the Construction of Pupil Identities

Table 10 indicates how teacher talk (in this case Ms Tripp) tends to be 'determined' by the timetable, mediated by the syllabus structure and differently distributed amongst pupils. In Form 1p, in the lesson described in Table 9, for example, John, Mary, Hugh and Heather (who we refer to as 'group' 2) and Jerry, Ryan, Rene and Liona ('group' 3) receive more public regulative talk than Mary, Naren, Abdul, Michael, Jenny ('group' 1) and Maureen, Lynne, Caroline, Odette, Peter, Paul and David ('group' 4), and also slightly more of the immediate instructional contacts with the teacher. We elaborate below on the nature of such 'groups'.

The 'groups' referred to in Table 10 are the fieldworker's constructions. Our interest in the steering group predisposed us to focus on how teachers distribute their attention across the ability range in mixed ability classrooms. Our first dimension, then, is the mix of ability as given on pupil records, by teacher ratings and standardized tests.

Table 10 Ms Tripp's talk in one 40 minute period

Group	Public regulative	Immediate instructional	Total
(a) *as percentage of teacher talk across four groups*			
1 (5 pupils)	5	24	18
2 (4 pupils)	32	21	25
3 (4 pupils)	37	26	30
4 (7 pupils)	26	29	28
	100	100	100
(b) *as average per pupil in each group*			
1	0.2	2.0	2.2
2	1.4	2.3	3.7
3	1.8	2.8	4.5
4	0.7	1.7	2.4

The second is how the fieldworker perceived the pupils' involvement in work or interest activity. And the third is the element of teacher interaction indicated by the fieldwork notes on what, and with whom, teachers talked. Figure 1 sets out a simplified form of the first two dimensions. It is clear that interest and work activity on the part of pupils is *not* reducible to differences in ability. Table 11 contains details of each individual pupil arranged within these groups.

Group 1 refers to a small group of five pupils, Mark, Naren, Abdul, Michael and Jenny, who, as we mentioned in the previous chapter, were characterized by their commitment to work, their ability and willingness to portray behaviours appropriate to the context defined by the scheme and teacher. This was reflected in the almost total

Figure 1 *Distributiuon of pupils by work and ability in Form 1p.*

```
                          More able
                             │
        GP1      (5)         │        GP2      (4)
     (Mark, Naren, Abdul,    │     (John, Mary, Hugh
      Michael and Jenny)     │      and Heather)
Work ─────────────────────────────────────────────── Interest
        GP4      (7)         │        GP3      (4)
     (Maureen, Lynne,        │     (Jerry, Ryan, Rene
      Caroline, Odette,      │      and Liona)
      Peter, Paul and        │
      David)                 │
                             │
                          Less able
```

Table 11: The composition of Form 1p (first year case study group) by work and ability

Pupil	Sex	Ethnicity	Teacher assessment effort–attainment[a]	NFER AH2/3 total	Reading age[b]
Group 1: able and independent					
Mark	B	WI/British	AA	A	12.0
Naren	B	Asian	BB	C	9.4
Abdul	B	Asian	BB	C	8.9
Michael	B	WI/British	BB	—	11.10
Jenny	G	British	BB	C	12.10
Group 2: 'able' but 'underachieving'					
John	B	British	CB	C	Above top
Mary	G	Wi	CB	E	11.4
Hugh	B	European	CB	C	10.10
Heather	G	British	B/CB	C	9.11
Group 3: less able/unwilling workers					
Jerry	B	WI	CC	—	7.11
Ryan	B	WI	CD	—	8.7
Rene	B	WI	CC	D	8.2
Liona	G	WI	CD	D	8.2
Group 4: 'normal', 'average' Sageton pupil					
Peter	B	WI	CC	C	Above top
David	B	British	BC	—	—
Paul	B	British	BC	C	10.3
Caroline	G	WI	CC	—	8.7
Odette	G	WI	CC	D	9.0
Maureen	G	WI	BD	E	9.11
Lynne	G	British	CC	—	10.5

[a] Teacher assessment: Autumn term school reports.
[b] Reading age: as determined by Schonell, R.3A Silent Reading Tests, administered by the school on entry.

absence of public regulative messages addressed to them. Mark, Naren, Abdul and Michael usually sat in close proximity to one another and their friendship spilled over into their playground activities. Jenny was much more of a 'loner' in the class though was sometimes found with Lynne or Heather. The comments of these pupils sum up the group's attitudes towards Ms Tripp, Mathematics and indeed their approach to schooling more generally.

> She knows that all four of us are really good children. We never muck about in her lesson. We always work as hard as we can (Mark).
>
> Yeah . . . and she gives us individual attention, . . . she knows that everybody else likes mucking about but she knows that us, right, will work, we're especially good because . . . um . . . from the start she knew that from the day we started we were really quiet and got on with our work . . . next time we were quiet again but others were really noisy . . . so she got to know we were going to be good (Naren).

In marked contrast are the pupils of group 3 (Jerry, Ryan, Rene and Liona) and group 2 (John, Mary, Hugh and Heather), whose behaviours were extremely problematic as the teacher endeavoured to maintain an appearance of classroom order and productivity. Between them they accounted for 69% of all public regulative messages. Between the excellence of the 'total worker' and the indifference ('interest') of groups 2 and 3 fell the behaviours of group 4. Less committed and difficult than either the pupils of groups 1 or 2 and 3, respectively, they achieved identities more anonymous (in the perspective of researcher and teacher) than those groups. They tended to be described by Ms Tripp as pupils 'normal' for Sageton, average in behaviour and attainment, and included Maureen and Lynne who achieved a far less favourable identity than was the case in Modern Language teaching.

The grouping described, however, belies any straightforward polarization of identity according to a behavioural/academic dichotomy. Pupils of group 1 were rated by the teacher assessments (and on NFER AH2/3) as amongst the most able in the class. They were able and willing to portray behaviours which facilitated the realization of their potential despite real difficulties that some (e.g. Naren and Abdul) might experience with the mode of transmission because of its demands on levels of literacy which, in respect of their reading age, were amongst the lowest in the class. Group 2, however, were similarly described by the teacher as 'able' pupils but were likely to be under-achieving on account of their perceived unwillingness to meet the behavioural requirements of the scheme. They were perceived far less favourably in Mathematics than in Modern Language teaching. Nevertheless, given their 'ability' and behaviour, such pupils were able to skilfully maintain 'successful' pupil identities in the perspectives of both teachers and their peers.[10]

John, for example, was considered by the teacher to be 'so lazy and difficult but could be very able'. He also enjoyed a close peer group friendship with Hugh, David and Paul and was often perceived as the catalyst in their 'interest' activity. Mary could sometimes be found with Liona, on other occasions with Caroline, Odette or Maureen. Behaviour and ethnicity appeared to form the bond between these pupils.

Group 3's observed pattern of work was a direct contrast to that of group 1. Whereas the former tended to work and see themselves as working solidly, the interest behaviour of the pupils of group 3 (the boys of which were often found sitting together, occasionally being joined by Peter) called for the highest proportion of both public and immediate teacher talk. In contrast to group 2, such pupils were defined as less able rather than unwilling to work independently. Consequently their progress was seen as dependent on teacher intervention.

Group 3, we suggest, is of some considerable interest. We suggest they constitute a 'counter-steering group', a group of pupils who because of their behaviour re-orientate the teacher's time and attention to themselves, the less able pupils in the class. This 'group' emerges as the teacher's problems of control, and in this context the pupils' learning difficulties tend to become surface features of interactions (see Edwards and Furlong, 1978, p. 133).

A crucial factor in this process is the time frame of SMP in which, for an individual, there is no specified lesson time by which the task must be completed. The constraints for teachers and pupils of finishing a topic within the lesson or the week are thus removed and transposed to the two or three years the department allocated for this form of curriculum material. In marked contrast to whole class method, (cf. Chapter 3 and Lundgren, 1977) with teaching governed by a tightly structured pacing of the syllabus, less able pupils are thus never removed from their learning problems with a particular topic. They never have the luxury of being removed from at least the surface features (in terms of a particular topic) of their learning problems as the class moves, *en masse*, to the next unit of curriculum. Pupil progress thus becomes more dependent upon an intervention by the teacher at the point at which the learning problem is experienced. In such circumstances, the learning problems of pupils who would under conditions of whole class teaching fall beneath the steering group and who would have missed out on learning, become more apparent to the teacher. Unable to progress without teacher help (perhaps constrained by content or, in respect of reading abilities, the written mode of presentation), their learning problems are increasingly expressed in 'active' forms of behaviour, to the extent that teachers are unable to meet (here, supplement worksheet instruction) their learning require-ments. In general, this behaviour then results in immediate instructional contacts rather than in the public regulative messages evinced in whole class method.

Ms Tripp with Form 1p was faced by these same constraints and limitations. She was relatively new to SMP but committed to the scheme, though with reservations. She found her actions bounded, in particular, by this group of pupils.

> SMP is supposed to be for mixed ability groups but there's about six pupils who are really weak. I can't get to them because it takes about 10–15 minutes each time. There's Liona demanding attention. I have to deal with her and I have to keep discipline.

We see, then, that despite individualization, there was a group of pupils towards the bottom end of a standardized ability range who thereby fall outside the curriculum content of SMP and whose needs cannot be met in the available time. Four of the six pupils referred to were pupils in the counter-steering group (the other two are Odette and Maureen). Their distinguishing feature was their tendency, unlike the other two pupils, to express their learning problems in active forms of behaviour. In turn these pupils rated themselves as below average in interest in the subject, in behaviour, work and ability. The teacher's and pupils' perception overlapped (though not totally) with each other and those of the researcher.

Piloting in Individualized Instruction

As mentioned earlier, the behaviour of the pupils of group 3 (counter-steering group) called for the highest proportion of both public and immediate teacher talk. Although the differences between groups in the amount of immediate talk received was only slight we are suggesting that even *comparability* is significant. That these less able pupils received as much (and more) of the teacher's attention as an 'able' child, constituted a significant re-focusing of teacher attentions when considered against the whole class method. A cursory glance inside individualized classrooms would then suggest that the 'less able' pupil is considerably advantaged in individualized mixed ability teaching. The pupils themselves, however, have a different view and they did not consider they received sufficient attention.

> Teacher should stay with you longer and explain things to you (Jerry).
>
> She doesn't help you enough when you can't do it (Liona).

In this respect it is clearly necessary to consider the duration as well as the incidence of interactions. A characteristic feature of immediate talk is its brevity (the great majority of events falling between 30–90 seconds duration). Indeed given the brevity of interactions and level of pupil ability, we would suggest that such pupils are involved in a process of individual piloting and meta-learning, i.e. they learn that they have received instruction but that they have still not understood, a process reflected in, and intrinsic to, their identity construction.

Jerry, for example, remarks of SMP,

> It's OK on the packs, but most of the time you forget afterwards . . . unless I get revision I can't remember what's been said.

and Peter, who gets far less immediate instructional contact than pupils of group 3, states

> she says she'll come back later but you don't get help . . . then once you do it you just forget.

The following sequences of pupil–teacher interaction are, we would argue, suggestive examples of the teacher strategy of individual piloting. They are presented somewhat tentatively because of the difficulties of generating data on teacher–pupil talk without recourse to techniques more sophisticated (and intrusive) than the paper and pencil method we adopted.

The first of these sequences of interaction involves a form of teacher talk to which we have already referred. It involves the teacher, in this case Mr Phillips, urging, reminding, restating the procedural rules for learning within an individualized scheme.

> Well if you try and look through the pack, always look back over the pack and I'm sure you'll find out how to do them.

This form of talk is a characteristic feature of individualized instruction (cf. Edwards and Furlong, 1978), at Sageton and elsewhere. As Stephens (1977, p. 3) remarks, 'all too frequently I have found myself reminding, urging or even directing children to read instructions carefully or to go back and read what the card says'. Whether this form of instruction is experienced as piloting, or a necessary prerequisite to learning in individualized instruction, will depend on the predispositions of the pupils concerned. As Stephens (1977, p. 3) goes on to say, 'but directing a child in this way is not encouraging him. Directing a child to read printed explanations and key statements may make the child appear to do just that. However it cannot make the child pay real attention to them'. Such statements assume that the pupil is predisposed with abilities sufficient to 'manage' the work sheet, e.g. levels of literacy, and the ability to work independently.

In the second example, Liona, a member of the counter-steering group, is working on the unit 'Shapes' and would appear to be completely stuck with the question 'A square is a special rectangle, what is special about it?' She attempted, briefly, to look through previous cards to see if some solution to her problem could be found. Failing this she put up her hand and waited for the teacher, her behaviour gradually becoming more pronounced, seemingly to emphasize her predicament. Ms Tripp arrived and took up a position over Liona's desk, examined her work and began:

Ms Tripp	OK . . . what's special about a square . . . that makes it different from that rectangle?
Liona	[glares at John and David who are not working] . . . It's got four sides!
Ms Tripp	. . . a rectangle is something like this . . . [points to a diagram] . . . but draw me a square.
Liona	[makes no attempt to start]
Ms Tripp	What would you do to make that a square?
Liona	[no response]
Ms Tripp	[now draws two lines on squared paper] . . . How many squares would the other lines have to cover?
Liona	[no response]
Ms Tripp	They'd be the same length. All sides are the same length . . . look back through the cards to see if you can find out . . . [departs to deal with John and David]

In this interaction, it is doubtful whether either party's understanding had been greatly furthered. The content of communication involved no real dialogue about what Liona was doing, had done, or any search for what kind of problem she was experiencing with the question. The teacher offered clues to imply and cajole without at first providing direct specification of what it is that defines a 'square'. But these were not grasped by the pupil who simply waited for further elaboration. Ultimately, in apparent contradiction to the investigatory ideals of the scheme but in recognition of demands (emergent, difficult 'interest' behaviours) elsewhere, the teacher simply had to resort, in the time available, to supplying an answer. The teacher had now 'solved' Liona's problem and she had learnt that she could progress with a task which was not really understood. Additionally, a significant pupil coping strategy has been learnt; that problems persist for only as long as s/he fails to secure teacher intervention. The implication for a teacher's classroom management are fairly obvious. As Lundgren (1977, p. 227) has pointed out, whilst this process may allow a pupil to progress initially, with the appearance that an effective instruction has accrued, in the long run, as pupils get further into material, given the cumulative nature of the subject content, this process is likely to become 'more and more meaningless for some students'. The realization may emerge for some pupils, that while they are receiving instructions from the teacher they are not learning. They meta-learn only that they have serious difficulties with learning within the existing context. As one pupil remarked, drawing comparison between his experience of classroom SMP, and that of small group remedial withdrawal within the Maths Department, 'In ordinary class . . . you think you can get on, but you can't (Jerry).

In the third example, Jerry is working on a pack from the topic 'Area'; Ms Tripp approaches, and instructs 'you see you have to measure the area of that shape . . . you've got to have a square the same shape . . .'

Jerry   [politely nods as if following the instruction]

Ms Tripp   You haven't measured this area . . . look you have to cover the shape with the squared paper . . . you cut out . . . mmm . . . Unless you haven't done it properly? . . . then count the number of squares in the shape . . . [departs to deal with the equipment]

Again this pupil was learning not about his problem with content but that his access to learning in SMP was limited by the demands made upon the teacher. He knew that he had received attention and that instruction was provided, but was left none the wiser as to how to solve his problem. He had, however, evolved his own coping strategy. As soon as the teacher departed, he left his seat and took his exercise book to Mark, a quiet 'total' worker, rated by the pupils as 'the cleverest' in the class. Standing alongside him, he politely waited for him to finish what he was doing then offered him his exercise book and workcard and asked for assistance. Delighted with this request, Mark took the book and quickly 'did' the offending task. Jerry received back the work, returned to his desk satisfied that his problem had now been solved.

It is to be stressed that we are *not* presenting the above exploits as examples of bad teaching. They are meant only to illustrate how, within a complex of interacting and limiting frames (of pupil identity, content, time, etc.), the tendency to teach and be taught in this way is immanent in the individualized mode.

You see I simply haven't got the time to give pupils the help they require. It's so much easier to say get on with so and so or give a brief explanation. I'd like to sit down and spend all day with some pupils but you can't. Sharon (class 1q) she had forgotten that along the straight line the 'angle' is 180°. It was all covered on the previous card but she must have just skipped over it. All my dealings with her were attempts to get her started. In the end I just told her she had to subtract from 180° (Mr Rees).

We see then that the language used by the teacher is not unlike that typically found in whole class teaching. It is

created by the conditions of teaching, and the functions of language fulfil the demands of this process. If the frames are constraining and the curriculum too demanding, it is clear that the nature of the language used will be such that the process can proceed with a minimum amount of disturbance. This type of language with its close emphasis on special terminology and procedure avoids the risk of problems arising and having to be faced, as there is not enough time to correct all gaps in the learning process (Lundgren, 1977, p. 226).

The following consequence emerges for pupil identity construction: because the language of teaching tends to be 'steered' by the context (the demands of the curriculum and the limits of time) rather than by pupil 'needs', initial individual differences among the pupils tend to be preserved and increased.

Evidently, not all pupils will experience this form of talk as piloting and will learn within the process, but they must have characteristics, attributes or 'abilities' which enable them to decide and fill in, with a knowledge derived from previous experience outside of the work pack itself, the instructional brief provided by the teacher. Pupils of the counter-steering group unable to do this are found by the teacher to be 'lacking in concentration . . . they're so easily disturbed'. The pupils in turn expect a teacher to impose concentration, 'she doesn't tell you to sit down . . . she just waits to let you make a noise and then when it gets bad she just shouts at you'. In Ms Tripp's view they 'give up so easily and waste time, if they can't do it they get silly half hours', or 'they just skim over the work and get annoyed when you tell them to go back and do it again'. In the pupils' perspective, 'if it's easy . . . it's not so bad, but when it gets hard you just give up and you just get fed up . . . muck about'. *Concentration* is one factor, then, *confidence* is another. 'They have to have confirmation of everything before they go on . . .' In whole class method such a group (the counter-steering group) rarely take up this amount of immediate teacher attention. They would exist below the steering group created by curriculum and time frames, though they might be the focus for public statements of a disciplinary nature. The refocusing of teacher attention in individualized instruction, however, as far as this is contingent upon behavioural nonconformity, occurs *pari passu* with increasing negative identification of such pupils as social types in a teacher's perception.

The behaviours thus described have their origins in the interplay of frame factors (time, control, content, etc.) and are, we are suggesting, context specific. Changes in frame signify changes in the learning opportunities experienced by pupils. This is illustrated in the identity of one of the pupils of the counter-steering group, Jerry. This pupil does not rate himself as below average in terms of ability, work, behaviour and interest in Mathematics. The more favourable self-conception can be explained by the learning opportunities made available during the Autumn term *via* remedial withdrawal. He himself noted the difference:

> you can't concentrate . . . you feel like mucking about. When you see someone mucking about you want to join in. In maths I work better out of class.

This raises the much broader issue of what abilities are required to work under mass schooling, even when the presentation is individualized. It is important to note that group 2 also received a high proportion of teacher attention. They were an abler group and, therefore, their difficulties of working in the classroom could not be just passed over as lack of intelligence. The interests and attitudes of such groups have received little attention in the literature. Their existence needs to be emphasized if only to prevent oversimple dichotomies being accepted uncritically. The pupils' explanation for their situation was made in terms of the softness of teacher discipline. Such incompatability between pupil outlook and teacher strategy may reflect a wider clash between home, and the expectations and conceptions of teaching and authority developed there, and schooling. The mother of one of the group 2 pupils says of the school on report evening that 'it's not strict enough . . . I'm very disciplined in the house so I can't understand how he's so bad'.

Finally, one further important comment needs to be made on Table 10(b). As has been noted, Ms Tripp gave disproportionate amounts of attention to groups 2 and 3. She also gave very similar amounts of total attention to groups 1 and 4. But the internal relations of the total is not the same in both cases. For groups 2, 3 and 4 there is a constant relationship between public and immediate talk. But group 1 was treated very differently from all the others: the experience of being able pupils was markedly more positive. This evidence is similar to that of other studies and adds weight to the picture given for other pupils.

Summary

The individualized curriculum in Mathematics was a better means of meeting the needs of the broad range of pupil abilities in the contexts of mixed ability grouping and of staffing problems. It served both to control teachers *and* facilitate structure, permitting teachers and pupils alike, consistency and support. This response to mixed ability grouping we can characterize as that of *adoption* (cf. Brickell, 1971), via the wholesale implementation of a publicly produced scheme and, at Sageton through the decision of one teacher, the Head of Department. As a result the scheme imposed a variety of constraints on the teacher's pedagogical role: instructional, disciplinary and administrative. Although *time* was individualized for the pupil, for the teacher in the context of such demands it remained (as in whole class method) a scarce commodity. Transposing the frame of teacher control to the worksheets shifted the 'authority of the teacher from themselves onto the materials' (Adelman and Walker, 1975, p. 163). Moreover, the worksheets in Maths (and as we see in other subjects) are no less direct or closed in terms of knowledge, than the systems explicitly imposed in whole class teaching. That is to say, they made little reference to and provided little access for the experiential knowledge of the pupils themselves. However, the authority of the teacher (repeatedly and explicitly announced in the 'centralized communication' structure of traditional whole class method) does become more oblique (cf. Edwards and Furlong, 1978, pp. 11–36). Adelman and Walker make the point that worksheets enable teachers to move away from a 'traditional' teacher role, 'to become "informal", neutral, seeming not to be constantly evaluating children's actions' (1975, p. 163). What we are suggesting is that an individualized curriculum limits a teacher's opportunities to be/do otherwise. Because the content of the syllabus is disparate and diverse and the worksheet mode mediates the pupil–teacher relationship, there is indeed far less opportunity than in other instructional modes for teachers to publicly announce their authority, positional status and control; to establish what D. Hargreaves (1972, p. 15) calls asymmetric teacher–pupil social relationships.[11] For some pupils, perhaps because their social milieux (in the familial, parent–child relationship) outside the school engenders expectations of authority and control at variance with those assumed and required in individualized modes of learning, the frame of teacher control in SMP could be problematic and a limiting factor upon their learning opportunities.

Teachers devise a number of strategies to deal with the variety of demands and problems they experience. In this endeavour however, as we have seen, they are constrained both by the expectations of significant others (e.g. the Head of Department) and the structure of the scheme itself.[12] For the most part, teachers either work from the front, do the rounds, or a mixture of both. Each may involve the process of individual or collective piloting. In the absence of required teacher attention, pupils devise their own coping strategies. They do as little work as possible, they copy, or get assistance from other 'abler' peers. They also use the work pack to search out answers subsequently given at a later stage, and they repeatedly demand the teacher's attention, knowing they may achieve 'instant solutions'.

All this generates an array of pupil identities certainly more complex than those represented in the literature. Reference to Model 5 (p. 48) may again help clarify how the process of their emergence operates.

To succeed, pupils need a range of predisposing attributes including appropriate prior knowledge in relation to 'new' content; they may find the latter at odds with their 'commonsense' conceptions or just plain difficult (factor i). Access to content is always via specific pedagogic modes (factor ii). Pupils may be able to handle the mode and work in the time available (factor iii) but fail to enter appropriately into the teacher's control set-up (factor iv), for example by failing, as in the case of group 2 in Maths, to work independently. Note that there is no clear distinction here between the individualized nature of SMP workcards and either pupil behaviour or what the teacher permits (Salmon and Claire, 1984). Failure to handle content and mode may certainly lead to pupil rejection of and difficulty with routine and boredom (factor v). It is clear that it is the pupils of group 3 who are most consistently required to endure these regimes. Unable to progress rapidly through content, such pupils consequently experience far less variety than the 'able' child. Moreover, in the third year upon setting, the 'able' top group experienced a greater variety of work and method, the blackboard supporting, sometimes supplanting the workcard as the main medium of transmission, while the remainder of pupils persisted in making their way painstakingly toward workcard completion.

five

Science:
Group Based Curriculum

As in the previous discussion of French and Mathematics teaching, two types of background information are necessary to any understanding of the examples of teaching provided: the departmental background of curriculum change and opinion and the nature of the Science course. All the lessons observed were those of first, second and third year classes (some 31 in total). As in Maths, Science featured mixed ability grouping to the end of the second year after which setting took place.

Departmental Background and Curriculum Change

The existing Head of Faculty of Science was appointed as Head of Science in 1956, soon after the opening of the school. He established a course which expressed current conceptions of science teaching and forms of organization.

> There were two science teachers here then. We did Biology with the girls and Chemistry with the boys. Then, we introduced General Science and Physics. The tradition was to keep boys and girls separate for Science and the boys from A and AB streams were put together and likewise with the girls. It was the same arrangement for the B and C streams. Each year for the first 3 years the boys had two terms in the General Science lab and one term in the Biology laboratory. The arrangement for the girls was just the opposite.

> In the early days, only the very bright pupils were put in for 'O' level Physics and Chemistry, the B stream course in the school consisted of a general science course grouped around a simple syllabus of electricity, chemistry, physics, mechanics and biology, with reference to our common life and natural occurrences.

Three years after comprehensivization the syllabus was again changed, this time to the current Integrated Science course.

In 1974 the Academic Board met and with a very narrow majority we went mixed ability. The decision was taken late in February and we were to start mixed ability in September. There was little money available and as far as I know there was no further discussion. I immediately applied to go on a summer course . . . mixed ability science . . . Nuffield . . . well there wasn't a single teacher in the department who knew anything about mixed ability or who had been 'brought up' in mixed ability. At the same time I wasn't all that committed to the idea. The great difficulty was staffing at the time . . . we had anybody; and to teach mixed ability you have to have good control (Head of Faculty).

Evidently, neither commitment (Hoyle, 1969), consensus (Bernstein, 1971), nor planning (Brickell, 1971) are consonant with the conditions of innovation in this setting. Faced with impending organizational change, for which the department was less than prepared, the strategy deployed (in contrast to the wholesale adoption of a course as in mathematics) was that of 'adaptation' (Brickell, 1971). Features of Nuffield combined science were accommodated within an existing organization and curriculum. The paradigm had shifted at least in the dimension of 'how to teach' science (cf. Ball, 1981). But little change had taken place along the dimension of 'what to teach', at least in the first three years of secondary school. All pupils experienced a series of topics in years 1 and 2 (many of which were retained from the previous general science course), while in the third year only the able pupils enjoyed the experience of a 'collection curriculum' (Bernstein, 1971) (they 'did' Physics, Chemistry and Biology) and the expertise of specific subject specialists.

The introduction of an integrated curriculum such as that described at Sageton is, Bernstein argues (1977, p. 104), likely to 'bring about a disturbance in the structure and distribution of power in property relationships and in existing educational identities'. As D. Hargreaves (1980, p. 135) points out, however, this analysis

more directed as it is to cross-cultural comparisons than to an historical account of the educational system in Britain . . . [is one where] . . . Bernstein does not deal very fully with the fact that the integrated code has been emerging in the secondary modern school *in response* to important structural and cultural changes. In the comprehensive school Bernstein's 'deep felt resistances' to the integrated code are likely to be experienced in the main by ex-grammar school teachers.

At Sageton, a 'new' curriculum was simply accommodated into an existing curriculum and organizational structure. In the prevailing conditions of high staff turnover such 'deep felt resistances' were less likely to occur. During the period of study, however, the teachers themselves did voice objections of a kind outlined by Bernstein (1977, p. 104). While generally supportive of the integrated course they expressed concern about the limited opportunities for career advancement which accrued to teachers by virtue of the integrated, organizational structure.

> Each subject should have a Head. We are as big as the History, Geography, departments. Then we could expect the school to prosper. It would never happen in a Grammar School. Maybe there is a need for one overall person but that isn't to say, there's no need for deputy heads. 'F' and 'T' schools still have heads. These scales have gone to the pastoral side. It's been overdone. The scale 2 in Physics, Chemistry or Biology, is the ultimate end. Where can we go from there? They have to be interested in the pastoral side . . . so their interest in their subject diminishes . . . the present new appointment is deputy head of science . . . and that's it. There should be scale 3's. We've remained the same structure as we were as a High School. Only the pastoral has changed. I only know about chemistry. I rely on their advice about biology etc., and they're only scale 2's. How am I expected to run a Biology Department without the experience? (Head of Integrated Science).

Problems such as these were likely to arise with the coexistence of two curricula (of 'integrated' lower school and 'collection' upper school), but with an organizational structure supportive of only the former.[1] Consequently, there was anger and frustration amongst teachers and an acute disjuncture between the personal capabilities of senior staff and their positional responsibilities. There was heavy reliance on unrewarded junior staff expertise. Inevitably, over time these staff were drawn into mobility upward and outwards from their department into expanding sectors of the organization – particularly the pastoral.

However, factors other than these also mattered:

> When we started, capital wasn't too bad but this is running out. We badly need replacements. It will start to effect the classroom soon. In the V and VI 'O' and 'A' level groups the more sophisticated stuff for upper school work you don't buy it. It's too expensive (Head of Integrated Studies).

and

> We were given (£x) capitation. That's not enough. Other schools of equivalent size get around £5000. It means we have to be so cautious with material. It can't be replaced. There has to be class demonstrations (Head of Faculty).

> It's getting worse and worse. There's not enough material available or apparatus for a lot of the work. We'll soon be reduced to chalk and talk (Science teacher).

Sentiments such as these were echoed time and time again within the department and now appear particularly poignant at a time of current cutbacks in education and assumptions that recent historical resource levels were adequate.[2] Although the strategies of allowing classes to take different routes through a topic reduced the problem, as we see, teachers nevertheless felt this constraint to be a source of imposition on their preferred (and expected) classroom practice. Problems related also to the availability of laboratory space,

> There is lab space for 160 lessons and 184 lessons to be taught (Head of Department);

staffing,

> this year the faculty has had to deal with 27 lessons (a week) being taught by supply teachers (Head of Department);

and to the availability of time, especially time to reflect upon and reproduce worksheets, which in their existing form were considered of questionable adequacy,

> They're such badly written topics.

produced with

> very little understanding of how to cater for the need of all the ability range (Science teacher).

> We need a lot more time for preparation, we need colourful, clear worksheets and instruction. Plenty of space for equipment (Science teacher).

> They are far from perfect. But it's having the time to do something about them. We all know they are not perfect but when you've got something that just ticks over and at the same time you've got a hundred and one other things to do, it tends to stay as it is (Head of Faculty).

The Integrated Science Course

The majority of the pupils were involved in an Integrated Science course based upon Nuffield Science[3] and it was intended that this course should bear many features of the parent scheme. Before looking at the teaching of this course, we will consider first these features as they were articulated in the 'educationist context',[4] that is to say, as defined in a policy document which contained a general description of the course and certain recommendations for its use. The analyses will identify certain 'tensions' inherent in the course which, we suggest, express a conflation of different paradigmatic[5] conceptions of Science teaching.

Independent, individualized instruction as found in Mathematics, where the aim was to have each child working on different curricular tasks suited to his or her level of ability, was not a characteristic feature of mixed ability Science teaching,[6] where content was topic centred and group based. Generally all pupils worked on the same topic although this in turn was further divided into a number of investigatory or practical activities. As in traditional Science lessons, groups were created as a common way of attempting to handle this activity, with pupils working predominantly from booklets. At Sageton, each of the three year groups covered a stipulated number of topics (seven in year 1, eight in year 2, seven in year 3) for example, on 'Heat', 'Water' or 'Measuring', on a rotational basis. Each topic lasted a period of five weeks. Topics were further subdivided into a number (usually 4–6) of investigatory or practical activities, 'stations' or 'units' (for example, the measuring topic consisted of 'stations' on weighting, time, length, balance, temperature), which pupils in groups or individually, worked through on a weekly rotational basis over the five-week period. There were 2×70 minute periods for first and second year pupils, 3×70 for third years. The course thereby imposed precisely defined time parameters within which teachers and pupils had to operate, creating for teachers and pupils alike problems of pacing and task completion. As with most science topic schemes (Sands, 1979, p. 618), those at Sageton lent themselves 'to the production of basic essential work which features on the first worksheets and work which extends the topic in depth or breadth but not linearly'. Each topic thus represented 'new' opportunities to succeed. In principle, children paced themselves within a topic, within the time parameters defined by the course organization. The 'able' pupils were allowed to move to another topic, 'perhaps to another laboratory' or onto 'more advanced materials', as they wished. The 'less able' did not perhaps complete each investigatory activity within a topic but, nevertheless sampled it, gaining access to its breadth of experience. As Mrs Turner remarked,

> it doesn't really matter if they don't finish a section before moving on, because the objectives of the work sheet is introductory to the concepts they'll need to know later. The poorer kids may only do the experiments and do little of the writing.

The course thus represented an intention to bring off a significant shift from traditional pedagogical practice toward the direction of what Bernstein (1977) calls an integrated curriculum, at least within 'Science'. This places less emphasis upon 'states of knowledge and the accumulation of "facts", than upon *how* knowledge is created' (1977, p. 102). As stated in the course outlined at Sageton: 'with this approach to learning, no longer do we expect students to learn things parrotwise, but we should teach scientific method and get them to investigate a problem and produce a solution'. Moreover, a common pedagogy is implied. The document prescribed how the course should best be deployed. As stated, pupils worked in groups or individually on investigatory or practical tasks with the worksheet or booklet mediating between pupil and teacher as the primary mode of transmission. Class teaching took place only during lead or introductory lessons and during end of topic (5th weekly) assessment periods. As in SMP then, the course imposed constraints too, on the teacher's pedagogical role. Teachers were compelled to deal with many things simultaneously, they were actively involved the whole time, and conscious of the need to progress swiftly around groups and to monitor safety (cf. Sands, 1979, p. 623). As in SMP, the traditional social relationship of teacher to the whole class as a social unit was broken up. The organization of the scheme required the provision of materials which has to be administered by the teacher. The management of classroom activities became more crucial and teachers felt, as we see, that their opportunity to establish effective control had been limited. With the scheme designed for pupils to work individually or in groups, there was increasing opportunity for pupils to indulge in peer group 'interest' talk. In the teachers' perspective, then, a distinction had to be made between conversation about work and such 'interest' talk. As in individualized schemes (though here within narrower time parameters) the course built in self-pacing by the pupil. Levels of involvement, attitude, motivation, ability to work independently, become more crucial to classroom management. There were inevitable tensions between the 'newer' conceptions of more pupil generated learning, emphasis on 'scientific method' and appropriate classroom control methods, and the sorts of pupil behaviours previously/ currently expected and the broader framework of parental and teacher expectations in which the department operated.

> In this school where there are disciplinary problems, I feel that we must be on top of the classes at all times. This does not mean that we need to have pupils sitting in silence at benches the whole time but neither must the method be used to cover up our inability to control our classes (Head of Faculty).

The significance of noise for the practical activity of teaching has been interestingly discussed by Denscombe (1980, p. 78). He suggests that a concern for 'keeping 'em quiet' may be particularly prevalent where schools exhibit a low achievement orientation. Innovations which involve the likelihood of increased amounts of noise pose particular problems in practice because their implementation potentially jeopardizes the appearance of control in the classroom and, with this, the image of teacher competencies. Science teachers at Sageton, therefore, worked within a framework of strongly contrary expectations, those intrinsic to the course and those of significant others within the faculty and institution whose prime requirement was quiet and order. They were faced with the task of defining behaviours appropriate to the scheme, which permitted 'greater freedom', which would at the same time be acceptable to those in positions *de facto* judging their competence as science teachers.

A further tension revolved around the conception of assessment embodied in the scheme. Checking on progress was an important part of the scheme. The process was complex and the criteria diffuse. On the one hand assessment took a form much the same as those used in homogeneously grouped classes, in multiple choice questions which were intended to test short-term recall. At the same time, assessment was to be systematically incorporated into the act of 'doing the rounds', where the focus was to be upon the behavioural features of a child's performance. In particular, 'their skills at handling apparatus, their interest in science etc. These will have the effect of making us as we walk round the groups, really look at the students, talk to them about their interests and ambitions' (Head of Faculty, Policy Document). The implications of this orientation for pupil identity, within integrated curricula, have been outlined by Bernstein (1977, p. 109):

> Weak frames enable a greater range of the student's behaviour to be made public, and they make possible considerable diversity (at least in principle) between students. It is possible that this may lead to a situation where assessment takes more into account 'inner' attributes of the student. Thus if he has the 'right' attitudes, then this will result later in the attainment of various specific competencies. The right attitude may be assessed in terms of the fit between the pupil's attributes and the current ideology.

For the teachers concerned, theirs was thus a task of retaining a 'process' orientation in classroom practice, with regard to method and outcome, at the same time securing transmission of content sufficient, at least, to provide evidence of success in terms of pupil learning and teacher competence at each predetermined point of evaluation. Conceptions of evaluation and method thus interacted to form further constraints on a teacher's pedagogical role. The reasons for this tension might be explained as a further feature of adaptation (Brickell, 1971),[8] a latent (traditional) conception of science teaching intersecting with a 'newer' curriculum model. Assessment is, however, also the point at which teacher perspectives and broader pressures and expectations of schooling intersect. Subject increasingly to the pressures for order and standards prevailing within the institutional and extra school context, Science teachers were encouraged by the Head of Faculty to pay far greater attention to homework, assessment and record keeping. Against this background, the course in general and the dual forms of assessment in particular, seemed to provide a solution 'to the goals of an educational system which are fundamentally contradictory'.[9] Liberal curricular intentions consonant with the course and current conceptions of science teaching were reconciled with the need to identify and select out children for success.

As prescribed in faculty policy documents:

> We must aim our teaching at the middle range of the IQ. We must not neglect the bright student. I feel that within this approach there is a tendency for the bright student to be neglected.

This is the kind of 'academic perspective' which Ball (1981, p. 175) discerned at Beachside, and 'which was concerned with "standards" and academic excellences, and where the focus was upon the "brighter" child and the importance of the subject'. Less clear in Ball's (1981) work, however, is an indication of how such perspectives are realized in classroom practice or in particular modes of instruction. While it was beyond the scope of this study to assess or determine the implications of this conception of instruction for the subject *content* of science transmitted,[10] an evaluation of the read-ability of worksheets was possible and undertaken.[11] This approximated a chronological age of 11. As 34% of Sageton pupils had reading ages on entry of below nine years, many were certain to find the material on the worksheets 'difficult' if not impossible to comprehend. Thus the Integrated Science course catered essentially for the 'average' child. It implied a particular level of skill predisposition both in association with the worksheet as a mode of transmission, the subject content, as well as the amount of time made available (i.e. requirements (i) and (ii) of the frame factors in Model 5 – see p. 48). It was to be expected therefore that a substantial percentage of Sageton children would have difficulties with completing the course and achieving any success in its terms. The steering group phenomenon was reproduced within an apparently 'new' curricular/pedagogical form. The course from its inception represented a considerable source of frustration to those pupils unable to meet its implicit requirements. We shall see that their chance of securing access to content sufficient to display evidence of learning and ability during points of ('traditional') assessment was severely restricted. Moreover, to the extent that pupils displayed frustration in active forms of interest behaviour, so too their failure to meet 'new' criteria of ability (of correct attitude etc.) further solidified their identities in the teacher's perspective as less 'able' pupils.

Teacher Strategies in Group Based Curriculum

Science teachers in their classroom practice (like those in other subjects) focused upon problems of pupil control. Only one of the first year teachers observed in 'initial encounters'[12] with first year pupils did not operate the course as the policy document recommended. He was a teacher new to the school taking responsibility for a class whose identity as a 'difficult class' had (partly due to staffing inconsistencies) already been established. He noted that

> I can't give these kids the time they need. If I could get around them all it would be OK. But there's always the problem of control. It's always there. If you're around everywhere you can't . . . they've got to be able to focus on you as a teacher . . .

Group work was avoided and class teaching preferred because it structured and limited opportunities for the teacher to establish the kind of positional relationships thought conducive to effective control.[13] The remaining first year teachers, however, endeavoured to introduce the course to pupils in a manner which approximated the intentions of its author. The normal practice was for teachers during week one of a topic to spend part or all of a lesson introducing its content to the pupils and reminding them how the course was to be operated. Groups of pupils, generally allowed to form on the basis of peer friendships, used 'trays' of resources provided to complete the tasks outlined for them in the booklets. 'Booklets' usually took three weeks for a group to work through, during which time the teacher moved around the room from group to group. The main body of topic work thus involved the teacher interacting at an immediate face-to-face level with individual pupils or groups, interspersed with the issuing of public regulative messages.

As in individualized instruction, with the booklet mediating between the teacher and the pupil, the centrality of talk via the teacher of whole class method was restricted. Occasions when it was required occurred during opening introductory lessons or opening phases of other lessons and during the fifth weekly 'test' periods.

A teaching pattern of this nature was, however, a first year, early first term phenomenon, its incidence decreasing as the year progressed. In the second year, the picture was overwhelmingly that of class teaching while in the third year only just over half of the lessons observed were 'group' based.

Mrs Turner and the pupils of Form 1p (the first year case study group) fit this pattern. This process of transition from group based to class instruction was indeed complex and some indication of its dynamics can be discerned from the practices observed. In initial encounters with the pupils of Form 1p, instruction was group based. Pupils had formed themselves into six groups and for the main body of topic work, appeared to progress largely independently of the teacher, using booklets as the primary media of instruction. There was, at least in early encounters, an absence of public instructional talk. The main body of the lesson proper involved the teacher interacting at an immediate level with groups or individuals interspersed with the issuing of public regulative messages.

While our data is not adequate to provide detailed analyses of the dynamics of small group interaction (cf. Barnes, 1977), it is highly suggestive of certain processes. A characteristic feature was the tendency within small groups for pupils to proceed at a pace defined by the more 'able' pupil. That is to say, the steering group phenomenon characteristic of whole class method was reproduced as an intra-small group phenomenon, but with an important difference. In whole class method the problem lies with the extremes of the ability range. The able pupil is held up while the less able goes unattended. In small group work, however, pacing of this kind does not necessarily signify exclusion from 'learning' for those pupils who fall below the steering group. Consider here the opinions of two pupils, Ryan and Caroline. Each was a low ability child as defined by teacher ratings;[14] both had reading ages (8 years 7 months) well below that required by the booklets to facilitate easy access to its substantive contents. Both portrayed 'interest' behaviours difficult for the teacher, although Ryan was considered the more difficult. Both expressed an emphatic preference for group work as the way of 'doing science'.

> I prefer working in groups 'cos then if you don't understand something you can get help from your friends (Ryan).

and

> I prefer working in groups because if you get stuck, like, if you don't know something, you can ask your friends (Caroline).

Ryan, previously identified as one of the counter-steering group in Maths, worked with Jerry and Rene (also of the counter-steering group) and Peter. The latter, who was more able than all three other pupils (as defined by teacher ratings and NFER tests), had a reading age (above 11) likely to make the mode of transmission more accessible to him than to each of the other pupils, with whom he shared a somewhat detached but definite friendship. Caroline and Odette worked together, neither considered 'able' by the teacher but rather, as in Mathematics, pupils 'typical' of Sageton, 'normal' and 'average' in behaviour and ability. (See Table 12 for the overall organization of Form 1p Science work-groups.)

Pupils of group 1 (which corresponded to the fieldworkers' total worker group 1 in Maths) had a stable relationship and displayed all the attributes of 'total' work here as in languages and SMP. All, with the exception of Naren and Abdul whose opportunities to achieve 'able' pupil identity were limited by their absence from many Science lessons due to their need for 'special English', were rated as able and 'well behaved' pupils by the teacher. Jenny, Lynne and Heather were in group 2 and similarly defined, the last two thus achieving an identity comparable to that in Modern Languages. Ability and ethnicity also featured in the grouping of pupils in group 3, John, Hugh, Paul and David. As defined by the teacher's ratings, this was a mixed ability group. John and Hugh were more able pupils with John being the more problematic in terms of behaviour. Paul and David were average and sometimes 'difficult pupils when they got together with John and Hugh'. For pupils of the counter-steering group, located mainly in Science group 5 there was little alteration in their perceived ability or behaviour in the perspective of their Science teacher. Each received well below average marks for behaviour and attainment in Autumn term ratings. Peter, a 'normal', 'average' pupil in Mrs Turner's

Table 12　The work group organization of Form 1p pupils in Science

Group 1		Group 2	
Mark	B–Br	Jenny	G–Br
Naren	B–As	Lynne	G–Br
Abdul	B–As	Heather	G–Br
Michael	B–WI/Br		
Group 3		Group 4	
John	B–Br	Mary	G–WI
Hugh	B–Eur	Liona	G–WI
Paul	B–Br	Maureen	G–WI
David	B–Br		
Group 5		Group 6	
Jerry	B–WI	Caroline	G–WI
Ryan	B–WI	Odette	G–WI
Rene	B–WI		
Peter	B–WI		

B, boy; G, girl; Br, British; As, Asian; WI, West Indian; Eur, European.

perspective (as previously defined in Maths and Languages), retained friendship with the group while maintaining a degree of isolation from their more extreme 'interest' activity. Liona (of the counter-steering group) was similarly defined as very difficult and 'less able'. Though she worked with Mary and Maureen, there was a degree of isolation between these three group members. Both Mary and Maureen achieved successful pupil identities in the perspective of the teacher, though Mary's behaviours were a frequent cause for concern. Maureen thus achieved an identity similar to that in French but significantly better than she managed as a mathematician and considered Science to be a subject in which she 'learns best'. Caroline and Odette achieved identities as 'average pupils', as in Maths.

For those pupils such as Jerry, Ryan, Rene and Liona who lacked the prerequisites necessary to work in Science (ability to handle content and MOT independently in the time permitted), group work seemed to provide a limited solution, both to the problem of their progress and to the teacher's contingent managerial demands. As Mrs Turner noted,

Kids can help each other. They often explain difficulties to each other . . .

Less than evident from our observations, however, are the kind of qualitative or co-operative interactions suggested by both teachers and pupils. More characteristic, perhaps, is Peter's retort to one of Ryan's comments:

Yeah . . . you just copy off me . . . [and] . . . you always look at what I've done, you don't do it yourself . . .

Nevertheless, we can see in group work what was a form of self-imposed individual piloting. This was a strategy by which pupils who otherwise found difficulty with attaining progress within the limits of time imposed by the scheme, could at least keep pace with the more able peers, but at a cost of understanding what it is they are supposed to be doing. Clearly this was a process which allowed pupils to give only the appearance[15] (and perhaps experience the feeling) of progress. Ultimately, as the process crystallized during test periods, it was an identity which such pupils were unlikely to sustain. Moreover, what was for some pupils an immediate way of coping, was (as we see in the statements above) for others (even close friends) a source of antagonism, frustration and friction. It seemed to infringe a pupils' code of conduct which valued learning as an independent, competitive and isolated experience.[16] Indeed, given the conception of pacing implied in the course (which allows the able to progress alone) and the absence of written material which encouraged co-operative endeavour, it would perhaps be more surprising if pupils expressed attitudes to the contrary.

As the term progressed, teachers (such as Mrs Turner) increasingly confronted problems of pupil control. In group based instruction as in the 'open' classrooms to which Denscombe (1980b, p. 67) refers, the boundaries between proper work and having a chat 'are blurred in a way which could be exploited in the negotiation of work'. Denscombe explains this tendency amongst pupils with reference to a disjuncture between the aspirations of open classroom teachers and the legacy of closed classroom instruction that children bring with them to the open classroom. What he fails to draw attention to, however, is the material (instructional/curricular) base which may underly and interact with a pupil's sociocultural choice not to work. An increase in pupil interaction and opportunity for 'interest' activity cannot help but evoke higher levels of noise and movement than in classes where the teacher is the only person who may legitimately talk. Within the broader framework of senior teacher expectations, increasing noise and movement was particularly problematic. It could, after all, be mis-recognized as a lack of control and invite hostility from those who regard it as a threat to the authority of the teacher (cf. Kohl, 1970). The teachers concerned (as in Mathematics) tended to explain their problems of control in terms of pupil ill-preparedness for work with the Science scheme.

> They're very silly and childish . . . waste time . . . they should be more serious (Mrs Turner).

> they started with a serious attitude but now they waste time chatting. S. should take herself more in hand and apply herself (Mrs Cooper).

> It's the attitudes that distinguish them and comprehension; negative attitudes to work, low ability, in reading and writing . . . very bolshy . . . terrible attitude. Mark is low ability but his attitude . . . is, well, so damn good. Chances are he will do well. I can't help them until I've got better control (Mr Pritchard).

Others located a pupil's inability to work appropriately within the course itself:

> I'm not prepared to work from the worksheets as they stand. Things are far too difficult. The pupils have been difficult. Some are quite able, most are not able to concentrate (Mr Lane).

> They need complete overhauling. There's not enough practical work. It's all such boring stuff . . . no diagrams to copy . . . not enough activity . . . it's all theory (Mr Lane).

or in the pupils' home backgrounds:

> Ability wise . . . there's Mark, John, Hugh others, all can think, largely,

they have the most articulate parents . . . they're sort of middle class
kind of people, Hugh's father has thousands of books at home . . .
Hugh can be troublesome though (Mrs Turner).

A failure to display the right attitude (and behaviour) was usually
attributed to a combination of factors: for example, the absence of
technical abilities (reading and writing) necessary for access to the
Science scheme, an unsupportive social class, home background, the
course material. All may be interpreted as contingencies producing
pupil inability to curb 'concentration from wandering' or the tendency
'to distract others' or 'indulge in silly escapades to relieve the
boredom'. They are 'not serious about Science'.

Pupils are distinguished according to their controllability (cf. Jenks,
1972), while the rhetoric of the Science course provides the necessary
constructs with which to explain their failure. 'The right attitude is
assessed in terms of the fit between the pupils attitudes and the current
ideology' (Bernstein, 1977, p. 109). That is to say, in defining pupils as
social types, teachers utilize categories drawn from their construction
of what a scientific approach to learning should be within the current,
paradigmatic conception of science teaching.

Faced with such problems of increasing pupil involvement in interest
activity, there was a concomitant increase in the amount of public
regulative teacher talk addressed to a small group of pupils causing
most concern. As an immediate strategy for resolving the emergent
discipline problems, Mrs Turner (as did many others) often adopted a
policy of intervention and isolation, removing the parties concerned
from their own to other groups more inclined in the teacher's
perspectives towards 'total' work. Rene (one of the counter-steering
group) began working with Jerry, Ryan and Peter. Increasingly the
teacher was drawn to their activities. Rene, who was found the 'most
difficult pupil, defiant, wastes time playing, distracts others. I'll exlude
him from experiments if he doesn't change', was removed and placed
with a group of workers Mark, Naren and Michael. This strategy
however was only partially successful. In the short term it reduced a
teacher's managerial problem, reducing levels of noise and movement
emanating from group 5. It did not, however, resolve Rene's learning
problems. Although placed with a group of workers, he was unable
(and made no great attempt to try, possibly because of the subcultural
significance of such an act) to penetrate the boundaries of their group
solidarity, and commitment to work (see Meyenn, 1980, pp. 108–42).
In exasperation, as they continued to ignore his presence he calls out
to the teacher 'they keep it all themselves'. His behaviour remained
problematic and he was continually drawn towards the interest activity
of his previous group of friends.

Within the broader framework of demands for order and control which teachers at Sageton had to work within, they had little opportunity but to invoke more dramatic and attested strategies of control. *They reverted to whole class method*, for example:

> I'm not going to let them work in groups again, until they want to learn. I can't allow them to be more independent (Mrs Turner).

> The class should be doing work on their own but I daren't risk allowing them to do it (Mrs Cooper).

This reversion to class teaching (evidenced in Table 13) was the product of teachers' identifying pupils as ill-prepared to work in the pattern required by the scheme. There was a perceived disjuncture between the behaviour of pupils and the conception of learning embodied in the scheme. Table 13 outlines how Mrs Turner's talk was differentially distributed amongst the pupils of Form 1p, over 4 × 70 minute lessons.

Despite the opportunities for group work presented in the booklet, in these lessons pupils enjoyed only 17 of a possible 280 minutes of practical activity for which they took responsibility. As indicated in Table 11, during these lessons John, Mary, Hugh and Heather (group 2) and Jerry, Ryan, Rene and Liona (group 3) received distinctively more public regulative talk than the 'total workers' of group 1, or the pupils of group 4 and also more of the instructional talk with the

Table 13: Mrs Turner's talk in 4 × 70 minute lessons, excluding beginnings and endings

Group[b]		Public regulative	Public instructional[a]	Total
(a) *as percentage of teacher talk across four groups previously identified in Mathematics*				
1	(5 pupils)	10	16	12.3
2	(4 pupils)	18	28	21.5
3	(4 pupils)	53	44	49.2
4	(7 pupils)	19	12	16.9
		100%	100%	99.9
(b) *as average per pupil in each group*				
1		0.8	0.8	1.6
2		1.8	1.8	3.6
3		5.3	2.8	8.1
4		1.1	0.4	1.5

[a] Refers to instructional talk in interactions between teacher and individual pupils, carried out publicly from the front of class position.

[b] As defined pp. 60–1.

teacher. When compared with individualized instruction (see Table 10) class teaching appeared to offer all groups with the exception of group 3 significantly less opportunity for involvement in instructional talk with the teacher, while at the same time increasing their experience of public regulative messages.

Despite surface changes in the organization of instruction, science teaching did not give pupils an opportunity to achieve significant alterations in their identity, as social types, as defined in individualized instruction. Only Naren and Abdul experienced any sort of shift in their identity, and were rated as slightly less able than in Maths, due less to their inability to handle content than the difficulties they experienced with the mode of transmission, because of their limited reading abilities. Consequently they were considered 'very enthusiastic, quite able, but they have difficulty with English, writing up experiments. But they're hard working . . . they enjoy science' (Mrs Turner).

The regularities to which Table 13 refers are then, we suggest, functional expressions of the situation in which the teacher found herself. On the one hand Mrs Turner controlled the teaching process at classroom level, having to resolve problems of discipline, pacing and content, but she was also 'controlled' or constricted by the interplay of pupil identities, content, time and MOT. Her disciplinary and instructional actions were concretely structured in interaction with specific groups of pupils. As we see in Table 13, group 3 pupils (counter-steering group) received significantly more instructional talk than other pupils as the teacher tried to manage their difficult behaviour, but this occurred *pari passu* with the negative identification of their behaviours as pupils.

Class teaching as represented here in the action of Mrs Turner was indeed for the teachers concerned a coping strategy, 'a creative response to problems and constraints that are externally determined' (A. Hargreaves, 1977). It was not a preferred way of teaching but was chosen because of its capacity to effect greater control over pupil behaviour, which itself was generated from a complex interplay of frame factors. As pupils related to content, time and MOT in group based learning, the learning difficulties of certain pupils (particularly the counter-steering group) were increasingly made apparent in interest activity which, given the degree of autonomy and self-direction presupposed and required by the group organization, was increasingly problematic for teachers. Class teaching which resulted was a chosen *second level* coping strategy, in which (cf. A. Hargreaves, 1979, p. 139) 'the moral aspect takes primacy. In this sense, social control becomes inseparable from curriculum planning, preferred styles of teaching and classroom organisation'. Group work was returned to only upon the re-establishment of the teachers authority, once the positional structural relationships of classroom life had been explicitly announced.

Right I usually do the experiments myself but today . . . we'll have a bash at it. We tried before . . . then it was chaotic. If you get stupid . . . there will be no practical work for you . . . for a long time (Mrs Turner).

Investigatory activity was, then, offered as part of a bargaining process: less boredom, more responsibility, in exchange for pupil conformity.

Class Teaching and the Limits of Control

This strategy of whole class teaching was, however, almost wholly unsuccessful. While it reduced a teacher's problems of transmission of *content*, in the limited time available it neither effectively reduced their problems of pupil control nor resolved pupils' learning difficulties. The reasons are complex and can be considered following some examples of class teaching, observed in years one and two.

Example 1: Mrs Cooper with Form 1s

The lesson proper begins with an eight minute introductory phase. The teacher, positioned at the front of class reads through the investigatory task which all pupils are expected to follow, and this is interspersed with question–answer sessions and the issuing of public regulative messages. A 15 minute writing phase follows: pupils copy out from the booklet the investigatory instruction and content statements. The teacher remains at the front of class, in a supervisory position. There follows a 3 minute organizational activity, pupils are asked to collect materials needed for the class experiment. A further 15 minutes are spent in practical work. In both writing and investigatory phases the teacher's concerns for pacing are manifest, in such statements as 'hurry up and finish. I'm eager to get on'. Ultimately, the problems of completion and 'understanding' seem to be resolved with the teacher spending 20 minutes dictating conclusions, using the blackboard, from which the pupils capture the salient points of the lesson for their exercise books.

Example 2: Mr O'Connor with Form 1q

Following an eight minute settling phase, in which the teacher orders pupils to 'come to the front with your chairs', the teacher systematically works through the content outlined in the booklet, for a period of 28 minutes. The topic is 'Heat' and the investigatory activity to be covered is intended to introduce the notion of 'conduction'. However, it is only via not inconsiderable skill on the behalf of the teacher, the use of a variety of control strategies and a subtle collusion with the pupils, that a semblance of order and productivity can be maintained. The teacher's problem is that of securing levels of attention and co-operation appropriate to class teaching and necessary if some degree of conceptual understanding of the content is to be achieved. This is pursued with the repeated issuing of disciplinary messages which continually breaks the flow of instruction, and the use of carefully directed instructional talk.[17] Using both public regulative messages and instructional questions addressed at 'problem' children, the teacher is able to contain but not suppress/correct pupil 'interest' behaviour. As a result he finally invokes a third strategy, that of indulgence. In this strategy 'Pupils are allowed to go beyond normally accepted bounds of classroom behaviour and teacher's decline to enforce general classroom rules' (Denscombe, 1980b, p. 65; Woods, 1977). Despite growing levels of indifference and interest activity from perhaps two-thirds of the pupils present, this teacher indulges such activity, issuing disciplinary messages only to define an acceptable threshold before proceeding with instruction. For example, after some 12 minutes into the lesson, he asks 'It says the word conduction . . . can anyone tell me . . . what is conduction?' Faced with a collective silence he again proceeds to read the definition provided in the booklet, a content which he later admits to finding 'far too difficult, that sentence I read, even I didn't understand it'. This is followed by more teacher instruction and a 'clarifying' investigatory task which the teacher completes against a background of indifference from the majority of pupils. At the end of this (28 minute) phase he instructs the pupils to return to their places and 'write up in your books what you think conduction is', a request to which a number of pupils retort 'We don't know do we!' and Mr O'Connor exasperates 'You've just done it!' The problem is resolved with the teacher using the blackboard, providing a series of concluding and descriptive statements for the pupils to copy into their books.

Example 3: Mr Khan with Form 2p

In this example, we find further instances of indulgence, as a teacher attempts to resolve his disciplinary and instructional problems. It takes some 15 minutes of lesson time for Mr Khan to regulate pupil interest behaviour: 'you know how much time you've wasted . . . we'll go on after school . . . I'm going to sit down and wait until you're quieter'. Despite the severity of these statements they are sufficient only to curb the level of pupil interest activity; many continue to ignore the teacher as he begins his class instruction. As the lesson proper progresses, for a period of 45 minutes, its salient feature is the teacher's tendency to direct his class instruction at those pupils positioned towards the front of class and his indulgence of those to the rear who are apparently content to ignore the teacher and class instruction. He intervenes in their activity only when their levels of noise and movement seriously impinge upon his instructional talk, or when they seriously infract the appearance of classroom social order.

Mr Khan	Will you shut up please.
Pupils	[burst out laughing]
Mr Khan	Look you've got to let me finish the lesson.
Pupils	[more laughter] . . . go on then finish the lesson.

Again, only in the closing phases of the lesson proper when the teacher concludes the lesson activity and pupils are required to put 'work in their exercise books' is the attention of all pupils ultimately achieved.

Many more instances of class instruction of this type (adopted by the teacher either because of their control problems or lack of resource) could be provided. However, sufficient has been said to evidence the occurrence of certain processes. The limited con-ceptual understanding which this approach produced in pupils contravened the intentions of both teachers and the Integrated Science course. We are simply suggesting that the solutions adopted represented a viable pragmatic solution to a teacher's disciplinary, control (or resource) problems. There is little to choose between group work and class teaching as a means of facilitating better conceptual understanding. We have seen that group work contri-buted to a teacher's disciplinary problems because of the learning problems it presented to children. It too allowed pupils to proceed without necessarily having achieved understanding. The difference between class based or group based teaching can be largely characterized in terms of their generation of collective or individual piloting, respectively. In the lessons described, it could be argued that pupils were merely negotiating forms of behaviour (interest activities and 'escape' from work) possible in group organization (see Denscombe, 1980b). Indulgence was apparent, in combination with the use of concluding statements, as instructional strategies, because they allowed teachers, in a context of constraining and limiting factors, to maintain classroom order and at the same time secure sufficient transmission of content to provide evidence, when required, of teacher competence.

Indulgence, however, also (as evidenced in Example 3) involved a structure of communication which makes explicit the boundaries of a classroom social structure within which the identities of the able and the less able are constructed and repeatedly produced. Figure 2 refers to the class teaching in Example 3, and the seating position of the pupils involved. Evident in this example is a degree of overlap between the focus of teacher instructional talk (which was directed to

Figure 2   Form 2p (case study group) seating plan in Science

B/B

_____ TEACHER POSITION

BENCH

AA	AA		BC	BB
X	X		X	X
m	m		m	m

AA	BC	BB	CC	BB
X	X	X	X	X
m	m	m	m	m

EE
X
m

CC	X			CC	CC		EE	DD
				X	X		X	X
m				f	f		f	m

CC	X		X	DC	X	CC		DD
							X	
m			f			f		f

BB	X		X					CC
f				BB		X		
			f					f

X, position; m, male; f, female; A–E, Autumn term teacher ratings: effort and attainment.

the front two benches), levels of pupil interest activity and, with the exception of two girls situated to the rear and rear side of the classroom who score BB on teacher ratings, ability as defined by both teacher ratings and NFER scores. In short, the strategy of indulgence in combination with class teaching, with the added feature of the teacher focusing upon the work progress of these pupils at the front to pace the lesson, celebrated both a steering group phenomenon and differential gender attachment to Science frequently noted elsewhere (Blackstone and Weinreich-Haste, 1980). (This was borne out in pupil questionnaire responses. Only two of 12 boys express below average interest in Science, compared with six of the girls for whom we have responses.) In general, a large number of pupils were disallowed entry into the learning process in Mr Khan's classroom.

If you don't want to work he'll just go on with the people that will work (Diane, Form 2p).

Some indication of what this process entailed can be gleaned from further analysis of the interaction of Form 1p (Table 13). Such an analysis reveals that girls accounted for only 3% of public regulative talk and 24% of instructional; that is, they appeared to represent less of a problem of control at this stage to teachers, but also received far less individual 'instruction' than boys with who the teacher interacted in the interest of order. However it would be invidious to blame the teacher in any obvious sense for causing the failure of the girls by virtue of entrenched stereotyped attitudes. Identity construction is not an inexorable outcome of labelling but a transaction that takes place as the teacher attempts to resolve pressing problems of order, time, content, etc.[18] Certainly expectations may predispose the teacher towards indulgence as s/he prospects the likely action of the pupil displaying difficult or indifferent behaviour. Some teachers, like Mr Khan with Form 2p, did express negative attitudes towards girls in science: 'girls are not really interested in the steam engine . . . boys are naturally interested' – such attitudes might well have contributed to the kind of indulgence exemplified above. As Denscombe (1980b, p. 65) suggests 'where they [teachers] come to regard the behaviour as "normal" for the particular pupil, there is a tendency to indulge the behaviour and cease attempts to remedy the normally unacceptable behaviour'. What we are stressing, however, is that the initial emergence of behaviours subsequently indulged by teachers have their basis in the material conditions of curricular and pedagogical practice to which teachers and pupils, with more or less difficulty, are subject and routinely relate. In the circumstances described it is thus more appropriate to view this stereotyped explanation as a feature of rhetoric which papers over cracks in performance, to explain disjuncture between course intentions and everyday practice. As Woods (1977, p. 288) argues, survival strategies have 'a rhetoric closely attending them', which in the context he describes

> asserts the peculiar characteristics of these pupils, personal, environmental, mental, which entitles them to special treatment, and the relationships they develop with the teacher concerned, which ensures the success of the survival manoeuvre is presented as evidence of the justification of the rhetoric. Thus the problem is collapsed back in the situation and contained within a solution that masquerades, very powerfully and convincingly, as education.

For those pupils unable to meet the requirements of doing Science, as defined by existing curriculum and pedagogical practice, unable to handle content, MOT (in group work), to work independently in an oblique frame of control within the time made available, Science teaching may represent a frustrating and unrewarding experience and they may by the second year no longer wish to take part in such lessons. In the view of first and second year teachers, such pupils were labelled as 'less able', 'most difficult', 'time wasters', 'not serious', they are 'unable to concentrate', 'don't listen', as 'very silly and childish', and 'immature'. The pupils of the counter-steering group of Form 1p, however, expected their teacher to take a firmer line, to be more strict: 'she doesn't make us work', 'she can't control'. Against the background of a frame of control which their teacher in class teaching subsequently invoked, these statements may appear somewhat contradictory, as the excess of public positional messages which the teacher issued could be seen to accord with pupil expectations and wishes. Yet their behaviour did not improve. There were a number of reasons for this, including the fact that the changing context of control did not alter their pedagogical or curricular opportunities for success at learning. Other reasons can be gleaned from the following statements of pupils of Form 1p.

> It's too boring . . . nobody likes science . . . it's not the teacher, it's just boring, you have to do writing all the time, it's boring (Caroline).

> We should do the experiments . . . what we are supposed to do . . . should learn science not writing and all that (Rene).

> If she left us alone to do the experiments we wouldn't be chatting, we wouldn't have time to chat. We would be working. Some of the teachers don't want you to learn. All we do is writing every day. Each time we come to science . . . if we do experiments . . . you know . . . she has to do it first (Peter).

> When you do it with the teacher you don't really get the experience. She tells you how it's going to happen (Ryan).

> If you don't do it on your own . . . if you do it on your own . . . you get to learn it for yourself . . . yeah . . . I understand it better then (Jerry).

Evidently, not only did the less able pupil find difficulty with content, MOT (given reading ability) and the frame of control, but also s/he was subject to a great deal of boredom and frustration. By and large, in the strategy of class teaching adopted by teachers, the pupils' role was relegated to one of passivity and conformity. Pupils placed a high premium on working in groups, on investigatory activity which was associated with doing Science and learning, even if, as we suggested, only of a limited kind. Consequently, while the frame of teacher control over pupil conduct *was* more publicly and rigorously exerted in whole class method, it occurred simultaneously with a reduction in pedagogical practices which, from the pupils' perspective, were regarded as legitimate, proper, science activity. *In effect, an increase in teacher control had a concomitant decreasing legitimacy*,[19] the upshot of which was an increase in pupil frustration, antagonism and alienation, and the placing of teachers in an extremely unenviable position.

Setting for Survival and Grouping for Control

The limited conceptual understanding which the approaches above produced in children contradicted the intentions of both teachers and course. We are not suggesting, however, that group work was a 'better' instructional form that whole class method, whether or not indulgence is a salient feature. Both instructional patterns allowed some pupils to progress without necessarily having understood, via peers in group work and the blackboard and concluding remarks in whole class method. In both, teachers were confronted with problems of pupil control, the development of which, we suggest, was located in the following process: In the first weeks of term as pupils related to the content of Science through the worksheet as a mode of instruction, within an oblique form of control, in limited time, learning problems were increasingly made apparent in active forms of behaviour which, against a wider frame of control in which teachers operate, are extremely problematic. Unlike the situation in Mathematics at Sageton, however, in Science these problems did not have to be resolved within the course structure. Conscious of the demands for good classroom control and pressured by the pacing implied in the course organization, teachers resorted to whole class method. This strategy was not chosen in a vacuum.[20] Teachers clearly drew upon skills and techniques derived from personal experience or professional training which, as the statements of the faculty presented earlier suggested and our data[21] bears out, provided conceptions of teaching, learning, etc. at variance with those embodied in the course. As far as these interactions were not intended practices of the teachers concerned, it is appropriate to regard them as coping strategies. 'They were "constructive and adaptive, creatively articulated solutions to recurring daily problems" ' (A. Hargreaves, 1978, p. 248). By class teaching, however, learning problems were not resolved but evaded and a steering group phenomenon, characteristic of whole class method, emerged. Problems of discipline and order persisted. Additionally this practice violated a pupil's expectation of doing Science and exacerbated rather than precluded a teacher's disciplinary concerns. Teachers were thus placed in an extremely unenviable position. To revert to practices in accord with pupil and course expectations was, *for as long as the conditions of curriculum and pedagogical practice remained unchanged*, simply to reproduce a teacher's problems of control. As we see, however, teachers had little opportunity because of wider frames of resource and time to effect changes in these conditions. A cycle of recrimination (of disorder and control) was set in motion in which both teacher and pupil identities were repeatedly and negatively reproduced and defined. Pupils were 'less able' and 'difficult', teachers were 'not strict' and 'don't want you to learn'. In these circumstances, unable to effect curriculum change, *setting* again (as in Languages) represented an immediate second level, organizational coping strategy.

During the period of study, a great deal of discussion centred on the question of whether to continue with the practice of setting in the third year, which had been introduced for the first time in the previous school year. A major split appeared between the majority of staff who favoured its discontinuation (and appealed for mixed ability even in the fourth year) and those (mainly senior teachers) who argued for its continuation. One of the latter argued:

> I'm happy now that we top and tail in the third year. It's good for the bod who takes the bright ones, but the ones in the middle, nobody, there's nobody to push them along. There are problems certainly. I would stick to mixed ability in the 1st and 2nd year for all sorts of reasons . . . but mainly social . . . the kids get together and help each other.

Another stated:

> Personally I'm in favour of this policy (of setting) . . . you can guarantee better results at examinations. On the other hand I would feel the same way as those who take the middle band, but it does safeguard the future of these pupils.

Despite the recognition that for the majority of pupils all was not well with the policy of setting, and the existing course content and presentation, both these teachers, senior in the Science hierarchy, are prepared to accept and support its continuation. Like Sharp and Green (1975) and A. Hargreaves (1978), we would suggest that the origin of these views need to be located outside the classroom, in the relations between teachers and, in the extra school context, in the identity of the school in the perspectives of interested outsiders (parents and feeder School Heads). In this situation teachers had to resolve a tension between their interests in realizing their subject principles, ideals of mixed ability grouping (social integration, co-operation, etc.) and the necessity to efficiently and reliably 'produce the goods', including selecting out pupils for the immediate purpose of providing evidence of teacher–school competence and in the interest of their future survival. Mixed ability grouping (in years 1 and 2) in conjunction with setting and the assessment inherent in the scheme, provide an immediate and functional means of coping. An image of social integration, progressive liberal practice and/or the effective selection of pupil ability, could thus be called upon to meet conflicting expectations of significant others. As one teacher remarked:

> at a Governors meeting the Head said he was firmly opposed to setting and that they only did it in Faculty of Social Sciences. The story is different when he's talking to white middle class parents who he can assure that their children could get into top groups and be fully catered for.

Setting here shares the characteristic imputed to all coping strategies, which contain

> the seeds of their own continuance and growth, often outliving their usefulness and festering, causing another problem, for which another survival strategy must be devised. They do not take the problems out of the arena as it were, leaving more room for teaching, rather they expand into teaching and around it like some parasitic plant and eventually in some cases the host might be completely killed off. Alternately they will appear as teaching, their survival value having a higher premium than their educational value (Woods, 1977, p. 275).

Although a highly overdramatic account of the significance of coping strategies, this pinpoints their possible outcomes. For example, Science teachers at Sageton lucky enough to teach top groups, as the above statements suggest, experienced an immediate reduction in their instructional and disciplinary problems. Such was the satisfaction to be derived from their experience that it encroached upon and challenged sincerely held principles opposed to selective grouping. Setting was consequently advocated as a viable solution to the problems of all teachers.

> Theoretically I'm totally opposed to it. The reality is some pupils have moved ahead at a faster pace than they would have done. I can't speak for the middle band but had some brighter kids been mixed up with some of the middle group pupils I wouldn't have been able to teach them. What I'm saying is, mixed ability is bloody difficult. I suggest, top groups on a rotational basis. If I was taking only the middle groups I would be against this (Mr Phelps).

For the majority of staff, however (as the statements below suggest), confined to teaching middle groups, opposition to the policy of setting centred upon problems of pupil discipline and poor motivation.

> Last year I enjoyed it when the class was mixed. Now they're missing the stimulus of the brighter kids. They know they are labelled (Mrs George).

> I can see the kids coming into the lower groups to see themselves as the lowest of the low (Mrs Turner).

People who take the top groups feel that pupils are gaining. T. is saying that her bottom groups are not too bad. The people who teach the middle groups . . . the majority . . . it seems they are missing out (Mrs Cooper)[22].

The deleterious effects of labelling, the absence of 'the stimulus of the brighter kids', underlay these teachers' demands for mixed ability grouping. The latter by implication is represented as a context more beneficial for the middle range of pupil ability, though our data lends this implicit claim little support. Table 13 suggests that it is pupils defined as 'average', a typical Sageton pupil, who are most disadvantaged (overlooked) in the classroom, mixed ability grouped or otherwise, and who received least instructional attention. However, removing from the class those pupils able and willing to succeed within the forms of teaching we have described, did pose for the majority of teachers considerable problems of instruction and control. Not only did setting aggravate their endeavours to secure classroom order, it also brought into focus (and called into question) the very credibility of the learning programme itself, as this exchange suggests:

Mr Lane	The topics we have are very advanced, they need to be revised.
Head of Faculty	[defensively] . . . They were written for mixed ability.
Mr Lane	Yes, but not with the top pupils streamed off.

The significance of a small group of pupils is thus revealed. These pupils sustained the image of mixed ability *teaching*, justified the continuation of the course (despite its limitations) and thereby ensured repeated failure of the majority of pupils. Their failure was ascribed not to deficiencies in the course but to qualities inherent in the pupils, their personality, social or material circumstances. The 'able' pupils provided the norm against which the actions of all other pupils were appraised and upon which the legitimacy of the teaching and curriculum on offer was sustained. For this reason, a narrowing of the range of ability presented to teachers was likely to, and eventually did, bring increasing pressures on senior staff to focus attention on and revise existing curriculum practice. Against the background of pressures to which we have alluded, and within a context of limiting frames of resource and time, these were demands which they were reluctant and unlikely to concede. They argued instead for a continuation of selective practices via setting in the third year as the more effective way of exploiting available pupil abilities. Hence, without curriculum and pedagogical reform, the problem of teaching and the cycle of failure to which we have referred was repeatedly and inexorably reproduced.

six

Social Sciences:
Individuated Curriculum

In this chapter we focus attention upon the activities of five teachers, Mrs Bodie, Ms Lewis, Mr Richards, Ms Newman and Mr Day, and the way in which they rather differently attempted to implement an individuated, Integrated Studies scheme. Attention is drawn to general features of teaching within the scheme, but important, if subtle differences in approach, are also identified. These arise from quite limited opportunities within the integrated course for teachers to impose personal goals, beliefs and principles and to realize idiosyncratic teaching styles.

The Integrated Scheme in Social Science at Sageton: background

Academic organization at Sageton took the form of a six faculty system. Each incorporated several departments whose autonomy flourished more strongly in the middle and upper school but which were curtailed in the pursuit of thematic 'relevance' in the lower. Such was the case in respect of the Social Science Faculty which in 1977 was constituted by the departments of RE, Integrated Studies, Geography, History and Multi-cultural Studies and contained 16 teaching staff, three of whom taught Social Sciences for less than half a full time timetable. The time allocated for 'Integrated' Studies in each of years one and two, and 'Related' Studies in year three, was 210 minutes per week. In year 1, upon which this discussion will very largely concentrate, the timetable was blocked to allow 6 × 35 minutes teaching units, organized by the faculty into a block of four plus two. The general pattern of teaching involved a lead lesson, always a film with a half year group of about 95 pupils. After the film the half year group divided into their respective tutor groups (e.g. Forms 1p, 1q, 1r,

1s). Each class then received 35 minutes each of General (where it was intended to follow up the film) and then History and Geography lessons. Later in the week each class received 35 minutes each of Multi-cultural Studies and Religious Education.

In year 2 a similar approach was adopted except that the timetable was not 'blocked' and the specialist subject requirements of the four departments (History, Geography, RE and Multi-cultural Studies) were accommodated by a complex alternation within a unit on a weekly basis. In year 3 the autonomy of subject departments was partially reaffirmed. Pupils received 70 minutes each of History, Geography, and either, Religious Education or Multi-cultural Studies, the latter sharing time on a half termly basis. Subject contents were 'related', that is to say drawn up in the knowledge of what was being taught in other departments, but the sequencing of units characteristic of teaching in years 1 and 2 was absent. In each of years 1–3 the curriculum and mode of presentation was *individuated*, that is to say, all pupils simultaneously had access to the same subject content within common prespecified time limits defined by the syllabus organization and timetabling. Pupils were expected to work alone, and largely independently of the teacher, through worksheets. The content of the courses in years 1–3 was at the 'newish' end of the spectrum and reflected aims more generally expressed in the wider subject subculture of social science teaching.[1]

> I think it's important to give pupils a world picture. We are so interdependent now. There's no point in concentrating only on Britain (Head of Faculty).

To this end, pupils were introduced, for example, to a Continent (with content contributed by each of the departments) and within this a theme or country.[2] In year 1, term 1, the first four weeks concentrated on the continent of Africa: the general theme was 'Tribes'. Each week was accounted for by an input (in the form of a worksheet) from each of the departments. Hence the week 1 lead lesson was a film on the 'Evolution of Life, Man'. Geography contributed, 'Map of Africa. Location of main tribes'. The History input was 'The Archaeologist, what he does'. Religious Education focused on 'Animism' and Multi-cultural Studies attended to 'Nomadic and Settled Culture'. Subsequent weeks had similar predefined contents for transmission, each embodied in the form of a worksheet. Knowledge within a subject was intended to develop cumulatively in breadth and depth but was not linearly sequenced from the point of view of any one of them.

From this brief outline we can see that the scheme imposed a variety of constraints on the teachers' pedagogic role. Not only was the curriculum predefined for them, but also the pedagogical mode of its transmission. The syllabus thus established for both teachers and pupils precisely defined parameters of time and content in which to work. Indeed, broad aims had been translated into a series of precisely defined contents for transmission. These in turn had been transposed to worksheets which in effect had become the syllabus, a situation not unlike that described by Hamilton (1976, p. 200). For the teachers concerned, theirs was a task of ensuring worksheet completion on a weekly, 35 minute unit basis in order to ensure simultaneous progress with adjacent subject contents.

Problems of pacing within the individuated scheme, given that pupils related differently to content in the time made available, were 'resolved' at the preparation stage, either by pitching work on the worksheets at various levels, or by providing additional tasks for the 'able' pupil to complete. Inherent to either resolution was a pacing of work which necessarily ensured that not all pupils could enjoy the satisfaction of worksheet completion. This problem was most acutely felt by teachers of first year pupils compelled to work within what was felt to be the insufficient 35 minutes per 'subject' imposed by the scheme. Achieving task completion amid increasing problems of control pushed teachers to articulate this problem of time as one of timetabling rather than that of curriculum organization. Consequently, its resolution was seen to lie in a future renegotiation of time made available (to allow 40–45 minutes) rather than in a reconsideration of the structure inherent in the syllabus itself. From the pupils' point of view, learning constituted getting to the facts presented by the worksheets in the limited time available. Each worksheet was self-contained though occasionally drawing on textbook material. Learning normally implied merely finding the answers by reading the material presented by the worksheet. Answers were already there, to be uncovered by reading the relevant text.[3] Sometimes this meant simply filling in the right word. Teachers were occasionally heard to indulge in the ancient rite of encouraging pupils to 'answer the question in sentences' but an overview of exercise books revealed a notable absence of this in practice. Within the frame of limited time and pressure for task completion the temptation to provide such material as to ensure 'progress' reduced knowledge in work books to a meaningless array of incomplete information. A situation not unlike that described by Birt (1976, p. 321) had arisen:

> Learning is essentially passive with pupils responding to the dictate of the teacher and textbook. The pupils' imaginations are not involved, thought is often unnecessary and personal involvement minimal. Nothing is done to increase the complexity of the child's thinking.[4]

However, if we are to understand the limits and possibilities of teaching and learning in 'Integrated' Social Science at Sageton we need, once again, to follow the paths of change and the conditions which influenced and framed observed practices.

Background to change: form before content

The integrated scheme described above was not the first attempt at integration within the Faculty of Social Science. A first phase of 'innovation' had taken place in 1975, one year following the inception of mixed ability grouping, with a move towards integration in the first year. A Head of Integrated Studies was appointed. In contrast to the history of change in both Mathematics and Science, the motivation for change did not emanate from senior staff (who rigidly opposed changes in curriculum practice within the Social Science Faculty) but from a group of enthusiastic and vociferous 'junior' staff. In consequence, the newly appointed Head of Integrated Studies was found in an unenviable position, of attempting to impose a 'new' integrated curriculum favoured by juniors on senior colleagues having deeply established and antagonistic subject identities.[5] Describing an early meeting with senior staff, he remarked:

> We had somebody in from the four departments, but we spent all our time arguing, the syllabus was a big problem. Nothing was produced. Everybody wanted more for their own subjects . . . Nobody wanted to give anything up. In the end I did it all and produced worksheets (Mr Campbell).

A year later, with the departure of this first Head of Integrated Studies and the appointment of a second, a further attempt to effect change was made:

> I got a totally different set up. I prepared things on a topic basis. I did the whole thing. In essence it was very good but too difficult. It was well accepted by staff but . . . problems . . . you had to have a box with 10 copies of each worksheet. Kids came up the front and said they wanted to do such and such a card. The problem was you had teachers who weren't committed to it so you got the box in a mess . . . By the end of the first term it had broken down. It was abandoned. Unless you had regular, committed staff it was going to be all ballsed up from the start (Mr Rice).

In January 1977 a new Head of Social Science was appointed. He was supportive of mixed ability and inclined towards curriculum change.

> I wanted to link together subjects. Where I taught before there was no

link up. I don't think there's anything to be learnt in isolation. There's
no point in doing different things, and at different times (Mr Frost).

He found, however,

things were in a mess. The integrated studies syllabus wasn't workable.
It was just a piece of paper . . . It was too difficult for the staff and kids.
We introduced a pilot scheme . . . changed about Easter, a kind of
introduction to what we were going to do. We had meetings, Head of
departments got together to discuss things. Geography was non-
existent, no syllabus, no books and X still here as a deposed Head. The
thing was, to have a framework.

The Integrated scheme (outlined in the previous section) was thus
adopted and it had several advantages. It enabled Mr Frost to realize
his intention of forging links between subjects. It also effected greater
control over other teachers. The initial concern was essentially
pragmatic, to impose a coherent framework on the anarchy of method
and content which had emerged. Hence the emphasis upon structure
rather than content:

This year we're going to get the structure right. Then we can sit down
and think about the content.

Moreover, the curriculum changes introduced avoided problems
associated with integration which had thwarted previous attempts at
innovation, that is to say, they allowed teachers 'to teach their own
subjects' (Head of Faculty), thereby retaining specific subject identities
and power domains. But demands of the timetable together with an
insufficient supply of teachers to ensure that each class could receive a
subject specialist on every occasion, still meant that teachers had to
teach a subject other than their own, with implications, as we see
below, for their instruction and control. However, the 'new' course
structure had neatly accommodated the authority of the Heads of
departments and the integrity and identity of their subject disciplines
along with Faculty management concerns for order and control over
more uniform teaching method and content. Thus there was little
initial opposition to the new course structure.

The innovation resolved these problems but others were immediately
created. The teachers themselves focused on the workload, the time
and exhaustion involved in establishing the course, particularly the
preparation of materials and worksheets, which meant they had
insufficient time to 'do a proper job'.

The aim was to have the whole first term work produced by the Summer
term. We had one and a half hours meetings a week to decide what we
were doing, then we just had to produce the stuff (Head of Integrated
Studies).

The large area (years 1–3) over which change was effected and the highly structured nature of the course (compelling the production of worksheets on a weekly basis) further exacerbated teacher problems of this nature. Even after the production of a sufficient quantity of materials to permit the introduction of the course, teachers remained concerned with what seemed to them an endless production of the next worksheet. As Mr Peters, a teacher of Integrated Studies remarked, 'the problems have remained the same . . . getting the worksheets in, preparation, getting them prepared in time'.

The significant point here is the way in which such problems, experienced in the management and preparation of a 'new' course, subsequently operated as frames or limits upon pupil and teacher *ability* in the teaching process. In Integrated Studies as in Integrated Science, the immediate tendency in the production of worksheets, was to reproduce within them a conception of ability and teaching characteristic of traditional whole class method. Teachers had neither the time nor the knowledge to plan and prepare otherwise. The solution to the 'problem' of mixed ability grouping was to produce class material pitched at the ability median of the class with *extra* materials (usually open-ended tasks) being provided for the able to keep them occupied until the introduction of new contents. The problem of 'pitch' also figured in the readability of the worksheets. Analyses suggested that they were suitable for pupils with a reading age of 12 and above. This difficulty was often compounded by the extremely poor quality of their legibility and presentation (itself largely contingent upon limited teacher time or technical inexpertise). As one teacher remarked: 'In the future we hope that all our worksheets will be typed' (Head of History). The scheme thus implied not only a level of pacing but also a level of ability/literacy required to work within the limited time available. As mentioned earlier, 34% of Sageton pupils had reading ages on entry of below nine, so many were certain to find the material on the worksheets difficult, perhaps incomprehensible and extremely frustrating within the pacing of the courses. In Integrated Studies, as in science teaching, beneath the surface appearance of innovation very little change had taken place either in teacher conceptions of pupil ability or in teacher ability to produce material varied enough to accommodate the abilities and interests of the majority of Sageton pupils.

However, factors other than time and expertise limited teachers' opportunities to invoke more substantial educational change. A further problem perceived by teachers was the level of resources available to them and the cost of producing sufficient material for each of the pupils to have 'their own worksheet'. In order to reduce demands of this nature a decision was taken to limit the production of worksheets (where possible) to a number sufficient for half of the pupils at any one time doing Integrated Studies (i.e. a half year group). This policy was possible in the first year as the pupils 'rotated' through each of the subjects. While two classes did History, another two did Geography, and then changed, and so on. While reducing preparation demands on the teacher, this practice simultaneously created further problems of teaching and learning within the classroom in respect of pacing, task completion and coverage, for with limited resource, pupils were often denied the opportunity to take worksheets home. But even when possible, this practice was often denied, 'shortage' being used as a justification when it was considered a 'risk' to allow pupils to remove worksheets from school. This meant that lesson time often had to be given to the task of 'copying out the questions for homework'[6]. This practice not only further encroached upon scarce time, but also removed from pupils their source of support and knowledge, necessary for later 'getting the right answer'. This was a further source of antagonism and frustration particularly for those pupils whose pace through the worksheet was such to provide limited access to its contents.

> When we have to do homework, right . . . we don't actually know something, right . . . well we just leave it out, and you know . . . right . . . when we leave it out we don't get a full mark for it . . . so we just leave it out (Caroline, Form 1p).

Time operated as a constraint in other ways. As Mrs Late remarked:

> What we do isn't integrated studies it's related studies. There is serious deficiencies of time, there's not enough time to talk about the scheme or the topics, or for departments to discuss how to draw out the interrelationships.

and Mr Lewis:

> Theoretically Geography, History lessons are based on the film, but there's no meeting for second year integrated studies teachers, so it can't be. It's a mess. So departments know who's producing the materials in their subject but don't know who's producing the other worksheets. You just go to the box and get it out.

The problems here are complex, and in part arise from a disjuncture between 'integration' as an idea (forced into coexistence with the 'traditional' subject based staff) and curriculum organization. Without an appropriate organizational structure supportive of new curricular intentions, opportunities for teachers to plan, develop and institutionalize integration in worksheet materials were severely restricted.[7]

Following the establishment of themes and structure at a senior management level, departments worked independently of each other producing relevant 'related' contents. In effect, the organization tended to ensure the systematic development of contents within departments, with only the most tenuous of links *between* subject contents. Consequently, the degree to which pupils perceived 'relatedness' in the course contents rested upon teacher endeavours to draw out their connection during lessons. As we see in the statements above, the teachers' opportunity to provide this sort of instruction was very limited. Without organizational means of departmental co-operation, yet with each teacher often expected to teach a subject other than his or her own, a tendency toward pedagogical instrumentality was inevitable. That is to say, teachers had little choice but to 'go to the box and get a worksheet', thereafter transmitting information which was precoded for them and about which little, if anything, was known.[8] Each subject remained effectively separated for teachers as for pupils.

For the pupils concerned, Integrated Studies certainly represented a frame (as limit) on ability not only in the form of time, level and quantity of transmission, but also in respect of its subject contents which together tended to lack sense, coherence and meaning. They provided a rich source of frustration and boredom.

> We work from worksheets all the time, every time, just like maths . . . work cards. All that rubbish . . . I don't like it . . . it's all muddled up . . . I don't understand it (Caroline, Form 1p).

and

> It's rubbish guy . . . jumble . . . I'd prefer to do history, geography and . . . like that (John, Form 1p).

These problems of integration experienced by teachers could be seen to go far deeper than that of the course *organization*. There was as yet no clear principles of integration to guide content selection such as would force departments together. Against the historical background of social science teaching at Sageton, however, this sort of luxury was not immediately possible, but was considered as a future focus for change.

> We have worked out the structure, now we can sit down and start to work on content, slant our work towards each others work (Head of Faculty).

However, as one teacher noted:

> At present the themes seem to be chosen by Departmental Heads and Faculty Heads. It appears quite arbitary. It might be better if we could reflect on the themes, why it's chosen. At present it doesn't appear that this is so (Mr Bird).

Integrated in name but not in organizational structure, decision making remained firmly in the hands of senior teachers. Teachers could feel remote from areas of decision making concerned with crucial matters of curriculum goals and course organization. They were expected to engage in intra-departmental co-operation concerning the production of worksheets and contents only after overall goals had been set by senior staff. Ironically, 'integration' of this form had made the arena of decision making more remote from teachers, the gap between senior staff and the majority greater than had previously been the case.

It is not surprising, in respect of what has been noted, that teachers of Integrated Studies were found to be experiencing problems of pupil control. The limits of time, presentation and content ensured that learning for some pupils was extremely problematic, a frustrating and unrewarding experience, as these statements (from pupils of Forms 1p and 2p) indicate:

> They're so short, you don't get time to finish the lesson. We're in the middle of a lesson and we're interested and we are told to go to see the film . . . then it finishes (Richard, Form 2p).

> They take the whole lesson reading out the worksheet and then the rest of the lesson is too short. If you had two lessons . . . normal like maths and English that would be alright (Liona, Form 1p).

Of course not all pupils experienced time as a frame in this way. Others, however, unable to enter successfully into the teaching process, increasingly expressed their disaffection in active and difficult forms of behaviours.

Physical contingencies further increased teachers' concerns for order. Organized into a main block of 4 × 35 minute units, in year 1 Integrated Studies created added occasion for pupil movement between lessons and increased interactional opportunities for indulgence in interest (i.e. non-work) activity during the merging of two classes for the lead (film) lesson. With the significance of the films shown not always apparent to children, and their growing awareness that the contents of subsequent lessons could be coped with largely independent of attention during film lessons, the teachers' problems of achieving pupil order became steadily worse, as even the first term in a year progressed.

> But after we do the film . . . not always . . . right . . . we don't do the same thing about the film because they don't talk about the film (Penny, Form 1s).

> But when they show the film if I'm not listening it kind of worries me because if someone else is talking, I start talking, the whole class talks. That's how it all develops (Ryan, Form 1p).

> It was more like Saturday morning pictures . . . You'd forget what the film was about (Elizabeth, Form 2p).

Teachers also focused on problems of pupil control, in and between lessons, as it related to other pressing concerns for time and task completion.

> At the moment there's a lot of time spent moving around . . . this isn't satisfactory, lessons are so short as it is (Mr Frost).

Problems of teaching, learning and control were thus established for teachers and pupils outside the classroom, at the Department and Faculty level of decision making. Mixed ability teaching as embodied in the syllabus realized a change in course structure rather than content. This change was necessary in order to effect control and some continuity over *teachers* and *method*. Given this structure, teachers understandably had neither the time nor the expertise to fully consider or appreciate what mixed ability *teaching* might mean in terms of an educational practice capable of reaching and teaching the full range of pupil abilities and predispositions with which they were confronted.

Teaching Strategies in Individuated Curriculum

In these conditions, teachers devised a number of strategies to reduce their problems of instruction, management and control. As we will see, within classrooms control was exerted through interaction in specific ways with individual pupils or with the class as a whole. Outside classrooms, for lead lessons and changeover, teachers vigorously 'policed'[9] corridor behaviour, while in some second year classrooms opportunities for movement were removed altogether, the teachers preferring to 'team teach' rather than provide occasion for disorder. The emergence of this latter form of 'new' teaching was thus motivated by concerns for control rather than by a more progressive pedagogical philosophy or any purely 'educational' rationale. Organizational decisions taken at levels outside the classroom thus became foci for the hidden curriculum.

In initial observations of classroom practice it was easy to be impressed less by the difference in teacher action defined in terms of their 'use of time' than by their apparent similarity. In total some 28 first and second year and 16 third year lessons were observed. On no occasion was a teacher of Integrated Studies observed to deviate from the course structure, or fail to use its 'recommended' mode of transmission. Table 14 provides some examples of the temporal structure in five first and second year classrooms. (The first year lessons lasted 35 minutes, the second 70 minutes.) Table 15 refers to contrasts in the talk of first and second year teachers in the settling and closure phases.

Table 14 shows quite clearly that pupil work dominates most classes in the examples given, and Table 15 that most teacher talk is immediate and instructional, that is to say, delivered to individual pupils (mostly at their own desks) rather than to the whole class. This is markedly different to that which we would expect in whole class teaching, though it reveals more teacher centralization of talk than is the case for the same classes working in *individualized*[10] instructional modes like SMP Maths. In second (as in third) years, with longer (70 minutes) work periods, there tended to be more class instruction, more teacher talk. Mrs Day with Form 2p is a clear case of this, dividing time evenly between introductory whole class instruction and pupil work (30 minutes each, Table 13) and also effecting more individual interactions in the hearing of the whole class during the introductory phase than were effected 'privately' in pupil work time, whether control or instruction oriented.

Characteristically, there was firstly a settling phase, establishing explicit positional teacher control, when worksheets were administered. Against this background there was an introduction of the worksheets to pupils. Their contents were read either by the teacher or

Table 14 Contrasts in the temporal structures of five first and second year teachers' lessons

Teacher, Form and lesson observed		Phases in minutes				
		Settling	Introductory	Pupil Work	Closure	Total
Mrs Bodie (Geography)	1s	4	5	20	3	32
Mr Richards (History)	1s	3	10	18	4	35
Ms Lewis (General)	1p	5	6	20	4	35
Ms Newman (Multi-cultural Studies)	2p	8	14	40	7	69
Mrs Day (RE)	2p	5	30	30	5	70

Form 2p was shared for Integrated Studies by Ms Newman and Mrs Day. Mrs Bodie and Mr Richards shared the teaching of Form 1s.

Table 15   Contrasts in the talk of first and second year teachers of Integrated Studies during the introductory (in brackets) and pupil work phases of the lessons described in Table 14.

Teacher, Form and lesson observed		Public regulative		Immediate instructional	
Mrs Bodie (Geography)	1s	(1)	4	(4)	10
Mr Richards (History)	1s	(2)	5	(5)	35
Ms Lewis (General)	1p	(3)	4	(8)	12
Ms Newman (Multi-cultural Studies)	2p	(2)	12	(—)	14
Mrs Day (RE)	2p	(4)	3	(20)	16

selected pupils or the task was shared and elaborated or clarified (usually to resolve problems of poor presentation) either through teacher talk or question–answer sequences. The latter displayed features typical of whole class method.[11] Questions were characteristically 'closed'. Answers could be guessed, or required little more than an ability to recall information previously acquired. Hence, a display of ability was contingent upon a willingness to conform to rules of attention/concentration. What counted as knowledge was confined to the parameters of factual content defined by the syllabus. Questions were steered by the teacher's concerns for what was functionally necessary to reduce immediate and pressing problems of instruction (pacing, coverage) and control. These features are further elaborated and exemplified below. This phase was followed by a period of individuated pupil work. In this respect (see Tables 14 and 15) Integrated Studies classrooms were far less 'busy' places for teachers than those of individualized instruction, e.g. in SMP workcard Maths. Generally, there were fewer interactions at an immediate face-to-face level and fewer public regulatory messages. Teachers tended to take one or two roles during this phase, first, and most prevalent, a supervisory role (Mrs Bodie with Form 1s, Mrs Lewis with 1p and Ms Newman with 2p), characterized by an explicit positional frame of control, the teacher taking up a front of class position, interacting with a few individuals when called upon to do so either in response to a pupils' appeal or 'needs' or their manifestly different behaviour. Secondly, as exemplified by Mr Richards with Form 1s, to a lesser extent by Mrs Day with 2p, the pupil work phase was characterized by a period of intense interaction or 'busyness' as the teacher did the rounds. These differences cannot simply be reduced to differences of teacher 'philosophy' in terms such as the traditional *vs* the progressive. Indeed, as we will see, the greater contrast in philosophy was between Mrs Bodie and Ms Lewis, whose classroom action was markedly similar.

Some examples from the practice of these teachers will highlight the relationship between the limits of curricula and the teaching process, and indicate the opportunities for the imposition of idiosyncratic teacher styles.

Mrs Bodie and Mr Richards, both senior teachers committed to further development of the Integrated Studies Scheme and (with some reservations) mixed ability teaching, were responsible for teaching the pupils of Form 1s. They 'team taught' only in 'Films', with Mrs Bodie subsequently teaching the General lessons, Mr Richards the History lesson, and finally Mrs Bodie returning to teach the Geography lesson. Eleven of the pupils of 1s had reading ages below 10, three of them Asian pupils with very little English. Both teachers were concerned about problems of instruction and pupil control. In lead lessons (films) they used a number of strategies to resolve their problems. The settling phase characteristically began with the teachers dividing their labour so that Mrs Bodie took up a supervisory role while Mr Richards ensured the readiness of the projector, etc. This was followed by a brief 2–5 minute introduction of the film contents, and involved little more than a quick reminder of what had previously been seen and what the day's viewing was to consist of. For example:

> Today we're going to look at Egypt, at the Egyptians, at the Oasis, all the people who live around them. How they live . . . methods of cultivation (Mrs Bodie to Form 1s).

This opening was followed by a further attempt to orientate the film (which tended to be of a general type covering an area of content far wider than prescribed by the syllabus) to contents known to be connected to subsequent worksheet contents, for example:

> I want you to note in particular . . . irrigation – why is it used? (Mrs Bodie to Form 1s).

This was followed by appeals for order, in the form of procedural statements:

> If you don't follow now you won't know what to do in the classroom (Mrs Bodie to Form 1s).

The structural constraints of the syllabus and a large crowd of pupils are being expressed in the form and content of teacher talk. The teacher defines what is to be learnt, what is valid knowledge, extracting from the range of opportunities presented by the films that knowledge which is of subsequent significance for worksheet completion. An extension of this strategy was observed in some second year classrooms where pupils were required to make notes on the film. Not knowing what to note and seemingly knowing the invalidity of subjective impressions, pupils compelled teachers to state what was relevant. Teachers responded in the manner 'we'll tell you when to write something . . . if it's important . . . just watch till then.' As teachers lacked knowledge of subsequent contents other than those for which they were directly responsible, teacher talk tended to be further restricted to specific subject areas. During a lead film, for example (with Forms 1s and 1q), communication between teacher and pupils took the following form.

Mrs Bodie	What's in the bags? If it's a hot climate what are you going to lose a lot of?
Lynne (1s)	Hair!
Mrs Bodie	Through the skin? . . . Salt . . . So what's going to be important?
John (1s)	Salt.
Mrs Bodie	Salt . . . Yes . . . So what do you think is in the bags?
Pupils	[in unison] . . . Salt.
Mrs Bodie	Yes . . . good . . . salt.

Pupil contributions are typically short, and guided toward slots in a developing exposition (Edwards, 1980). In an obvious sense, these features of talk in lead lessons resolved both instructional *and* regulatory concerns. Classroom order related to the teachers success at establishing the significance of lead lessons for subsequent lessons. Nevertheless, some pupils recognized the limited importance of these lessons and increasingly displayed difficult behaviours. Indulgence of such behaviours (facilitated by the darkness demanded by films) emerged as a supportive controlling strategy.

General lessons, which preceded or followed lead lessons emerged as occasions of strategic importance for teachers such as Mrs Bodie and Mr Richards. This time was used either to reintroduce worksheets previously unfinished or introduce a worksheet for completion in subsequent lessons. Rarely was time used as intended to 'follow up', i.e. to discuss the contents of films observed. This strategy reduced a teacher's problems of pacing and task completion but, interposed between lead and follow up History and Geography lessons, further undermined the significance and coherence of the work in the pupils perspectives (see Penny's comment, p. 107)

Factors other than time, however, influenced a teacher's decision to use lesson time in the manner described. Mrs Bodie notes:

> Ideally this period would be used for discussion of the film, but you can't do that with pupils like Lynne and Brian present. They are so unpredictable . . . you can't risk it.

Control was sought in those activities which offered greatest structure and opportunities for surveillance of pupil behaviours by the involvement of *all* pupils with the worksheet, rather than in the single person verbal exchange of whole class 'discussion'. Occasionally, however, the latter was attempted (by Mrs Bodie).

Mrs Bodie	In the film we saw some mounds, what were they called . . . Brian?
Brian	Pardon Miss?
Mrs Bodie	[repeats]
Brian	Dunes.
Mrs Bodie	Yes . . . why can't people go around in bare feet?
Brian	It's too hot . . . they get burnt feet.
Mrs Bodie	Yes . . . [elaborates].

This somewhat mechanical questioning of pupils continued for 25 minutes. There was no exchange of information or expression of opinion on the part of pupils and consequently no indication or impression of the problems they may have experienced with the film. The orientation in the teachers response was towards assessment, rather than reply.[12] Insight or 'knowledge' was not required of pupils beyond levels of attention to, and recall of, previously accumulated contents. Moreover, a cursory glance at the distribution of communication in this lesson revealed that the 'able' child (as defined by teacher ratings) accounted for the greater part of individual communication with the teacher. Eight pupils accounted for 26 of the 39 'bids' or responses to teacher questions, while another six took the remaining 13. The latter pupils, amongst the least able and most problematic to the teacher, were controlled by teacher-initiated involvement in instructional talk. Individuating the curriculum brought about few changes in the structure or content of classroom discourse. It was (as we saw in Languages and Science) controlled by the teacher and steered by the syllabus content, its pacing defined with reference to the able child. Individual differences amongst pupils brought to the context were thus likely to be confirmed.[13]

Subsequent History and Geography lessons taught by Mrs Bodie and Mr Richards had many of the features previously described. In their History and Geography lessons described in Tables 14 and 15 the introductory phase was characteristically short, though Mr Richards spent almost twice as much as Mrs Bodie in this phase. Little attempt was made to show connections between specific worksheet contents and the structure of the course as a whole. Talk was restricted to clarifying immediate contents, to ensuring sufficient understanding for 'progress', i.e. worksheet completion, in the phase of pupil work. Pupil progress was further facilitated by teachers 'doing first questions' or even all of them, on the worksheet, the teacher either providing answers or stressing how or where they may be found in the text. In this way teacher's immediate management problems were reduced.

In the phase of pupil individuated work, however, differences between Mrs Bodie and Mr Richards emerged. Mrs Bodie's approach was characterized by a supervisory role. Once the introductions phase had been completed, she assumed that the worksheet content was sufficient for pupils to progress. She 'did first questions', thereby reducing immediate demands upon herself to resolve individual learning problems. Further problems had little scope in which to flourish as a particular worksheet 'lasted' only for a single period. Next week brought a repetition of the same limited sequence in which this teacher's concern focused predominantly upon maintaining classroom order. In the lesson described (Table 15), she interacted with nine of the 20 pupils present for instructional purposes on ten occasions during the pupil work phase. Throughout the lesson, pupils were left in no doubt as to the asymmetry of relationships which obtain between them and teachers *and* her commitment to imposing the course upon them in its existing form, of 'making it work'. In the settling phase, for example, talk was characterized by harsh imperatives and positional appeals.

> What a stupid lot you are . . . sit down . . . am I going to wait for you to settle down? Hurry up . . . OK . . . turn to your worksheet.

Thereafter 'silence' was called for while selected pupils read the text. In contrast to this somewhat autocratic approach, the actions of Mr Richards appeared as altogether more 'liberal'. Control (to use Bernstein's (1977) notion) was less visible, boundaries between lesson phases were more obscure and hold over pacing, within the limited time permitted, more relaxed. For example, in an introduction phase, the teacher announced:

> OK . . . those who wish to read . . . listen now . . . if you're happy carry on . . . If not listen.

By allowing the 'able' to proceed alone, the less able received the necessary clarification of content, though their problem of worksheet completion was still not resolved. Furthermore, in the interest of maintaining order and securing completion, this teacher placed a premium on interaction with all pupils at an immediate face-to-face level, as can be seen in Table 15.

Both teachers expressed a commitment to mixed ability grouping, Mrs Bodie because of

> the detrimental effects of selection on those who don't get into the top streams,

and Mr Richards, because in

> mixed ability, you've got to teach as a class of individuals. They've got to be known and related to individually . . . but the possibilities of this? The amount of energy needed is terrific. How to recognise 2 or 3 pupils all likely to be control problems, Fiona for example . . . you let them get on with it a little in respect of the group and you come back to them . . . to get them going.

We might infer that Mrs Bodie believed the 'work' of mixed ability innovation to be accomplished when streaming was abolished. Nothing else followed in terms of a need to alter pedagogy. Mr Richards' justification for mixed ability was in terms of the utility of a more individual pedagogy and an attempt was made to reform teaching action in consequence.

Time was an acutely scarce commodity for Mr Richards. Given the pupil demands emergent in his classroom context (with a weaker frame of control than Mrs Bodie), his ideals could hope to be realized only via the expenditure of considerable energy and an amount of 'indulgence' of otherwise deviant behaviours. This teacher was 'oriented towards being a class teacher' and to getting things moving via his own initial talk in which a display of teacher enthusiasm was perceived as crucial to pupil motivation. It was in the act of 'doing the rounds' that he consequently attempted to achieve a great deal of immediate individual contact only to be inevitably constrained by the worksheet. As Barnes (1977, p. 137) points out, worksheets 'interposed between the teacher and the pupil will tend to minimise the likelihood that the teacher's interests in the subject matter will be communicated to his pupils'. In doing the rounds (and during introductory phases which were longer than those of Mrs Bodie) a 'performance' was given in which the salient qualities appeared as dynamic enthusiasm, humour and interest for the subject.

The behaviour of both these teachers represented strategic responses to shared structural problems, mediated by individual perception. Both teachers were 'successful' both in establishing order, and in the appearance of productivity within the structure of the integrated course. Mrs Bodie 'contained' learning problems expressed in difficult behaviour by public regulation rather than instructional intervention. Mr Richards, in contrast, used a wider variety of strategies. He, like Mrs Bodie, established a positional frame of control in which teacher authority and the asymmetry of pupil–teacher relationships were clearly and publicly defined. However, within this frame, he relaxed control over pacing, displayed interest and gave help at an immediate level. Thus he was able to facilitate a degree of progress amongst all pupils, though of a limited kind given the brevity of such interaction, and to weaken the constraints on pupil achievement which the structures of the scheme imposed.

Ms Lewis with Form 1p, in contrast to each of these teachers, equated mixed ability with 'a more flexible structure'.

> If a child asks a question and it doesn't know the answer, it doesn't seem relevant . . . and it could contribute . . . it could be a learning situation for all of them. Then I think you should accommodate it.

At the same time she was aware of constraints in the form of a wider framework of expectations which defined teaching and learning in a way contrary to her own and which limited opportunities to effect this sort of teaching.

> The only problem in mixed ability is very . . . sort of . . . tends to be very informal way of teaching. To teach informally you have to have an informal structure. This school doesn't have that. It's very formal. If your children are noisy in a lesson or if they seem to be enjoying themselves then people who are passing your classroom might say that you had no discipline.

In contrast to both previous teachers mentioned, Ms Lewis in initial encounters with the pupils of Form 1p tried to use General lessons as intended in the course.

(A)	Ms Lewis	Today . . . I don't want to do any writing . . . we are going to have a discussion. I want to know what *you* thought about the film.
(B)	Jerry	[copies the teacher] . . . I want to know what you thought about the film?
(C)	Ms Lewis	Ryan! What did you think of the film?
(D)	Jerry	It was about Egypt and the river Nile. How people get water from the river.
(E)	Ms Lewis	. . . right . . . yes . . . what did the water do for them?
(F)	Jerry	Grow crops.

(G)	Ms Lewis	Good . . . is *he* right? . . . We saw it was barren, in the desert, you can't just produce water. How did they get water?
(H)	Liona	I don't know.
(I)	Ms Lewis	Look listen . . . listen to what others have to say.
(J)	John	It was rubbish.
(K)	Ms Lewis	Why is it rubbish? . . come on . . . that's a silly thing to say . . . give a reason . . .
(L)	John	I can't understand a word they're saying.
(M)	Ms Lewis	What did you see?
(N)	David	It's a stone age country.
(O)	Ms Lewis	Explain . . .
(P)	David	They didn't wear modern clothes, they were primitive people . . . they lived in mud huts.

(The teacher has to intervene in the growing non-work activity of pupils. 'I'll wait a minute to see how quiet you can be, Ryan can't be quiet . . . OK. Odette give out the folders . . . I wasn't going to do any writing but you can't be quiet'.)

Ms Lewis attempted to use the time available for lead lessons in a way quite contrary to that of Mrs Bodie. Her actions reflected her belief that it was important to define the situations in such a way that more 'open' forms of communication were possible. Indeed, difficulties with content were revealed in John's answer (L) and in David's (N) reply, which would not have surfaced in more typically 'closed' communications. It became apparent, however, that as the frame of teacher control over knowledge was relaxed, disciplinary problems increased. Engaging in this form of communication, Ms Lewis assumed that pupils are able and willing to interpret this form of questioning as meaningful and therefore act in the desired way (cf. Salmon and Claire, 1984). While some pupils were able to respond in the desired way, others found such talk tangential to the task of getting work done. Jerry remarks:

> we didn't do any work just talk . . . and then she's always moaning at you.

Ironically, such teacher action *generated* difficult behaviour, and it was to these very pupils who expected a strong positional frame of control (in this case, the least able pupils and those pupils defined by the teacher as able but difficult and underachieving), that such 'open' questions were addressed, in an endeavour to *maintain* order. Consequently, in subsequent lessons observed, the teacher was less inclined towards this form of discussion, there was more work from worksheets, discussion of a type earlier outlined, and a supervisory role similar to that of Mrs Bodie. In the General lesson outlined in Tables 14 and 15, for example, Ms Lewis interacted with only ten of the 19 pupils for instructional purposes on 12 occasions during the phase of pupil work. Her actions were steered by the disciplinary problems presented by the less able (Jerry, Ryan, Rene and Liona) and the able but difficult pupils, particularly John, Heather and Mary. These two categories account for over half of the immediate contacts, while David, Paul and Caroline, less 'able' and also behaviourally difficult in the teacher's perspective, received the remaining individual contact.

Thus Ms Lewis' endeavours to step outside the structure of the scheme with Form 1p were limited not only by content and time but also by the pupils themselves. As Barnes (1977, p. 127) has noted, they have learnt during the years that most teachers only wish to hear the expected reply, that they do not want discussions 'that include divergent viewpoints and which raise different questions from theirs'. Given that the pupils of 1p experienced routinely a supervisory style of teaching in Integrated Studies and with other subject teachers, it would be most surprising if this teacher were able to 'bring off' successfully the kind of approach she ideally desired.

The problems of control which Ms Lewis now faced were not unlike those experienced elsewhere by 'idealist' English teachers, observed by Caroline St. John-Brook (1983). She found that teachers' attempts to 'resist the common sense assumptions that children go to school to have facts put in their heads' met with little support from some, particularly less able, working class children. As the Sageton data suggests, some 'able' working class children fail to learn because of a mismatch between theirs and the teachers' conception of appropriate classroom, teacher–pupil relationships. The 'problem' lies with the teachers' frame of control rather than with their conception of knowledge.

In Integrated Studies, once the course content was produced in the worksheet there was nothing else for teachers to do other than secure its transmission, revise or improve its contents. As Mr Frost noted:

> Well it seems to have become a bit too easy . . . You get teachers just going to the box before a lesson and taking a worksheet . . . That's it.

Once established, the courses took on an existence largely independent of teachers, who were required only to oversee their servicing and management. Ms Newman had played no part in course formation and the production of worksheets and because of this, and because most of her teaching was done in other sectors of the school, she had little interest in its practical or pedagogical outcomes. In these circumstances she ritually went through the motions of implementing the course as she received it. As Tables 14 and 15 suggest, her lesson pattern was straightforward. During the introduction of a worksheet, in order to keep control, the teacher took full responsibility for its 'reading'. This was followed by a lengthy period of pupil work in which a generally supervisory role was assumed. With little investment in such actions, the outcome was as unsatisfying for Ms Newman as it was for the pupils concerned.

For teachers such as Ms Newman with 2p and Ms Lewis with 1p, the curriculum package along with the expectations of pupils and significant others within the organization, could arguably be seen to have had a deskilling effect upon them. Certainly neither was able to teach in a way they would like. However, given the general conditions of schooling, the inflexibility of the timetable and pupil expectations, limited resources, pressures for control and effective evaluation, the limited expertise of teachers with pupils of heterogeneous abilities, the success of the new curriculum would have required much more than new skills of management or control (see Apple, 1980). The adoption of such new curriculum forms can and should constitute a more general reskilling of teachers, not only in terms of classroom practice, but also in the organization of curriculum (time, content, pedagogy) at departmental and faculty level.

Each of the observed teachers was reduced to using available coping strategies to try to resolve problems associated with a course which they had rapidly constructed, or had been constructed for them, to meet specific organizational ends. None of these teachers would consider themselves to have achieved effective mixed ability *teaching*.

Differences in the approach of each of these teachers were reflected in the pupils' perception of them. In order to succeed in this context, pupils had to be able to cope with content, *more or less independently* within quite limited periods of time, working from a worksheet which then required a level of literacy quite above that which most of the pupils possessed. It is not surprising therefore that in Form 1p, Jerry, Ryan, Rene and Liona, along with Paul, Caroline, Odette and Maureen, found the setting problematic, expressed their frustrations in difficult behaviours and were imputed deviant, as well as less 'able' or 'just average' identities. The setting was also difficult, however, for Abdul. Given his reading ability, his opportunities to achieve an 'able' identity are also made difficult. He remarked:

> They're so short . . . you don't get time to finish what you're doing, we should have longer like in English.

Unlike pupils of the counter-steering group, however, such problems were expressed in further work commitment rather than interest behaviour. Consequently by the summer term this pupil, along with Mark, Naren, Michael and Jenny had achieved the success he desired. Amongst the pupils of group 2 (see pp. 60–2) only Mary portrayed an improved attitude and behaviour, reflecting perhaps her expressed interest in the subject. The remainder, while recognized as able by the teacher, were considered underachieving due to their 'inconsistent effort' while the pupils themselves focused somewhat cynically, on the teachers frame of control:

> Yeah . . . Ms Lewis . . . she's the best [laughter] It doesn't matter what you say (Paul).

> I suppose she's good really . . . she won't embarrass you . . . she'll take you out and tell you . . . and make you come back after school . . . a bit soft (David).

Amongst the pupils of group 4, only Peter and Lynne achieved favourable identities in the teachers' perspectives. Both in behaviour (as observed by the teacher and the researcher) and in the teachers perspective, these two achieved identities more typical of those of group 2. Both were considered 'able', 'mature', especially Peter, though he lacked the 'consistency' of the successful pupil. (Lynne was also referred to as 'giggly', only 'works when she wants to'.)

For Ms Lewis, the difficult behaviours were explained with reference to a variety of 'learning problems'. Problems centred significantly upon the independent work demanded by the worksheet. Ms Lewis, for example, remarked of individual pupils:

> Odette can hardly write, Caroline can't express in writing, David technical difficulties, slow, learning problems, Ryan restless, can concentrate . . . disruptive, Rene has to be given attention.

They are 'not mature enough'. Here is a clear recognition of problems generated by the mode of transmission though there is a tendency to psychologize the problem rather than to locate it in the immediate conditions of curricular practice.

For the first year pupils of Mrs Bodie and Mr Richards:

> If you're not learning, a good teacher, she'll come up to you and tell you . . . really get the meaning of it . . . Like Mr Richards . . . nice . . . if you didn't hear it he don't go really mad, he just explains it to you (Lynne).

> yeah, but most teachers, like Mrs Bodie she don't, she just tells you off . . . really aggravates . . . she should just say I excuse you or something . . . like that or I'm sorry and do it or start all over again . . . but she just gives you one perfect answer and then you got to stick to it (Tony).

> Mr Richards alright . . . he finds things more interesting. He teaches so all of us can understand (Claire).

Mrs Bodie's not very good, because if you can't listen to it the first time it's just tough luck (Brian).

Similar comparisons are drawn between Ms Newman and Mrs Day with Form 2p, the latter whose approach approximates that of Mr Richards.

Mrs Day gives us interesting work . . . interesting to learn. That helps you . . . she gives us exciting work . . . most of the time (Narayen, Form 2p).

She makes us laugh . . . makes us understand it . . . Ms Newman, just says it . . . If you ask Ms Newman a question she just says it, she'll just say this and that . . . you say pardon . . . she'll just say, I've told you that (Rosa).

And in comparison between Ms Lewis and another teacher responsible for teaching the pupils of Form 1p with a supervisory approach, pupils of 1p remark:

Mr F, he's strict while you're doing your work he comes over to see that you're working . . . he just says get on with your work . . . or stand in the corner with your face to the wall (David).

None of the teachers really help you . . . Ms Lewis doesn't really help you . . . she just says put up your hands and you put your hands up for the whole lesson. She doesn't come . . . and when you shout she puts you on a piece of paper. F . . . he don't help you . . . if you make a noise, gee (Maureen).

It is perhaps not surprising then, that the successful teacher in the perspectives of pupils is a teacher neither 'radically' inspired (who attempts to step outside the structure of the course and generate 'new' knowledge) nor overly 'autocratic' (able to impose the course in its existing form, upon pupils), but whose 'liberal' endeavours permit pupils a degree of success within the limits and constraints on ability imposed by the course organization and structure. Mr Richards with 1s and Mrs Day with 2p provided interesting work, help and understanding, broke the routine of work with their enthusiasm or humour and thereby facilitated some degree of progress. Of course, not all pupils experienced each of the conditions of learning as restrictive. Those who had the predispositions to work within the frames imposed tended to appraise teachers positively. For the able pupils of Form 1p, for example, Ms Lewis is neither considered too soft, nor unable to provide the required attention (even though during classroom time they receive less attention than the less able and active).

She's the best . . . kind . . . she's nice and makes us think we'll learn good things . . . doesn't just keep on saying shut up and be quiet all the time (Naren).

For those unable to meet the requirements of learning, however, and dissatisfied with the teacher's approach, the unchanging conditions of practice give rise only to a mutual and negative identification. Pupil deviance and alienation in this context stems not from a confrontation with reified knowledge, but their problems of *access* to it. Hence, the 'good' teacher performs in such a way as to provide 'help' and 'understanding' of contents and her control is 'fair' and 'strict'. As we saw in some Science lessons, a strong positional frame of control, (the 'strict' teacher), may not be 'fair' because the teacher is not concomit- antly providing a valid learning environment. His or her humour also needs to be sufficient to break much of the routine and boredom associated with learning. This conforms quite closely to a growing literature (cf. Furlong, 1976; Gannaway, 1976) on pupil perceptions of teachers and teaching process. But as we have elsewhere stressed (Evans and Davies, 1985), these teacher behaviours are not simply reducible to attitudes of individuals' personalities, they are structured responses to concrete situations. They *can* be planned for and produced.

A Note on Teaching and Learning in Withdrawal Groups in Social Sciences

As in Mathematics, 'less able' pupils were withdrawn from the mainstream Integrated Studies lessons to small remedial classes organized within the Faculty of Social Sciences alongside mainstream Integrated Studies. With only limited space and staff available and a desire to keep groups small, not all pupils with learning difficulties could be removed from the mainstream classes. Ability (or rather lack of it from the teachers point of view) *and* behaviour thus tended to operate as criteria for the removal of pupils. The more difficult the pupil's behaviour the greater her or his chances of being extracted from the mainstream lesson. In Form 1p, Jerry of the counter-steering group was one such pupil withdrawn as the term progressed to the small remedial class. Other pupils in Form 1p had reading ages below nine, but were not withdrawn because their behaviour tended to be less problematic. In consequence, these pupils continued to find the mainstream setting difficult.

Remedial teaching in the Social Sciences is of particular interest because it once again evidences the way in which changes in the 'frame' of curriculum organization and transmission could signify changes in the learning opportunities experienced by pupils (such as Jerry of the counter-steering group). In withdrawal groups, teachers confronted with six to eight pupils were able to pitch and pace their presentation (usually a great deal of teacher talk supporting worksheet instruction) at the level of time taken to complete a question or read the text *by individual pupils*. This served to emphasize (to the researcher) how difficult, frustrating and unrewarding the mainstream classroom was in the experience of these children. Moreover, in withdrawal classes, the levels of concentration required of these pupils to deal with the text was often expressed in brief periods of 'respite', when pupils were content to listen to the text rather than follow. On such occasions their behaviour often took a form (for example, a relaxed, 'layed back' position on their seats, hands behind head) which in 'normal' classroom settings could be interpreted as illegitimate interest activity, 'being away', 'not listening', or a rebuke to teacher authority. In this relaxed frame of teacher control over pacing and behaviour, not only were a broader range of behaviours considered legitimate, but there were occasions in teacher–pupil talk for more 'spontaneous side involvements' when pupils could take the lead, and inject into the discourse elements of their own interest, knowledge and biography. For example, in a second year withdrawal group:

Ms Jones	What senses had they developed?
Caren (2q)	They could hear noises.
Ms Jones	Yes . . . hearing.
Jerry (2p)	Strong bones.
Ms Jones	What else?
Greta (2q)	Spears, arrows.
Ms Jones	No . . . but strength . . . yes . . . it's all very well to see and hear but you also have to catch the animal.
Jerry (2p)	Do you remember that boy last year who did the high jump?
Ms Jones	No.
Jerry (2p)	He jumped every one.
Ms Jones	Oh.
Jerry (2p)	. . . Yeah . . . barefooted.
Ms Jones	Painful . . . you think he was strong?
Jerry (2p)	Yeah guy . . . over the gravel.
Ms Jones	OK, I think you can do question one now . . . Does anybody need help with spelling?

There is little doubt that many pupils found such occasions more rewarding than their experience in the mainstream classroom. Jerry (1p), for example, remarked of Integrated Studies: 'Sometimes I like it . . . when I'm with Ms Jones in the small group you do the work better . . . before the others do it.' Consequently, this pupil was better behaved and achieved a more positive identity, as an 'able' child and as a worker. A similar sentiment was expressed by two second year pupils, both of whom had experienced learning in withdrawal groups and also in the Remedial Department. In the following statements, their thoughts on withdrawal groups are also generalized to the opportunities presented by the Remedial Department.

Rachel   If somebody gets stuck on a question there's 31 in one class and seven in the other. By the time they've done it we would have read the worksheet, and by the time they've finished we've just started and it would be the end of the lesson.

Robert   In the class, right, teachers just shout and talk. They [other pupils] start laughing at the words.

Noel   It's like when you go back from Ms Crocker's class [Remedial Department] it's like stalemate, the end of fun. In the other class you have fun, then it stops. Like the programme on telly. They go into this fantasy land and have a whole lot of fun, and when they come back, they're back in bed.

The latter comment requires little elaboration. It is a valid representation of the difficulties these pupils experienced, which highlights less their problems than those of pupils with similar 'disabilities' for whom remedial withdrawal was not available. Their success in these situations could represent a severe contradiction to teachers' assumptions about the nature of ability and curricular practice. The curriculum and pedagogy of withdrawal groups and remedial extraction provided pupils with an experience of schooling widely at variance with that of the mainstream classroom. This made the stated policy of reintegration highly problematic and infrequently realized. With only limited opportunities to effect change in the curriculum and pedagogical practices of the mainstream classroom, in Integrated Studies as in Science, attention was increasingly drawn (at the senior teacher level) to finding better forms of evaluation and assessment rather than curriculum reform. Both the History and Religious Education Departments did, however, increasingly draw upon the Remedial Department for help with worksheet production. Unsurprisingly, teachers increasingly appealed for an expansion of remedial work and the Remedial Department. As far as this attitude deflected attention from the conditions of existing curricula, and provided a means of accommodating the range of abilities made available, this orientation appeared to be little more than a second level coping strategy.

seven

English:
Mixed Curriculum

English appeared to represent the other end of a spectrum to Mathematics, Modern Languages, Integrated Studies and Science at Sageton. Teachers were far less obviously confined within the limits of a precisely defined syllabus or pedagogical mode of transmission. Indeed, until the period of study there did not seem to be any syllabus at all.[1] Teachers would seem to have an autonomy with which to impose idiosyncratic styles or approaches far greater than was evident in the actions of other subject teachers. As the comments of a teacher indicated,

> I have total control over what I do and there are no effective checks. Vague oral guidelines come from Mr Poulton but he doesn't know whether they're followed. Texts used depend on availability and somewhat inconsistent booking systems. There is general agreement on areas of work to be covered but this is informal (Mr French).

As we see, however (and as suggested in the statement), this autonomy was not unrestricted.

Background

Mr Poulton, the Head of Department, arrived at Sageton in 1974 (Summer Term) as deputy Head of English, Scale 3, and was appointed Head of English soon afterwards. He knew little of the initial motivation for mixed ability grouping and like all other senior teachers were thoroughly unprepared, given the nature and timing of the innovation, to meet the change.

> I'm not sure why it happened I joined at the end of the Summer Term after the decision had been taken . . . when I returned from my Summer holiday . . . they had gone mixed ability. Since then we've attempted to cope with it . . .

Although wholly supportive of mixed ability grouping,[2]

> it overcame the negative effects of the old system and it produces a
> positive challenge to teachers, to stretch the brighter and cater for the
> lower ability pupils . . .

the immediate response to the grouping policy was to retain a syllabus,
which was based on selected textbooks and which emphasized the
development of technical language skills. In Mr Poulton's view:

> a traditional system, orientated to the needs of external examinations
> and . . . very much class based.

Departmental support for mixed ability grouping was also apparent
in the general perspectives of its members and could be inferred from
the retention of mixed ability in the third year, with 'flexible' grouping
for 'O' level and 'CSE' work in year 4. But the idealist perspective[3]
identified by Ball (1981) and St. John-Brooks (1983) in English
departments elsewhere, was *not* a generalized feature of the perspectives or practices of English teachers at Sageton. The Head of
Department, as the above statement indicates, expressed concern for
the 'traditional'[4] aspects of English teaching in mixed ability grouping,
and for the welfare of the able pupil. This attitude comes closer to
Ball's 'academic' rather than idealist perspective.

> In terms of written skills I'm not sure . . . there's a tendency perhaps not
> to stretch the bright ones . . . [and] . . . It's almost impossible to teach
> these technical skills in the mixed ability we have . . . We have very few
> classes with an even spread. We need to prepare material for written
> skills. We don't have these . . . to teach paragraphing formally isn't
> possible . . . only the bright ones would get it (Mr Poulton).

In this 'traditional' situation teachers were expected to meet a broad
range of curriculum specifications laid down in a new framework
introduced by Mr Poulton. To

> read one class novel per term. Pupils should also read two private
> readers. Both imaginative and critical writing (and occasionally language
> lessons, e.g. vocabulary) as well as discussion will come from these
> activities (syllabus, working party document).

In addition,

> Source books or language books were to be used so that pupils
> completed at least one composition per . . . fortnight and two
> comprehensions. Other regular work was to be discussion, improvised
> drama and the use of the T.V. system (syllabus, working party
> document).

And within this syllabus variety teachers were to

> concentrate on the basic failings of our pupils, in punctuation, spelling and simple grammatical errors in their written work.

at the same time remaining sensitive to the

> non standard forms used by our pupils, recognise and respect them for what they are, part of a separate grammar, and initiate into standard forms in a pragmatic way (syllabus, working party document).

This framework of curriculum content and intention was made public by the Head of Department in a syllabus working party document, during the period of study only under increasing pressures for accountability from the wider social context. The document indicated that, although in comparison with most other curriculum subjects English lacks a definite 'subject matter', there was thought to be an extensive body of knowledge and technique for the teacher to convey to pupils (for example, technical skills of punctuation, paragraphing, spelling, etc.), as well as a wholesome diet of literature. Control over what counted as knowledge was to remain firmly in the hands of the teacher. As we see in later discussion, opportunities for pupils to achieve successful 'able' identities were determined by their capacity to meet these 'traditional' (or formal) criteria. However, the range of options available to pupils in terms of what and to some extent how they wrote, read or said things, was wide when compared with other subjects (Ball, 1981, p. 231). As Mr Poulton noted:

> In language teaching it is possible to reproduce stimulus for each of your classes, either for individuals, groups or the class as a whole, which will be of immediate interest to them – using photographs, newspapers, etc.

In this manner in English teaching the frame of teacher control over knowledge tends to be weaker in the Bernsteinian (1977, p. 89) sense, creating a greater opportunity for correspondence between common sense and subject content or school knowledge.

At the time of study, however, three years after Sageton had begun mixed ability grouping, this curriculum underwent a period of 'modernization'. Commercially and departmentally produced individualized and individuated (theme based) instruction materials were introduced. The decision to reform practice arose from a complex of factors. Within the department, the teachers themselves focused on the inadequacies of existing curriculum, pedagogy and resource. Limitation of 'space in which to centralise resource' (textbooks, class readers, etc.) and 'competition amongst staff for scarce good class readers' in particular had led to a 'breakdown in the system of class sharing' (Mr Poulton). Criticism also focused upon limitations inherent in the teacher-talk method itself, as one English teacher, Ms Thompson remarked:

> It's the linguistic level at which you have to talk to them. If you give individual instruction it's OK, but if you talk to the class as a whole . . . it has to be at the lowest common denominator. Worksheets overcome this problem . . . in part.

And another, Mrs Ashton:

> The range of ability is so great. To invent mixed ability material is difficult, near impossible. We haven't the materials ready prepared for class readers, so we hit the mythical middle with the worksheets we produce.

Within the frames of limited resource, limited pupil ability, (and as we will see, limited professional knowledge), the autonomy granted to teachers of English was experienced as a limited kind indeed. In acknowledgement of the constraints of existing pedagogy (teacher talk, or worksheets which tended to 'hit the mythical middle') there emerged growing opposition to 'autonomy', and appeals for greater, more co-ordinated departmental action. As Mr French remarked:

> it's too much to expect individual teachers here to plan and organise mixed abilities in the class. It needs departmental organisation.

At the same time the department was even more subject than most to pressures to 'improve' standards. It tended to come under fire both from senior teachers (Head, Deputies, etc.) and from other subject teachers. With the general response to mixed ability grouping taking the form of worksheet instruction, greater emphasis was placed upon levels of literacy. With only limited opportunity or knowledge to improve this condition of learning within most subject areas, the onus was placed upon the English Department and the remedial facilities to provide the necessary *remediation*, i.e. the make-up of skills not yet learnt, but crucially significant to a teacher's concern for instruction and control (Corbishley *et al.*, 1981). In this context, and with no school policy on language across the curriculum, the English Department and *its* failings tended to offer an immediate explanation and a scapegoat for the failings of other subject areas. Against this background all eleven[5] department teaching staff were 'removed' *en masse* during the Autumn term (1977) to undertake a week long course on mixed ability teaching. As a department, they appeared no more or less capable of making the transition from mixed ability grouping to mixed ability *teaching* than any other. Although the majority supported the policy of grouping into the third year, few expressed satisfaction with their personal ability to effect mixed ability teaching. Only three teachers indicated that their professional training had prepared them for this. The majority had a university background, one year's teacher training (PGCE) and based their knowledge of mixed ability on 'experience' and 'trial and error'.

The upshot of all this was a *gradual* introduction of 'new' content (individuated, individualized, partly theme-based work, and material concerned with the 'technical' aspects of language, grammar, spelling, etc.) into the existing curriculum framework. The syllabus, however, remained 'a source of ideas, alternatives and agreed procedures' rather than a definitive (and didactic) statement of contents; a broad framework in which teachers themselves 'find the most suitable "technique" to teach that particular class at any time' (Mr Poulton). For this reason the English lessons observed varied more in format and style than those in other subjects and therefore the presentation of a typical or representative lesson is, as Ball (1981) also found, very difficult indeed.

Teacher Strategies In A Mixed Curriculum

Table 16 Contrasts in the talk of first and second year teachers over one period of 40 minutes each, excluding beginnings and endings

Teacher/Form		Public regulative	Immediate instructional	Mode of instruction
Mr French Ms Pym	1s	12	39	Individualized
Mrs Cable	2p	3	12	Class teaching
Mr Dean	2p	10	23	Individuated
Ms Pegler	1p	13	3	Class teaching

In total, 35 English lessons were observed. Mr French and Ms Pym 'team taught' the pupils of 1s.

Tables 16 and 17 suggest that there are marked dissimilarities in the interaction patterns in first and second year classrooms (cf. SMP), as great between teachers (Table 16) as within the practice of any one teacher (Table 17). Each class in years one and two received 4×70 minutes of English a week and could be taught by one or more teachers. Mr Dean and Mrs Cable, for example, shared the responsibility for teaching the pupils of Form 2p. Mr French 'team taught' with Ms Pym, a member of the Remedial Department, and introduced an

Table 17 Contrasts in the talk of Ms Pegler during three 40 minute periods, respectively of class teaching, individuated and individualized instruction, with Form 1p

Teacher B Form 1p	Public regulative	Immediate instructional	Mode of instruction
Lesson 1[a]	13	3	Class teaching
Lesson 2	17	18	Individuated
Lesson 3	29	22	Individualized

[a] The same lesson as shown in Table 16 above. These lessons are expanded in Table 18.

individualized scheme, constructed together for the pupils of 1s. Mr Claxton and Ms Pegler taught the pupils of 1p, Ms Pegler taking them for 3 × 70 minute periods, and provided a diet of class reading, writing, individuated worksheet tasks and, later in the term, a period of individualized instruction. (Greater detail on each of these classroom activities is provided below.) Generally, all pupils experienced one (or more) periods of class or individual reading followed by a period of writing, based on the reading, per week. Each pupil was also usually involved in a worksheet task, which could constitute a theme (e.g. 'Kidnapped' or 'Passports') lasting two or three lessons.

Normally pupils worked alone from worksheets or text books though occasionally, in third year lessons observed, they were involved in collaborative exercises, e.g. constructing a 'play' from a series of photographs. There was little evidence of 'discussion' work and none of drama, which was avoided because of the limitations of space, expertise and the problems of control associated with it.[6] Many lessons did, however, involve the reading of the story by the teacher, or the reading of poetry, and grammar work. 'Doing English' thus describes a variety of different kinds of learning experience and opportunity on the pupils' part (cf. Ball, 1981, p. 230).

In class teaching, the traditional social relationships of teacher to the whole class as a social unit remains intact. Teacher authority is repeatedly made explicit in the 'act of speaking' (Edwards, 1980), in positional location (teaching from the 'front of house' position), achieving a centralized communication structure, and in a variety of control strategies: lining up, supervised entry, registration. Consider Ms Pegler (a young but experienced English teacher with a few years teaching experience at Sageton) and Form 1p in the following example:

Ms Pegler arrived in the classroom prior to the arrival of the pupils of 1p. She busied herself with the task of ensuring that classroom and text books were in a general state of orderliness and preparedness. She turned to the blackboard and wrote up a series of questions related to the class reader. As the pupils arrived she positioned herself in the doorway. Pupils lined up, she chatted to the early arrivals, waited for all to appear, then chaperoned them into the classroom. Positioned in front of the blackboard she waited for all pupils to take up their seating positions, for the noise to reach an acceptable conversational level, turned to the register, slowly, methodically, called out each pupil's name, demanding silence while the task was completed. This accomplished, with her again positioned in front of class, one of the pupils is asked to distribute books; she recapped (2–4 minutes) on the story, and began to read. This phase continued for some 40 minutes. Ms Pegler's reading was colourful and dramatic. For a further 17 minutes pupils worked at the tasks provided on the blackboard, and Ms Pegler took up a supervisory role.

In this example of Ms Pegler's teaching, a cluster of routines and procedures are effectively used to establish order, to clearly demonstrate boundaries between corridor 'interest' behaviours and classroom 'work' behaviour, and to announce basic social structural arrangements. Such actions are an important means by which teachers defend themselves from pressures, in this case of dealing with a large number of children (see Pollard, 1980, p. 43).

Within the constraints imposed by resources, pupil ability, and their own expertise, teachers persisted with whole class method (and within this the use of the class reader) as an effective coping and controlling strategy. Fifteen of the 35 lessons observed, for example, were of this nature. Ms Pegler was one who acknowledged the limitations of this type of activity (e.g. reading for 40 minutes) for the pupils concerned but recognized its potential for social control.

I'd like to do more discussion but you can't do it . . . it's a bit risky.

Another English teacher, Ms Simms, said:

I usually read for about 30–40 minutes normally. About half a dozen of them speak so little English, I read *to* them because they can't follow. And, it's much less of a strain when I read. I can never get them all together otherwise.

That class teaching provided individual pupils few opportunities for immediate contact with the teacher (either face-to-face or publicly) was evident in the action of Ms Pegler and Mrs Cable (see Table 16). Ms Pegler's lesson in Table 16 refers to a period of class teaching described above, followed by its reconstruction in individual work. For Mrs Cable, class teaching, and a general use of text books or class readers, was a means of coping with the limited time to prepare 'more suitable material' which accrued owing to the pressure of dual pastoral-teaching responsibilities, rather than from a concern for control. Authority vested in senior pastoral positions like hers and repeatedly announced in the broader school context, ensured a 'passivity' amongst her pupils uncharacteristic of their performance in other classrooms.

While reducing a teacher's instructional or disciplinary concerns, class teaching simultaneously limited the learning opportunities of many pupils. (In the case of Mrs Cable, question–answer sequences tended to be dominated by the pupils defined as 'able' by the teacher.) The pace of instruction (as in French) was defined by the teacher, even if only by reading the text. Given the aural and reading abilities of many pupils, the tasks of attending and listening could prove frustrating and unrewarding occasions to all but the able pupils. It was perhaps for this reason that in Ms Pegler's classroom Jerry accounted for four of the 13 control messages and Rene, another three. Our earlier discussion of withdrawal group extractions emphasized how laborious and painful a task reading could be for such pupils. Related problems, however, could be experienced by 'able' pupils.

> We like reading the books best but the trouble is we read on faster than the teacher. Ms Pegler is always stopping to tell the boys off for mucking about. Then we all get told off because we don't know where we are (Mary, Form 1p).

For 'able' and 'less able' alike, class teaching thus represented an opportunity for the imputation of negative pupil identities to the extent that frustration was revealed in difficult forms of interest behaviour. Within the frame of control invoked by both Ms Pegler and Mrs Cable, however, there was reasonably successful containment of such behaviours and differential involvements, thus maintaining an appearance of order and productivity.

Mr Dean (Table 16) and Ms Pegler (Table 16, Lesson 2) give us examples of individuated lessons using worksheets with content designed by teachers which are thought to be of interest to the pupils concerned. Mr Dean's worksheet, entitled 'Kidnapped', contained a variety of tasks, requiring both creativity and the practising of grammatical skills, e.g.

> Draw a picture of each of the crooks. Underneath describe what they are like . . . [and] . . . This is a letter which Vanessa's parents received from the kidnappers: write it out in your book, and correct the crooks' bad spelling and punctuation.

The general pattern of teaching on these occasions involved a period introducing the worksheet and 'discussing' of its contents, followed by a period of pupil independent work. Ms Pegler's individuated lesson (Table 17) proceeded through a 17-minute introductory phase, followed by 34 minutes of pupil work. The worksheet was entitled 'Record Breaking' and the following extract is taken from the introductory phase:

Ms Pegler	OK, I'm going to give you two sheets to look at . . . I'll explain what they are for . . . [distributes worksheets] . . . OK, can anyone tell me if they know of any records that have been broken?
John	I broke a record.
Ms Pegler	You did . . . what was that?
John	The Osmonds.

Fully exploiting an ambiguity in the text, this comment raises a laugh[7] from the rest of the class. So early was it in the lesson proper, however, that the teacher treated it lightly, but as no small threat to classroom order, and quickly took responsibility for the task and continuing reading. As the teacher continued there were further interventions:

Ryan	I don't believe that . . . how could anybody do that?

The teacher smiled, but proceeded without further comment. Moments later she again invited comments. This time Ryan responded with a story about 'milk bottle balancing', but as he proceeded other pupils now interjected to challenge the credibility of his account. Ms Pegler responded:

I'm tired of this rudeness . . . you speak one at a time. Ryan was trying to say something. When someone is talking you listen . . . Ryan . . . [Ryan continued].

Relaxing the frame of teacher control over knowledge does then implicate what Edwards (1980, p. 241) has called 'the ownership of instructional talk' which he argues 'is displayed through a general pre-allocation of turns' and is founded upon a teacher's claims to prior knowledge. In the above sequence, instances occurred when the subject content failed to concur with the pupils' common sense notions of what was possible. As a result, albeit momentarily, the teacher was in danger of losing control over the communication structure. At Ryan's story, conversation took a form of natural out-of-classroom talk. It was spontaneous and conflictual. The teacher was forced to announce rules of discourse (turn-taking) characteristic of whole class teaching, and soon desisted with the activity altogether.

Even a small shift in the frame of curriculum, including the greater use of worksheets, generated new demands of teachers and 'new' requirements of pupils. While this could, as we see later, signify more enjoyable learning for pupils, it simultaneously caused problems of control and management for teachers. For this reason, far less time was given to 'discussion' (introductory phases) than to dependent pupil work. Worksheets, commanding independence and involvement in unambiguous, discrete curriculum tasks, offered far greater potential for order and control than the precarious and unpredictable outcomes of class discussion. This tendency was evident even in the teaching of Mr French and Ms Pym. Although their instruction was individualized, they intended to use the latter portion of each lesson for class activity, 'discussion, group work, or drama'. However, during the 420 minutes of their lesson time observed, only 60 minutes were given to activities of this nature. For Ms Pegler with Form 1p and for Mrs Cable, the phase of pupil independent work meant they took up supervisory roles. Behaviours were contained within precisely defined, and narrow parameters of acceptability. In the individuated lesson exemplified on p. 137 Ms Pegler interacted *instructionally* with only nine pupils on 13 occasions during their independent work. The interactions were brief, seemed sufficient to allow progress, and were largely accounted for by the less able and average pupils. Jerry, Ryan and Rene of the counter-steering group received by far the greater proportion of the teachers time. This is not unconnected, as we see later, to the pupils' positive rating of the lesson. Whereas this teacher's approach was consonant with school-wide expectations, Mr Dean experienced them as a severe constraint upon his own preferred classroom approach.

> Mixed ability is used here as much as an instrument of control as an instrument of education and there's side-effects to that. You need more tolerance of noise in mixed ability. Once the Head looked in and we were doing a class play. He came in and asked what we were doing. This is always the background. It's such a different style of teaching . . . getting amongst kids. A much deeper idea of how kids learn is needed. You need to know the kids so well . . . know how they work.

This teacher neither desired nor attempted to effect the kind of control over pupils which characterized the actions of both Ms Pegler, and Mrs Cable with whom he shared the teaching of Form 2p for two periods a week. His strategy of control approximated more to what Woods (1977) has termed 'fraternisation' than the kind of supervision displayed in the actions of Ms Pegler and Mrs Cable. Pupils were allowed a far greater measure of liberty than was customary, and the girls were even allowed to continue knitting.[8] However, in this endeavour, to develop good personal relations with pupils, Mr Dean found himself constrained not only by expectations defining appropriate pupil and teacher conduct prevailing in the broader setting, but also by the way in which such expectations further restricted curricular activities which he thought would facilitate interpersonal contact.

> I want to take them on a trip, perhaps one a term. They could then feel
> ' secure that you cared and wanted them to learn, but the hassle, it was
> unbelievable, nobody would give permission. The Head finally let us go
> but he gave them all a lecture in the hall on how to behave.

He was also constrained by the expectations of pupils themselves which were at variance with his conception of teaching (see St. John-Brooks, 1983). This disjuncture was compounded by the system of class sharing. As Denise remarked:

> gee, he can't control guy, he should be more like Mrs Cable.

> In the teacher's perspective, however, such pupils 'lack confidence, it's
> as if they've been brought up on tests. They want confirmation that it's
> going to be right before going on . . . Naren, Louise, Simon and
> William won't chance it at all . . .' (Mr Dean).

Relaxing the frame of teacher control over pupil conduct exposed the way in which pupils differentially related to individuated learning. Problems of pacing were sharply represented to the teacher and in time led to a reconsideration of appropriate curriculum.

> At the beginning of the year I used worksheets but it's a problem finding
> stuff that will satisfy everybody. Worksheets are OK, but they must be
> more open ended. Worksheets that develop into something more
> complex would be good. This *is* my first go at mixed ability (Mr Dean).

In the lesson described (Table 16, Mr Dean), the lesson proper began with the teacher attempting to introduce a new worksheet to the class as a whole. He announced his intentions and began his introduction. However, throughout this phase, a number of pupils ignored his instruction, instead turning their attention to completion of the previous lesson's worksheet. Appeals for attention were ignored and, finally, in order to resolve his growing control problems, he transferred his introduction to an individual level. Asking pupils to carry on independently as he did the rounds, he ensured that the few ready to start the new work progressed. Thereafter, as pupils related to the context or content of learning and expressed their problems in active forms of behaviour, Mr Dean intervened at an immediate level. In a period of 40 minutes he interacted with some 12 of the 22 pupils on 23 occasions, and it was the less able, and able but teacher–dependent pupils who enjoyed the majority of interactions.

In marked contrast, in the classroom of Mrs Cable, one 30 minute period of pupil work observed (not one of those referred to in Table 16) found the teacher interacting at an immediate level with only six of the 22 pupils on six occasions. This teacher tended to take a supervisory role, working from the front, calling on pupils to check work at her direction. Problems with content or context were made explicit only within the limited opportunities for contact presented by the teacher. In contrast to Mr Dean, whose intervention and help was contingent upon active 'behaviour', with Mrs Cable it was mostly chance seating positions which determined a pupil's opportunity for assistance. Within the frame of control activated by Mrs Cable, the context resembled that of collective piloting. These differences in approach were clearly perceived by the pupils. Mrs Cable was generally considered a teacher who could control but not provide an 'interesting' learning environment. Mr Dean, to the contrary, provided interesting work but could not control. Both teachers experienced difficulties achieving successful identities in the pupils view. In the case of Mrs Cable it had much to do with her pastoral commitments and limited knowledge of mixed ability teaching; for Mr Dean it was much more because the expectations of children and other teachers contradicted his view of competent teaching.

The *individualized* instruction of Mr Frost, Ms Pym and Ms Pegler deployed schemes which consisted of individual graded readers,[10] each with supporting worksheets or cards commanding a variety of tasks suitable to the level of reading ability associated with the text. As we noted in SMP, transposing the frame of teacher control over knowledge to worksheets in individualized instruction, tends to break up the traditional social relationships of teacher to the whole class as a social unit. The opportunity for teachers explicitly to announce their authority is reduced. This has implications for control. As we have seen (cf. Gannaway, 1976; Furlong, 1976), among the criteria pupils use to assess teacher effectiveness is that of their ability to keep order and establish control. In English lessons, however, an individualized curriculum represented only *one* of a variety of ways of learning experienced by pupils. So such lessons often took place against a backcloth of structural meanings explicitly announced on other occasions. Ms Pegler, for example, as others, tended to persist with controlling 'settling routines' (lining up etc.) despite the opportunity presented by an individualized scheme to desist with such activities. None the less, individualized instruction represented a context more difficult to manage and control, at least for Ms Pegler, than either class based or individuated instruction (see Table 18). This problem was 'reduced' in Mr Frost's and Ms Pym's classroom by a division of labour, Ms Pym taking a supervisory role while Mr Frost did the rounds.

Table 18: Contrasts in the distribution of Ms Pegler's talk between pupils over 40 minutes of the 'lesson proper' in three lessons (introduced in Table 17) of class (1), individuated (2), individualized (3), instruction with Form 1p.

Pupil	Sex	Lesson 1 class teaching	Lesson 2 individuated	Lesson 3 individualized
Mark	m			!
Naren	m		X	! X
Abdul	m	!		
Michael	m		X	Absent
Jenny	f			X
John	m	!!	!!!! (X)	!! X
Mary	f		X	!! XXX
Hugh	m	!		XXX
Heather	f			
Jerry	m	!!!! X	!!!! XXX	!!!!!!! XXXXX
Ryan	m	Withdrawn, remedial	(X)XX	Withdrawn, remedial
Rene	m	!!! X	!!!!! (X)XX	Absent
Liona	f	Withdrawn, remedial	Absent	Withdrawn remedial
Peter	m	X	(X)	!!!!! OX
David	m	!	! X	!!!! XXXXX
Paul	m	!	(X)	!!!!! XX
Caroline	f		!	!
Odette	f		! X	!
Maureen	f		X	
Lynne	f		!	

		Reg.	Instr.	Reg.	Instr.	Reg.	Instr.
Totals		13	3	17	18	29	22

X refers to immediate instructional talk with an individual pupil.
! refers to public or immediate regulative talk with an individual pupil.
(X) refers to public instructional talk with an individual pupil during the phase of class discussion.

It is evident from the case of Ms Pegler, that problems of interaction vary not just between teachers but within a teacher's practice (see Tables 17 and 18). Lesson 1 refers to the period of class teaching alluded to, lesson 2 to individuated and lesson 3 to individualized instruction. In all three, Ms Pegler's time was not evenly distributed amongst pupils. Boys characteristically received more time and attention than girls. Teachers respond to pupil behaviour not to pupil learning, as Jackson (1968) makes clear. Moreover, in both class teaching and individuated instruction it was Jerry, Rene and Ryan of the counter-steering group who received the greater proportion of the teacher disciplinary and instructional attention. In lesson 3, however, with the absence of pupils Ryan and Rene, other 'less able' pupils emerged as a problem for the teacher, particularly David and Paul. The following sequences are taken from this lesson.

The period of settling and administration of the scheme took some 15 minutes. This left 50 minutes of lesson time (Table 18, lesson 3 describes a 40 minute phase of pupil work within it).

1.   Ms Pegler   How nice to be able to say nice things to your parents about your work . . . OK . . . if you've got all you need, you know you should be working. There's a lot of noise . . . the work that you do now when you're not talking is far better than when you're talking.

Public messages such as this, addressed to the class as a whole, were few and far between. More common were instructional and regulative messages issued at the immediate level and which functioned to control pupil pacing and retain the appearance of social order. This is well illustrated if we chart the interactions between Ms Pegler and David and Paul.

2.   Ms Pegler   Have you finished your worksheet yet?
3.   Paul   It's too easy.
4.   Ms Pegler   OK, I'll expect you to finish it in about 5 minutes then.
5.   [Minutes later, recognizing interest activity of David and Paul]   Ms Pegler   I'm timing you!
6.   Paul   I've finished that one.
7.   Ms Pegler   Come and get another one then.
8.   [Paul goes to front and collects another]
9.   [Eight minutes later]   Ms Pegler   [to both David and Paul] . . . You're both being silly . . . I'll have to separate you.
10.   David   I've finished.
11.   Ms Pegler   Good. That only took you about 4 weeks to do. Come and get a piece of paper . . . Right, copy down the questions on the blackboard.[11]

12. [One minute later]
    Ms Pegler   Where's your pen David? . . . [separates David and
                 Paul]

13. [Five minutes later at David's desk]
    Ms Pegler   Do you know what you're supposed to be doing?

    David   How many more weeks to the end of term?

    Ms Pegler   Four . . .

    David   I'm not going to do another book then.

    Ms Pegler   Come on you've got plenty to do.

14. [15 minutes later]
    Ms Pegler   [returns to David noticing his 'interest' with Paul]
                 . . . Tell you what, if you don't feel like doing that
                 book you can get another one . . . but remember
                 you'll have to do the worksheet questions the next
                 time.

Although individualized teaching appeared to give pupils more choice in the selection of material and the speed of working, it was Ms Pegler who remained in control of the amount of knowledge to be 'got through' in the lesson,[12] though as we see, this now has to be negotiated with the pupil. Control over pacing was merely transposed from the public to the immediate level of interaction. Both David and Paul failed to display the kind of qualities required by an individualized scheme, and this (as in SMP) tends to explain the higher incidence of public and regulative messages. Neither pupil immediately turned his attention to the task. The teacher recognized this and attempted to motivate them (as evidenced by interactions 2, 4, 5). Nevertheless, interest activity continued, possibly relating to Paul's completion of his work, and the teacher was forced to intervene at an immediate level (12) and separate the pupils. This was only partially successful, the teacher again having to intervene (13 and 14) in order to get him started. In interaction 14 the conflict of interests between pupil and teacher were finally resolved. David confronted a task (writing) which, given his reading ability (although we do not have a score for this pupil, his work and his withdrawal for remedial help suggested great difficulties in this respect), was likely to be problematic. He avoided work in the interactional opportunities presented by the more open (cf. Denscombe, 1980b) context of individualized instruction, in favour of more interest activity. In recognition of such activity, and of his difficulties, Ms Pegler, in the interest of order, steered David away from the problem he experienced with the task. The pupil had successfully 'negotiated' a delay in involvement with a potentially difficult task. The pupil's learning problems were thus made apparent at the surface level of interaction with the teacher. And they were revealed, as such, in active forms of behaviour *and* through the medium of peer group relations. The situation was indeed comparable to that described in SMP and by Walker and Adelman (1976, p. 146) where they, with reference to 'informal classrooms', argue that:

> sub-culture relationships become part of the lesson itself. Friendship groups become an important element in the organisation of schoolwork, both through the division of labour and through the differentiation of allocation of tasks. The teacher in an informal situation does not encounter friendship groups as a hidden adendum but as part of the surface structure of the situation. In a sense he is trapped in them for they are the social system of the class within which he has to work and he can do little to change them.

We are not, however, suggesting that an individualized curriculum can be defined as an 'informal setting' (if this is taken to imply some kind of symmetry in the social relationships between pupils and teachers). In individualized instruction, there is indeed little class instruction and as a result teacher authority is less public than in other instructional modes. Control over pupils merely becomes more oblique, as it is effected at the level of immediate interactions. However, in these circumstances, as pupils confront problems with the content or context of learning, and express them in difficult forms of interest behaviour, often within their peer group, teachers are 'compelled' (because of the individualized nature of the content and therefore the child's problem) to intervene at an immediate level.

Teacher and Pupil Identity in Mixed Ability English

Mixed ability English encompassed a variety of different classroom practices and ways of organizing learning. Even within the particular mode of presentation (e.g. individuated) subtle differences in teacher approach presented pupils with different learning experiences and opportunities to achieve success or 'able' pupil identities.[13] It was correspondingly more difficult to locate generalized pupil attitudes towards English teaching, though differences in perspective were clearly evidenced. For the pupils of 1p, for example, English teaching represented a varied instructional context with a strong, precisely defined frame of teacher control over behaviour, and a tendency for the teacher's time and attention to be directed towards the less able pupils as the latter expressed their learning problems in 'active' behavioural forms. Consequently, in the pupils' perspectives,

> The English teacher . . . is best. It's interesting, she lets us read . . . She's kind, we do different things in the lesson (Maureen and Lynne).

I like English. Sometimes we have difficulties and I ask Ms Pegler and sometimes I try my best to carry on . . . When I'm really stuck I go to Miss (Mark and Naren).

She makes it sound good, makes a different voice (Caroline).

She's nice, she's the best. When there's lessons we don't like, we mess about, but lessons we do like, we take an interest . . . She explains everything . . . she does it fairly (David and Paul).

We do workshop, reading books, writing out stories, comprehension, it's good (John and Hugh).

The class keeps quiet . . . she's not really strict . . . she gives us good work things that excite us (Ryan).

She's kind . . . everyone works very hard for and they respect her (Jerry).

She was able to meet the children's criteria of the 'good teacher' by providing interesting work, help when needed, being strict but 'fair'. Even for those pupils whose behaviours might suggest an anti-school attitude,[14] e.g. Ryan and Jerry, this teacher, and 'doing English' was positively appraised. Such pupils are, however, less favourably considered by the teacher. They were pupils who 'find difficulty concentrating', were 'always quarrelling', were 'easily distracted', 'moody' and 'inconsistent'. However, given the written standard English criteria invoked by the teacher to define 'ability', even for those pupils willing to display behaviours appropriate to the setting, the difficulties were considerable. Only four pupils received from Ms Pegler an above average rating for attainment: Heather, John, Mary and Peter (and for the latter this was a significant improvement in identity when compared with that achieved in other curriculum areas). The other three tended to be considered as 'able' in other subjects but often also underachieving because of their failure to 'behave properly'. The frame of control which this teacher operated, facilitated, at least for these pupils, access to more successful pupil identities. These pupils 'write well, fluently'.

Despite the 'intelligence', 'lively imaginations', 'enjoyment of writing' displayed by Mark, Naren, Abdul, Michael and Jenny (the 'total workers') they remained in the teacher's perspective 'able' but limited by an incapacity to 'write well', 'punctuate properly'. They are 'untidy', had 'difficulties' in 'reading', and 'spelling'. However, unlike pupils of the counter-steering group, their potential for achieving more positive identities was recognized, and seen as contingent upon their possession of appropriate behavioural predispositions such as their ability to 'work hard' and 'concentrate'. Opportunities for mobility within the classroom social structure were thus differentially represented to pupils both in school reports (from which these statements are taken) and in the kind of interactional sequences we have described.

Mr French and Ms Pym were far less favourably considered by pupils. These teachers operated a jointly constructed scheme which tended to be considered as a 'pilot' scheme for further individualization in the department. The scheme as implemented did indeed involve some weakening of the frame of teacher control over pacing. Pupils could take as long as necessary to complete a reader or worksheet. But as Ball (1981:225) similarly emphasizes:

> even with regard to pacing, it is important to make the distinction between long-term and short-term control over pacing of knowledge. Mixed ability teaching based on worksheets often appears to give individual pupils more choice in the selection of questions and the speed of working on each worksheet, and sometimes between one worksheet and another, but in most cases it is the teacher who decides when one topic is to be discontinued and another begun.

Mr French and Ms Pym attempted to structure the phase of individualized instruction by clearly stipulating '20 minutes reading, 20 minutes writing and 20 minutes class instruction'. This temporal structure tended to be retained without variation during the week. Consequently, and somewhat ironically, what was for the teachers a 'novel' project involving quite dramatic shifts in the mode of presentation was considered fundamentally otherwise by the pupils of Form 1s themselves.

> It's so boring, when we first started it wasn't boring, he kept on about it being us the only ones doing it (William).

> At first it was good . . . but then . . . first half you do quiet reading and in the second half you do quiet writing (Tola).

> Everything we do is the same thing all the time, they don't change it, it's reading for 20 minutes, writing for 20 minutes and something else (Jane).

Despite individualization, school time, in the pupil perspective, remained teachers' time not pupils time (A. Hargreaves, 1978a, p. 90) and was experienced as a direct imposition. As William of Form 1s remarked:

> If you have a book and you enjoy it, at the beginning it's OK then it gets boring and you start getting lazy and get restless. If you ask for a change they say, try and finish it off.

and Sammy:

> First time, I thought it was going to be nice then I got stuck on a book for eleven weeks. It got so boring.

As described in SMP, pupils experienced fewer opportunities than in class teaching to escape or avoid difficult or uninteresting work. The implications of this for teachers' classroom control and management were all too evident and are suggested in the above pupil statements, as well as in the definitions of identity imputed to pupils by the teachers. In Form 1s, twice as many pupils achieve negative behavioural identities (i.e. are rated as average or below for effort) than in Ms Pegler's classroom.

The abilities of pupils were thus differently framed and formed over many lessons, according to how teachers responded to the broader constraints within which they operated organized learning and superimposed their own preferred styles of teaching. But despite quite dramatic changes in the 'surface appearance' of teaching (those for example between lessons 1, 2, 3 of Ms Pegler or between Mrs Cable and Mr Dean), opportunities for pupils to achieve successful or 'able' pupil identities were not dramatically affected. It is true, however, that differences between lessons 1, 2, and 3 above, for example, do reveal differences in the *degree* to which learning difficulties were made apparent, *when* they were made explicit, and *how* they were consequently treated. 'Difficult' behaviour in lesson 1, for example, was met with *public* regulative action but in lesson 3 by immediate *individual* instruction. However, these interactions were brief and procedural rather than diagnostic. Ms Pegler had little opportunity to spend the kind of time with individuals, particularly the less able pupils, which would narrow existing differences between them and their more able counterparts. A rather jaundiced interpretation of the positive way in which these pupils perceived the skilful activities of Ms Pegler would be to say that in her lessons less able pupils were simply provided with the conditions in which they could better enjoy their failure.

While then many of the English teachers (like those in other subjects and in other schools doing mixed ability) felt that they had achieved a significant change in teaching methods and curriculum from those of selective grouping and class teaching, analytically and indeed in the pupils' perspectives there was little evidence of dramatic change in the learning opportunities provided, though as we have seen some teachers (such as Ms Pegler) were able to make learning more enjoyable and rewarding. It would, however (as was stressed in our discussion of Integrated Studies), be highly inappropriate to criticize the department for not taking more immediate and 'radical' steps to reform their curriculum. The teachers viewed change as essentially evolutionary (or what Ball (1981) has termed 'gradualist and improving'). The momentum was sporadic, uneven, its motivation and thrust arising from disparate factors rather than co-ordinated 'rational' decisions on the part of teachers and department. They did seek better ways of producing worksheets improving the readability of the text; they formed workshops, examined the use of available literature, the media, themes, etc., all of which provided material which slowly filtered into practice rather than radically reformed it. When the system of constaints (resource, knowledge etc.) which impinge upon the teacher's practices is taken into account, the possibilities for more radical types of change in teaching methods are seen to be very limited indeed.

eight

Conclusion:
Innovation without change?

Research on ability grouping in schools has undoubtedly contributed towards a debate amongst teachers and politicians about which form of grouping is better and how teaching ought to be organized. Contradiction and ambivalence abound, as in the recent ILEA report[1] which in one breath acknowledges the absence of evidence 'which conclusively demonstrates that a particular form of pupil grouping is associated with higher achievement or better performance in public examinations', while in the next recommends 'mixed ability grouping especially but not exclusively in the first three years of secondary schooling', without specifying why, in which subjects, or how such conclusions can be confidently drawn. This adds little to anybody's understanding of the kinds of problems or possibilities which teachers and pupils themselves may experience when caught up in the process of mixed ability innovation. Against the background debate about mixed ability grouping and comprehensive schooling the Sageton study set out to concentrate attention on the teaching process and in particular to focus upon the ways, if any, in which 'teachers perceive pupils differently, interact with them differently and convey to them different conceptions of personal worth' (Ball, 1981, p. 279). Admittedly we have only touched the surface of this kind of question. We are more than aware of how limited, partial and selective are our descriptions of the working lives and perspectives of Sageton's pupils and teachers. Not every Sageton teacher, pupil or subject is represented in this account and the focus has often been more upon the departmental response rather than upon the complexity and nuance of individual teacher action within mixed ability grouping. Much data remains the subject for analyses and later reporting (see Davies *et al.*, 1985). We have also revealed little of the interplay between the social world and peer group relationships of pupils (cf. Davies, 1982; Turner, 1983; Salmon and Claire, 1984; McPherson, 1983) and their success or otherwise at learning within the variety of curricula which teachers provide in response to mixed ability change. Even so, the analyses presented are suggestive of certain processes, and these we will try and summarize below.

If nothing else, the Sageton data has surely stressed how fruitless is the task of drawing easy conclusions from research which has simply surveyed and/or compared the outcomes of different forms of grouping or teaching without, at the same time, saying anything about their respective histories, organizations, current or developing states of curriculum and pedagogical practice. Innovation is, as Esland (1972, p. 103) had pointed out,

> a social process. It takes place through time and is part of the social reality of a community of people. Although the innovative idea is in individual consciousness, it nevertheless remains a product of social interaction.

At Sageton, as at Beachside (see Ball, 1981), the teachers themselves considered innovation to be an 'evolutionary' process, a transition (from mixed ability grouping to mixed ability teaching) fraught with unforeseen complications and unintended consequences. Certainly, to look upon the Sageton data as providing examples of an accomplished *product* called mixed ability *teaching*, rather than as an innovation in *process*, would be both to misrepresent the genuine endeavours but sometimes limited successes of the teachers concerned, and to grossly misunderstand the nature of educational change as it is evidenced in British schools.

We have seen that the decision to 'go' mixed ability can be motivated by concerns far removed from the sort of egalitarian motivation often imputed to the practice by opponents and proponents alike. Nevertheless, the adoption of mixed ability grouping with comprehensive schooling does obviously represent a major change in the organization of schooling, a change with significant implications for teachers and pupils. Faced with a heterogeneous range of pupil abilities inside their classroom, teachers are immediately forced to consider the question (even if only to the point of rejecting it outright) of how to provide for the educational needs of *all* pupils. From the point of view of some educationalists (e.g. Kelly, 1978, p. 43) an opportunity for the realization of a system of mass education and for the development of a common education for all, would appear to have at last arrived.

But characterizations of the egalitarian nature and outcome of mixed ability teaching, worthy as they are, hardly correspond to the everyday reality of practice and perspective amongst teachers and pupils in many British secondary schools. Indeed, on the basis of the

Sageton experience we would contend that comprehensive teaching, and mixed ability grouping in particular, is replete with both innovation without change, and change without innovation.[2] Stratification, social division, inequality of educational opportunity stand largely unscathed, despite the hustle and bustle of curricular activity which on the surface suggests that substantial educational innovation is afoot. We would argue like Ball (1981, p. 285) that it is misleading to look at comprehensive education or mixed ability grouping as effective techniques of social engineering. 'The rhetoric of comprehensive education is concerned with equality of opportunity but this is not the same thing as saying that comprehensive schools are being set up and run to achieve this aim.'

The Sageton change to mixed ability grouping, as elsewhere (cf. ILEA Inspectorate, 1976), was represented as a desire to get away from the worst effects of streaming. It was supported in the hope that it would bring about an important improvement in control over pupils and persisted because as an organizational practice it also provided the means (a space) by which the job of identifying and exploiting available, but scarce, talent could be more efficiently (and humanely) carried out. The achievement of a new social order was not a primary concern. However, given the manner in which mixed ability grouping was introduced (as in so many other comprehensive schools (cf. Reid, 1981)) and insufficiently planned-for reorganization was subsequently enacted at Sageton, it is hardly surprising that this innovation was not wholly successful in achieving even the lesser goal, of pupil order. At the drop of an organizational fiat (in its overnight mixed ability change), the conditions were immediately created in which certainly no single class (at intake) presented teachers with insuperable problems of instruction or control. But by 'spreading the problem children', teaching had instantly and routinely been made difficult for more teachers in all classes. This hardly represented the achievement (or imposition) of effective control of pupil behaviour. Those practitioners or politicians searching in mixed ability grouping for a solution to intractable problems of pupil control would be well advised to look elsewhere. Classroom teachers themselves rarely saw mixed ability grouping as a solution to the problem of pupil disorder or as a means of effective control – a function sometimes attributed to the practice in action by analysts (cf. Ball, 1981). In this respect it is not insignificant to note that only a small number of Sageton teachers had experienced the control problems associated with the previous homogeneous grouping at the school. Only 16 of the 45 teachers from whom we have questionnaire responses had taught at the school prior to mixed ability grouping. The initial school management motivation for change was thus unlikely to sustain the innovation in its original form in the perspectives of 'new' Sageton teachers. They wanted and expected curriculum reform not simply as an answer to a control problem which few of them had witnessed.

It is thus hardly surprising that we find in schools which have undertaken change of this kind, at great pace and with insufficient planning or discussion, teachers thoroughly unprepared and unable to provide the expertise for curriculum or pedagogic reform of any sort. In these conditions at Sageton teachers expected leadership in these areas, not least from the new Head, but instead got only top down pressure for concentration on control and more rigorous assessment procedures. These circumstances meant disaffection, even alienation amongst teachers, a desire to leave Sageton rather than indulge in the (unsupported) search for curriculum change. To talk only of changing teacher attitudes or of improving the mechanism of decision making (the kind of prescription found in Reid *et al.* (1981), for example) as the means to effecting better mixed ability teaching seems shallow. Given the material and social conditions of a teacher's practice, constrained by the pressures of parental expectation, demographic trends, LEA policy, and the immediate and wider evaluation systems these are ritual and cosmetic acts of window dressing, unhelpful and potentially misleading for teachers wishing to improve or undertake an innovation of this kind.

In the specific Sageton educational experience we see the implications for an educational system caught up in the process of change, necessarily orientated (at local level) towards the immediate goals of its own survival, forced to contend with the wider (and antagonistic) demands for the identification and development of pupil excellence, success and/or orderly failure. In this situation teachers had rapidly to improvise change but they lacked the wherewithal, having neither vocabulary nor practice to effect a local version of mass education. Their actions consequently presaged new disorder.[3]

The Sageton innovation, in common with most others of its type, including that researched by Ball at Beachside, introduced mixed ability grouping rather than mixed ability teaching. The content and organization of classroom methods were left to be resolved at the departmental level or by individual teachers, the latter more or less willing or predisposed to respond to the change. For each department the change to mixed ability immediately demanded a quick and ready resolution to the practical problems of teaching groups containing the complete conventional range of pupil ability. However, the curriculum adopted, as in Maths and Integrated Studies, first and foremost met the needs of effective control over teaching method and curriculum content. There was little opportunity for any of the departments to consider the relative merits or otherwise of their innovations or to think out their implications for pupils or themselves. Perhaps we should have placed more emphasis on the pressure within most of the subjects for further reform and revision from junior teachers, initiatives which were generally deflated by the caution of their seniors. Neither 'side' showed the slightest tendency to behave either like deskilled dopes or system dupes as portrayed in the 'golden age lost' view of Apple (1980) or the even more overdetermined accounts of Marxists such as Sharp and Green (1975). It really is important to insist that macro-inspired generalizations about teachers' work frequently look like nonsense when the social and material conditions of curricular and pedagogical practice are faced up to in detail. The practices of mixed ability teaching that were implemented at Sageton corresponded to what the teachers thought possible given the limits of time, knowledge and resource within which they worked. The imperatives of mixed ability 'theorists' (such as Elliot, 1976, or Kelly, 1975) remained essentially irrelevant. There was an absence of dramatic or 'real' educational change.

Centrally, mixed ability teaching *has* brought about a significant change in some of the surface features of the technology of teaching, rather than a basic departure from assumptions embodied in whole class method and homogeneous grouping. In several subjects the written word, transposed to the worksheet, has increasingly replaced teacher talk as the primary means of making knowledge available to children. This in itself is not insignificant, but this mode is no more or less capable of overcoming instructional limits than the latter, in respect of 'teaching' the majority of pupils. Literacy rather than listening has achieved an added importance.[4] At Sageton there was a tendency for teachers to reproduce within the worksheet (both in the mode and the content of presentation) the same instructional limits that have characterized whole class method. Instruction was orientated towards pupils of average and above average ability. Many 'less able' pupils (if defined only in terms of their reading ages) found it extremely difficult entering into and achieving success at the learning process and their difficulties were often exacerbated by the pressures of pacing imposed by the syllabus. It is hardly surprising therefore that the material conditions of pedagogy and learning generated a degree of frustration and anger which in some pupils was consequently expressed in 'difficult' forms of behaviour. Where the instructional mode (as in SMP) allowed for the expression of such behaviour a counter-steering group emerged. Pupils not usually the focus of a teachers attention *vis-à-vis* the pacing of instruction (in whole class method), forced themselves upon the teacher's attention, and 'challenged' conventional interaction patterns. Learning difficulties were therefore more readily and explicitly revealed, albeit briefly, but at the cost of achieving 'deviant' pupil status. Mixed ability grouping with individualized and individuated instructional mode is not therefore an easy solution to the difficulties of less able pupils who continue to see themselves as failures, badly taught and badly behaved.

Reference to the genuine learning difficulties which these pupils (mainly boys in this study) experience and express, makes it extremely difficult to talk simply of (or represent) such behaviours as indices of an anti-school attitude[5] or as a rejection of middle class school knowledge.[6] Reference to each of the subjects and different modes of presentation has indicated that we cannot properly talk about pupils rejecting knowledge which they have not in the first place been effectively offered (Davies and Evans, 1984). The 'problem' of pupil 'failure' in schools cannot neatly or wholly be reduced to the nature or origins of school knowledge but must also be seen in terms of the means and opportunities of giving/gaining access to it (see also St. John-Brooks, 1983). Given the material conditions of learning which many pupils consistently experience in comprehensive schools (and the Sageton experience is not untypical – cf. Reid, 1981, or Ball, 1981) it would be more surprising if their behaviour were other than difficult. The less able pupils in Form 1p, particularly those of the counter-steering group, had reading ages well below their chronological age, and well below that required to cope with most of the content of all but the best worksheet systems. Their disaffection with their lack of learning, and their related difficult behaviours, provide little support to the evidence from Beachside or Banbury that less able children are more content with their situation in heterogeneous grouping. Only when and where the curriculum and pedagogical condition of learning were sufficient to allow at least a sense of progress, such as in Ms Pegler's English lesson and Mr Richard's Integrated Studies lessons, could heterogeneous grouping be associated with anything that looked like contentment amongst pupils. But to talk in terms of degrees, of more or less contentment or disaffection, would be neither meaningful nor helpful to pupils or teachers (for whom comparison is not possible) forced routinely to contend with their teaching and pupil learning problems in one particular form of ability grouping.

The emphasis we have placed upon the learning problems relating to reading age experienced by pupils, is consonant with claims often made in the Special Education literature, that reading difficulties and learning disabilities in particular are responsible for school failure and deficiencies. As West (1979, p. 135) remarks, 'a high percentage (50–75%) of officially incarcerated delinquents are reported as having reading problems'. But although these suggested links between learning disability and deviancy are plausibly suggestive they can, as West goes on to point out, without due caution disturbingly embody, an all-too familiar psychologising which individualises the problem in such a way as to deflect attention to the significance (or otherwise) of social class or 'cultures', as a factor in the success or failure of Sageton pupils. Sageton was predominantly a black working class school. But, to have reduced the success or failure of pupils simply to a class or culture explanation without reference to the material condition of teaching and curricular organization, would have risked gross over-simplification. Class and culture do not explain the differences in success and failure of Sageton pupils. Class, like gender or race or even ability, does not enact itself straightforwardly in the classroom, either through the form of a teacher's reified expections or any other single mechanism. To an adult observer, Sageton teachers appeared neither consciously prejudiced in their perspectives nor in their overt practices. It was rather the absence of a professional knowledge of a pedagogy which could reach and teach the full ability range which often made them appear so in the pupils perspectives. Moreover, while there was little obvious racial disharmony in any of the classrooms observed, there was little in the curricular activity of teachers to encourage the kind of inter-racial co-operation which is often found in more collaborative learning environments (cf. Salmon and Claire, 1984). Indeed, but for the pupils (boys) in group 1, in Form 1p, where 'ability' and commitments seemed to override ethnicity, there was remarkably little social interaction between the different racial groupings. Teachers' views of pupils and those of the professional authors whose texts they used, were mediated in the language of worksheets (especially manifested in their level of difficulty and in the standard forms of English). Teachers simply lacked both appropriate professional knowledge and also the time and resource to produce material which surmounted these difficulties. Much of the material which teachers use in mixed ability classes is of a printed or duplicated kind. It is obviously important therefore that teachers should select material which is comprehensible to their pupils. Both the Bullock report (1975) and Rampton (1981) stress the need for language development, in a way in which we as teachers ought not to dismiss as official rhetoric.

> In the course of the child's life in school there should be a gradual and growing extension of his powers of language to meet new demands and new situations and this again takes us firmly to the need for an explicit knowledge of how language operates (Bullock, 1975, p. 143).

But how are teachers to achieve this? To assume that teachers have the skills to 'competently teach not merely all levels of ability but all levels of ability together is simply fatuous'.[7] Within the limits of time, resource and professional knowledge which teachers, such as those at

Sageton routinely work, all too often in worksheet regimes, lessons appeared to provide little opportunity for the development of language of whatever form (standard or non-standard). If nothing else, successful mixed ability teaching, even evaluated only in terms of teacher and pupil expressed preferences, calls for a greater flexibility and variety of classroom organization than has characterized homogenous grouping and which has also tended to feature in the mixed ability classroom at Sageton and elsewhere (see Reid *et al.*, 1981; DES, 1978). It is understandable that the pupils of 1p generally defined 'English' teaching, represented to them by Ms Pegler with increasing variety of content and method, as their most favoured and rewarding lessons. More generally, however, pupils, particularly the less able, could be subject to the routine and boredom of a particular mode for long periods of time (e.g. three years of SMP work cards) unless they were removed for what often turned out to be a satisfying remedial break. They were generally subject to demands which they experienced as *restrictions* upon their ability, demands generated by the particular mode of transmission and its requirement, which they could not serve and which inhibited access to the opportunities inherent in the mode. Here is a poignant form of the catch 22 in education; if you can't do the practices required by the learning mode, you don't learn; and if you don't learn then you can't do the practices required by the learning mode. Literacy, definable in very particular reading age terms, was an inescapable demand of the work card. Failure to 'have it' meant failure to gain access to the procedures and knowledge content embodied in the material.

The ability to produce more 'open', linguistically sensitive, better prepared and more varied material is of crucial importance in mixed ability grouping. Ironically, it may in current financial and economic circumstances be increasingly difficult to achieve. Conventional pedagogy, i.e. whole class teaching is, as Bernstein (1977, p. 134) has argued, a 'remarkably cheap' pedagogy, requiring only a small space and a table, book and chair per pupil. In mixed ability classrooms, alternatives or supplements to whole class method and the class based text need to be sought but the costs of producing worksheets, packs, visual aids, occasional visits, etc. are not inconsiderable. The relative status of different subjects determines the ease with which preferred instructional strategies can be adopted. Levels of resource made available by the school mediate wider financial and economic restrictions, help or hinder favoured educational programmes. Our discussion of Science and Integrated Studies evidenced this concretely, showing how physical resource sets limits to the possible actions of teachers, obstructing opportunities for group work. The limits of time and resource also effect significantly the quality of instruction. The production of workcards by teachers is extremely demanding, not only of financial resource but also of a teacher's *time*. Projects need constant supervision, servicing, additional materials, and gathering of resources. Strains on the organizational powers of teachers are considerable. The quality of instruction which teachers are able to provide for children is thus necessarily related to wider arenas of decision making relating to (and determining) available levels of resource (time and money) and embodied in the timetable. Yet the availability of timetabled time for instruction preparation and planning is neither a feature of teaching in Sageton nor has it ever been in secondary schools in general.

In most mixed ability classrooms at Sageton, teacher control over knowledge so characteristic of whole class method was largely untouched. It was simply transposed to the worksheets. There was no basic shift away from a transmission model of teaching. Pupils worked mainly from worksheets and were less obviously doing teacher-controlled work in that they no longer had to work at a common pace and could often choose whether or not to enter directly into interaction with the teacher. Nevertheless, 'they were still moving into the teacher's meaning systems and leaving it relatively undisturbed' (Edwards and Furlong, 1977, p. 142).

Conventional injections of 'greater variety' or 'more relevance' in terms of the curricular diet of secondary schools would not in itself be sufficient to secure the educational advancement of many children. The Sageton data has emphasized the necessity and validity of making a distinction between the *content* of a learning task and the *communication* of the task (cf. Mehan, 1979). Both need to be borne in mind not only for the purpose of analyses but also during any process of curriculum reconstruction. This allows us to differentiate between how a pupil's relationship between either factor may be framed (limited or facilitated) both within and also at levels above the teaching process. In modes of transmission other than whole class method access to the substantive content of a learning task may, as we have seen, be less dependent upon a pupil's capacity (and willingness) to listen, than upon levels of *literacy* with which the pupil is predisposed.[8] Hence, whether the worksheet is experienced as a limit or possibility *vis-à-vis* successful learning outcomes depends on a complex interplay of pupil predispositions with the quality of instructional mode, especially in terms of its suitability for the range of pupil characteristics and the amount of time available. For many pupils time and content interact to frustrate all hopes of academic success or recognition. These factors are in turn related to the wider contexts of decision making concerning the allocation of resource and time in which teachers operate. Accepting this, it is possible to conceive of pupils' failure in the educational process as, to a degree at least, independent of their experience of the hidden or overt curriculum. Pupils may fail or show disaffection because of the way in which learning is organized, rendering them unable to achieve because of a complex interplay between personal predisposition, levels of resource, the form and quality of instruction and the teachers' perception and management of these factors.

It would not be accurate to present the use of worksheets which dominated the Sageton mixed ability setting as an insignificant shift in the mode of transmission, without implications for the teachers and pupils concerned. As pupils relate directly to the mode and its contents, they are less dependent on the teacher at each stage of acquiring the relevant material, but differentially so, according to whether they have the necessary predispositions to work independently from the worksheets as constructed. Those with these dispositions are not always, as we saw in Form 1p, the 'able' children. It becomes possible for some pupils at least to feel more in control of what they do and when they do it. Pupil progress is clearly not only a matter of having the necessary technical skills (i.e. learning ability), but also the kind of social and emotional predisposition conducive to working confidently in relative isolation from the teacher's attention (and control). In general, to be schooled is to have the cognitive aptitude, social interactional skills and emotional attitudes prerequisite to learning in large classes. But within classrooms, different modes of transmission make different and differential demands upon children and produce specific effects. Teachers need to consider what processual skills and attitudes are constantly and differentially required by pupils to facilitate movement into the curriculum content and mode. Mixed ability practice makes different demands on both pupils and teachers and the evidence we have presented suggests that we need to make more complex our ideas of what it is to be an able pupil or teacher in schools.

Both Mr Richards and Ms Pegler, for example, were able to achieve 'successful' teacher identities in the perspectives of the pupils of Form 1p because each was capable of providing not only an interesting (in Mr Richard's case) and varied *content* but also because they created the conditions or *context* in which pupils felt they could progress and learn. Both teachers were quite explicit about the demands they were making of children, the nature of the task and the relationships which were to exist between themselves and their pupils. Neither teacher's 'control' could be said to be 'informal' or authoritarian. The pupils perceived them both as strict but fair. The rules and requirements of their classrooms seemed quite 'public', rational and unambiguous. They defined quite precisely the boundaries of acceptable social and learning behaviours. In these classrooms there seemed to be a high degree of consensus between the teachers' and the pupils' definition as to what was required of the 'good' teacher and what had to be done in order to learn. The boys and girls of 'groups' 2 and 3, for example, generally expected teachers to control, but 'fairly', to provide interesting work and to 'make' and 'help' them 'understand' in order to learn. From the *point of view of these pupils it was the teachers rather than their own responsibility to ensure that this would happen*. Thus they were dissatisfied with the actions of Ms Tripp in Integrated Studies. Despite her valiant efforts to bridge the divide between school knowledge and the pupils' experience, she was unable (like Mr Dean) with Form 2p) to provide the instructional mode or means by which this could be achieved with *all* the children. The provision of 'interesting' work *alone* in the pupils view was no more an acceptable or legitimate condition of their 'doing work' than the unaccomplished imposition of 'effective', strict (but 'unfair' because of the absence of an interesting content) control.

However, the Sageton data does not lend support to the views (see St. John-Brooks, 1983; Salmon and Claire, 1984) that working class children are purely instrumental in their attitudes to school learning, and that they separate this learning from their 'intimate' personal experience. The working class pupils of Form 1p, on the limited occasions (in remedial or extraction lessons and those of Ms Pegler, Mr Richards and also Ms Tripp) when the boundaries between school knowledge and pupil experience were noticeably blurred, seemed equally capable of enjoying the teachers incursion into their private lives as any other pupil. However, this could only be attempted once the pedagogical conditions of learning had successfully been established. It was the failure of Ms Tripp and Mr Dean (with Form 2p) to attract and keep the interests of all pupils which often created the appearance that some children could not, would not, be content with the *content* of the teachers 'instruction'.

Pupil responses to, and opportunities within, the variety of curricula which they received in mixed ability innovation, was complex, transient and varied. For this reason it is extremely difficult to summarize the findings in terms of whether mixed ability grouping benefits or dis-benefits the able or less able child. The most cynical overview would be to claim that their abilities and differences are left relatively untouched. As we have seen, all pupils, whatever their ability to cope with the *content* of the curriculum, *could* find difficulty achieving success in some subjects because of their inability or unwillingness to work within an independent mode. For some pupils (the able but underachieving), getting started meant waiting for the teacher to direct and *demand* their attention to the task at hand, for others, getting unstuck and making progress also meant continued dependence upon the teacher's consistent assistance and help. However, individual help from the teacher was not (*could* not be) always forthcoming, at least in a form which facilitated either the teacher's or the pupils' full understanding of the learning difficulty. Instruction in worksheet modes tended to be brief, and very often seemed sufficient only to allow pupils to enjoy a sense of progress. Pupils were involved in 'individual piloting and meta-learning'. But in marked contrast to whole class method, where teacher control and collective piloting generally obscures pupil difficulties with learning, worksheet instruction at least has the potential for making explicit the learning problems being experienced by pupils, at the point at which they are experienced. Indeed, when these different pedagogies are compared, whole class method does begin to look like the 'concealment caper of all times' (Davies and Evans, 1984).

In common with many other classroom studies (see Stanworth, 1981) the Sageton data reveals that it is boys rather than girls who are most frequently perceived by the researcher and the teacher as most 'difficult' and who consequently command the greatest proportion of the teacher's instructional and regulative talk and time. Only one girl, Liona in Form 1p (though Mary and Heather were also difficult), showed anything like the extremes of behaviour which could be displayed by pupils such as Jerry, Ryan and Rene. At Sageton, boys and girls tended to be differentially treated in terms of the amount of teacher time they received and were rarely seen to engage in social, let alone collaborative or co-operative 'learning' interactions. However, this evidence does not suggest that the educational opportunities which accrue to boys are necessarily greater or 'better' than those experienced by girls. We need to look carefully at the nature and quality of instruction being received by these less able and difficult boys and girls. Given the range of demands made upon teachers by mixed ability (and the absence of appropriate prior pedagogical expertise), only limited opportunities accrue to such pupils for the resolution of their problems. The explanation of difficult behaviour and deviance requires no positing of prior pupil values. Difficult pupils seem rational and explicit concerning the difficulties which they encounter in getting at classroom knowledge. Teachers are appraised and valued according to their ability or (perceived) willingness to make this possible. The 'motivations' and 'attitudes' which teachers ascribe to pupils are best thought of as disposition generated by experience of specific school-provided learning conditions rather than initial causes of competence or performance. Admittedly this research has touched only the surface of such processes as collective and individual piloting and meta-learning, processes which we can see are sub-strategies within particular modes of curriculum organization. But the analysis does lend support to much recent classroom research (see Westbury, 1973; Denscombe, 1980a; Lundgren, 1977; Woods, 1977, 1980a) which has suggested that *teaching* is certainly not always as it seems (i.e. a process effecting *learning*, in the conventional, knowledge acquisition sense of the word). Both teachers and pupils are found in a position of having to 'cope', in order to protect their fragile educational identities in circumstances which routinely provide opportunities for their evaluation and demise. Together (as was most vividly attested in Science and Maths) they create in a complex process of interaction, the appearance that teaching and learning is occurring. This is no secret either to teachers, abundantly aware of the gross inadequacies of what they both say and do to provide a very limited form of instruction, or to the pupils who consequently routinely experience the feeling that they have been 'taught' but yet again have failed to learn anything of significance. Pupils who begin by explaining such failure disparagingly with reference to teachers are innured into going on more damagingly to complete the explanation with reference to their own ability or selves. When faced with a novel mode, it is, indicatively, 'the teacher' who takes the praise or blame from children.

Mixed ability teaching does not then, at least in the early states of its development (as currently found in our schools), seem to involve any radical change in the learning opportunities presented to pupils which lie at the heart of schooling. The 'organising notions' (Ball, 1981, p. 286) embodied in the teacher's and likewise the pupils' attitudes and view of the classroom remain largely unchanged. Teachers at Sageton, as elsewhere, after all are deeply socialized into the practice of whole class teaching, with its reliance on common pacing, skills of listening, recording and responding to directed questions. They are not prepared (nor could they have been expected) to think out in advance the implications for themselves or the pupil of doing teaching differently. Teachers are not socialized into the minutiae of what a particular mode of instruction presupposes of children, into what it takes for a pupil to be in a position to reveal competence. At Sageton, as at Beachside, most of the teachers continued to think of the children in terms of conventional ability types. They viewed mixed ability groups in terms of an *a priori* normal distribution of ability into bright, average and less able. However, the straightforward polarization of pupils across an ability/behaviour continuum was not in evidence. Able but difficult pupils represented a severe problem to teachers, particularly as the teachers were concerned for achievement and academic success. All the departments worked under constant pressure to assess fully. Teacher perceptions of senior teacher and parental pressures for academic excellence (in a context of falling rolls), were clearly a major consideration in the classroom selection of appropriate curriculum and teacher strategies. They also influenced the return to class teaching (as an assured way of getting at least some pupils to success) and the policies of setting. Although, then, the initial move away from whole class teaching did give rise to new ways of teaching and altered content, it also gave rise to new sorts of problems of instruction and control. In this context much of the reversion to mixed ability grouping in our secondary system (and there has certainly been a recent increase in the tendency to top and tail where it is practised – Reid *et al.*, 1981) can be seen as an acceptance of pedagogical failure. Setting for many schools and subjects is an organizational coping strategy, all that is possible given the conditions of work (curriculum, resources, etc.) and prevailing pedagogical expertise with which teachers operate. The continuation of mixed ability innovation (at Sageton, a creditable even astonishing expression of commitment) can, however, lead to a gradual evolution of alternative teacher strategies. These represent, at least in their current form, a widening of the definition of what constitutes appropriate teaching, and occasionally they have given rise to a heightened awareness of what abilities are required to work within such 'new' instructional modes (if only in terms of crude notions of reading ability or 'independence'). This is progress by default, because at Sageton it was not the intention behind mixed ability innovation to complexify ideas of pupil ability, but to exploit old forms in new ways (Davies and Evans, 1984).

This emphasis upon the identification and categorization of pupil differences so persistent in British schools has ensured that selection is a fundamental part of the mixed ability classroom. Differences between children are formalized in interaction patterns and communication structures which produced at Sageton a four-fold division of pupils clearly demarcating the able, able underachieving, average and less able. Given the constraints on teaching (the demands of time, the curriculum and evaluation system), the language of classrooms remains restricted and steered by the demands of the context, rather than by immediate pupil needs. This often differentiates learning outcomes among the pupils. Initial differences among the pupils are preserved and increased (Lundgren, 1977, p. 227). Differentiation is further compounded and institutionalized upon grouping by setting, not least through the syllabus structure. At Sageton, as at many other comprehensive schools (Reid *et al.*, 1981), mixed ability grouping was retained (in some subjects) only to the end of the third year. At this point (if not before as in Sciences, Language and Integrated Studies) pupils experienced different career routes in the form of differentiated curricula, and often differentiated teaching methods. As Ball (1981) has similarly noted, even with mixed ability grouping, setting introduces an element of early sponsorship into some subjects (particularly in foreign languages). Apart from these mechanisms there remains a whole range of selective processes resistantly rooted in the material world of school which convey to pupils their respective status, ability and personal worth.[9] The demise of selective forms of schooling and grouping does not necessarily signify anything like the end of selection and differentiation in schools and classrooms. It would be surprising if this were otherwise given that mixed ability as an organizational form has appeared in our schools for reasons which have had little to do with the provision of an appropriate pedagogy, curriculum, or educational equality of opportunities, but everything to do with system management, evaluation, efficiency and control needs.

Notes

Chapter 1

1   Bellaby (1977) and the recent work of Ball (1981) are notable exceptions. The latter, for example, provides 'an intensive study' of one institution by non-participant observation.

2   While Ball's (1981, pp. 278–9) work says much about classrooms both banded and unstreamed, he concedes that ' "certain effects" brought about by mixed ability grouping might not be explicable without longer term and more intensive observation and analyses of teacher–pupil interaction in the mixed ability classroom'; see also Edwards and Furlong (1978).

3   NFER AH2/3 tests were administered by the research team with the help of teachers to all pupils in years 1–3, in full knowledge of the 'cultural' limitations inherent in both test and testing procedures. However, it was felt that the information gained from such tests could be used cautiously along with other sorts of data gleaned from teachers, or school assessment procedures, to provide some indication as to the nature and level of pupils' 'ability'.

4   As Edwards and Furlong (1978) point out, in the most common form of classroom research, that of systematic observation, a manageable record of what is said depends on extracting the essential features from an otherwise overwhelming stream of talk. This is usually done by coding the talk into a number of categories which are claimed to abstract these essentials from the surrounding noise. The interaction can then be "tallied and plotted on a matrix to present an objective picture of the verbal patterns" so that, systems for analysing classroom talk can tell us what actually occurs in classrooms' (p. 39). See also McIntyre (1980) and Delamont and Hamilton (1976) for critical discussion.

5   A full discussion of the limits and possibilities of Systematic Classroom Observation is provided by McIntyre (1980).

6   A number of recent empirical studies stress a similar view (e.g. A. Hargreaves, 1978; Sharp and Green, 1975; Ball, 1981), but often with little reference to the way in which similar factors may be differently realized, i.e. perceived as a constraint or possibility by the actors.

Chapter 2

1   A more detailed historical account of Sageton's development can be found in Evans (1977) and Leavold (1977).

2   The current ethnic representation at Sageton, as subjectively appraised by the Head, Mr Fillmore, was around 60% West Indian, 20% British, 15% Asian, 5% other.

3   For further discussion of the previous Headmaster's perspective at this time, see Leavold (1977) or Evans (1977). As an example of the view taken, the Head stated 'I would always push for middle class values because I always thought they were better'.

4   A straight comparison on the same test is not possible. IQ scores for the first year of entry as a secondary modern categorized on a 10–20–40–20–10% distribution (from low scores to high, left to right) were 2–23–71–3–0. In 1977–8 the first year intake on the NFER/AH2/3 (general reasoning) scored 30–32–28–7–2. These differences are unlikely to be the product of test differences.

5   This would be expected by Monks and is, we have suggested (Corbishley and Evans, 1980), a feature which is significant when reading teacher's comments, especially on the balance or split between pastoral and academic.

6   That is to say, as defined in the staff guide; for example Heads of Schools were expected to take responsibility for both 'the academic and social welfare, well being and control' of their respective years.

7   It might be added, however, that even under the previous organizational structure these Heads of School did not have the 'academic well being of pupils' amongst the role responsibilities which were formally defined for them. However, given the status then imputed to their positions (and the organizational structure), they evidently saw themselves as mini-school Heads with concerns which encompassed *both* the pastoral and academic well being of their pupils.

8   For a further discussion of these difficulties with specific reference to pastoral care see Corbishley and Evans (1980).

9   See also Hunter (1979).

10 The Head renewed emphasis upon senior management meetings in an attempt to redefine and establish their importance, following a period of growing disenchantment amongst the senior management.

11 As Rutter and his colleagues (1980) found, the 'balance' that was most important to the successful school was in ability, and rather less so but still significant, was social class. Mr Fillmore was acutely aware of both.

12 Tests were administered by the school during the first term.

13 This perhaps evidences the longer term intentions of the Head for curriculum reform (albeit of a highly centralized kind). While the proposed changes represented quite dramatic structural novelty and created opportunity for curriculum reform, little if any debate concerning its nature was conducted at the senior management, pastoral or

academic meetings. Discussion tended to centre on the implications of changes from a four to an eight period day for control. The inseparability of social control from curriculum planning was repeatedly made explicit. See also A. Hargreaves (1979, p. 139).

14   See A. Hargreaves (1979, p. 140): 'The orderly organisation and spatial distribution of pupils is the essence of good policing.'

15   Ball (1981, p. 186) uses the term 'restricted autonomy' to refer to an autonomy restricted from three sources, all of which engender limitations on classroom practice: (1) subject subculture, that is the tendency for styles and methods available to the subject teacher to be defined by what counts as 'good practice' within the subject culture; (2) the culture of the school as a whole, which defines 'acceptable practice' in terms of classroom style and control relationships; (3) external constraints, for example, public examinations, and broader parental expectations.

Chapter 3

1   Wringe (1976, p. 51), however, comments without specifying which year groups he is referring to: 'In 1962 only twenty five percent of children in England and Wales were learning a second language.'

2   The 1970s began to see the introduction of new commercially produced language courses, though generally these received less dissemination or publicity than 'new' curricula in Maths, Sciences or the Social Sciences.

3   His had been one of the published schemes which had aimed at 'the great majority': see the note below.

4   Hawkins and Howson (1974–9).

5   See Wringe (1976, pp. 25–35) for a critical view of this emphasis.

6   See Evans (1982, appendix 4) for list of books recommended by the Head of Department for 'average and less-able pupils' in the third year.

7   *Longman's Audio Visual French Course* (Antrobus and More, 1967, the principal course adopted prior to mixed ability grouping at Sageton.

8   Modern Language teachers, as most other teachers at Sageton, considered themselves to be working with a pupil intake skewed towards the average and lower levels of ability.

9   A disjuncture also noted by the H.M. Inspectorate in DES (1977, p. 2).

10   See Denscombe (1980a, b, c).

11   Warnes (1975, p. 97) is very critical of language departments on these grounds, but his view is certainly a minority one among language teachers (quoted in Ball, 1981, p. 180).

12   See also A. Hargreaves (1978, p. 82) on the organization of staffing in middle schools as a coping strategy.

13   German was taught only to the top groups of pupils in year three, who did two periods of French and one of German. It was the Head of

Department's intention to expand the teaching of German into the second year if more staff could be added.

14   See Woods (1977).

15   See Blake and Davis (1964).

16   In Evans (1982) we refer to three 'levels' of decision making; the first is the classroom context of teacher–pupil interaction; the second the broader school context of department, faculty, management meetings etc.; and the third, the broader LEA and community context of decision making.

17   A point made by both A. Hargreaves (1978, p. 81) and Woods (1977).

18   See also Ball (1981) on language teaching.

19   As Wringe (1976, p. 59) notes: 'In streamed or setted *classes* but otherwise progressive departments, a standard procedure is to work over each new piece of material orally, this usually being followed up by various kinds of written work, often done at home out of class time. For sheer efficiency it is difficult to see how this can be bettered. This however is a class teaching approach *par excellence*.'

20   See Rubin (1977) and Hawkins (1979, p. 74).

21   See Ball (1981, p. 211).

22   A typical feature of whole class teaching. See Edwards and Furlong (1978).

23   See Hammersley (1976, pp. 104–15).

24   See Edwards (1980).

25   A feature also described by Ball (1981, p. 211).

26   A feature also of traditional mathematics teaching in whole class method. See Lundgren (1977).

27   The more damaging effect of a *public* labelling of pupils is discussed by D. Hargreaves (1976). What these pupils are learning is not French but the product of the teachers' strategy of control. Their difficulties are 'due' to a personal failure to conform to rules of behaviour. They are learning about their own learning: 'meta learning' (Lundgren, 1977). The consequence is reflected foremost in their low opinion of their ability at French.

28   See Bernstein (1977, pp. 116–47) on 'interrupter systems'.

29   See Wringe (1976, p. 63) on the use of European Studies.

30   For a discussion of this issue see Wringe (1976, p. 55).

Chapter 4

1   The public sector of schooling was in something of a turmoil at this time. It was a period of dissatisfaction amongst teachers over pay scales, differentials and job responsibilities. The Houghton pay award helped alleviate some of these frustrations.

2   This is but one form of SMP. In the main, SMP relies upon textbooks and traditional modes of transmission (class teaching).

3   A discussion of the limits and possibilities for variation in teacher style within SMP is found in Buswell (1980, pp. 293–307).

4   SMP Teachers' Notes, p. 7.

5   The term immediate is preferred to personal because the latter (invoking Bernstein's (1977) personal-positional dichotomy) tends to imply a significant change in the form of pupil–teacher relationships and control. Our data suggests, however, that public *didactic* pedagogical talk tends merely to move to the immediate level. Control over pupils, therefore, does not necessarily become more implicit, as the relationships realized in the form of talk (at least from the pupil's position) are quite explicit. Like King (1979), however, we would suggest that the teachers' control of children's classroom behaviour is better described as oblique (as distinct from direct), rather than implicit. Certainly it appears as such to the rest of the class and to the researcher.

6   Interest behaviours are akin to what Goffman (1963) describes as 'side involvements' and Stebbins (1975) as 'away behaviour'.

7   Teachers in the Fife Mathematics Project (Crawford, 1975, p. 108, 68) also focused on discipline as more problematic in an individualized curriculum.

8   The use of 'hard' data here, however, is somewhat misleading, as the fewer regulative messages tended to reflect acceptance of higher thresholds among teachers, rather than improved behaviour from second and third year pupils. It may also be worth noting here that the incidence of public and regulative teacher talk decreases with the age of the teacher, and length of stay at the school (and hence experience with SMP cards).

9   See also the Fife Mathematics Project (Crawford, 1975, p. 99) where some teachers assessing the project drew attention to a similar emphasis upon the socialization of pupils into the scheme; also, in an individualized Humanities scheme, see Edwards and Furlong (1978). Given the analysis offered in later discussion in this chapter, it is possible to reconsider some of this data as instances of collective/individual piloting.

10   Only recently in the literature is the full range of pupil identities being given enough consideration. See, for example, Hammersley and Turner (1980) on 'conformist pupils' and the D. Hargreaves (1979) discussion of 'four ideal type pupils' and his stress on a consideration of the 'indifferent' or 'instrumental types'.

11   D. Hargreaves (1972, p. 15) argues that teacher–pupil interactions are typically 'asymmetrically contingent: the pupils' behaviour is much more contingent on the teacher's behaviour than the teacher's behaviour is contingent on the pupils' behaviour'.

12   'There's not enough time for us to cover all these topics they should have finished by the third year. They are too slow in the 1st and 2nd years. This is the thing with cards, they got fed up and there's periods of turn off. But then of course if you do something else, blackboard work, they are not doing the cards. So it's a vicious circle' (Mrs Tripp)

Chapter 5

1 See also Hamilton (1976).
2 A. Hargreaves also draws attention to the import of 'material' constraints on classroom practice.
3 Nuffield Combined Science (1970).
4 We use the term here to refer to the formally organized contexts of decision making above the teaching process and not as implied by Keddie (1971) to invoke a largely unconscious disjuncture between teacher words and deeds (see Evans, 1982).
5 See Esland (1971) for further discussion of this concept; also Ball (1981) for its application to the study of teaching.
6 See also Sands (1979).
7 B. Bernstein, (1971) 'On the Classification and Framing of Educational Knowledge', in Bernstein, B. (1977).
8 Adaptation according to Brickell (1971) is 'not so much a shrewd redesigning of an outside program to fit special local contours as it is a matter of knocking the corners off trying to get it through the doors of the school' (p. 399).
9 A point argued by A. Hargreaves (1978) who presents 'guided discovery' as one common solution.
10 Shayer's (1978, 1981) work approaches such questions, examining the relationship between pupil abilities and content levels of difficulty, etc. of 'new science schemes'.
11 Using Fry's Readibility Formula. A selection of worksheets from each subject is provided in Evans (1982, appendix 3).
12 Ball (1980), from an interactionist perspective, stresses the significance of initial encounters in the developmental nature of teacher–pupil relationships (following Lacey, 1970).
13 D. Hargreaves (1972, p. 204) notes that the most experienced teacher insists that if he is to survive he must 'define the situation in his own terms at once. Basically the initial definition is not so much a statement of the rules that will govern the class but rather a clear indication that a teacher is completely in charge and not to be treated lightly'. We do not think, however, that this analysis pays sufficient attention to the way in which a teacher's opportunities to effect the appearance of authority are structured by course curriculum organization or subject definitions of appropriate method.
14 And as defined by Primary School Test Scores (NFER Verbal Reasoning D.), both are amongst the lowest ability in the class. (We could not administer NFER AH2/3 tests to these pupils.)
15 'Front', as Woods (1980c) argues, which implies a kind of deception (here, self-deception), is an important feature of strategies.
16 Compare with the findings of Galton *et al.* (1980). It is worth mentioning at this point that of the 18 pupils of 1p for whom we have questionnaire responses only four expressed a preference for co-operative group work

as a mode of instruction. The majority advocated either 'working by yourself' or 'working by yourself in a group'. In effect this may be little more than confirming preferences/experiences gained at junior school.

17   As Hammersley (1976, p. 108) notes, teachers use questions not to get answers but as a summons and to imply to the pupils that they know when they are not attending them even though 'they might not show it'. Their 'concern with the establishment and maintenance of pupil attention underlies and interpenetrates even those classroom activities that are apparently concerned with the transmission of knowledge'. This strategy explains why the pupils of Group 3 (Table 13) experience a higher incidence of instructional talk than all others.

18   See Sharp and Green (1975).

19   Atkinson and Delamont (1976, p. 139) make the point that 'guided discovery is difficult to sustain at the best of times. If the nature of this management is not respected by any of the parties then trouble can ensue'.

20   A. Hargreaves (1978) emphasizes the significance of teachers' 'experience' in coping strategies. See also Mardle and Walker (1980) on professional socialization.

21   The modal teacher, constructed from questionnaire response, is an ex-grammar school pupil with a specialist degree training, one year PGCE and little knowledge either from personal experience or professional training of how to teach in mixed ability grouping.

22   It is, of course, somewhat ironic that teachers experienced greatest problems of control with those pupils for whom the course was originally designed to cater (see p. 98).

Chapter 6

1   See, for example, Williams (1976).

2   See Elliot (1974) for a critique of this form of 'integration' and the role of Geography within it.

3   See also Edwards and Furlong (1978) who portray this form of learning as a feature of first year Humanities teaching at the Abraham Moss Centre.

4   Birt (1976) further argues that *textbooks* in secondary History classes all too often reveal (a) demands for simple recapitulation of fact; (b) 'mechanical' questions, sometimes with a simple comprehension element, e.g. 'fill in the bands'; (c) non-questions, e.g. 'How many masts does the ship in the picture have?' These characteristics were frequently displayed in the worksheets at Sageton, which were also technically far less well produced than textbooks might have been.

5   As Musgrove (1976, p. 134) points out, 'subjects are not only intellectual systems they are social systems: they confer not only a source of identity in their members they confer authority and they confer power'.

6   A. Hargreaves (1978, p. 92) discusses the use of homework as a coping

strategy. Without sufficient resource and opportunity to set homework, teachers at Sageton were limited in their capacity to use this means of coping.

7 Hamilton (1976) discusses the problems of managing 'mixed' integrated and collection curricula in Integrated Science teaching.

8 In this way worksheets provided a necessary substitute for any 'deeper' integration, forming the point of contact between departments.

9 The elements of which are described by A. Hargreaves (1979, p. 146).

10 In individualized instruction where all pupils are working on worksheets or cards on potentially different topics at their own pace, class instruction is rarely possible. Much of a teacher's time is spent interacting with individual pupils 'privately' at the pupil's or the teacher's desk.

11 See Edwards and Furlong (1978) for a discussion of what research has shown to be the characteristics of classroom talk.

12 A characteristic feature of transmission teaching (Barnes, 1977, p. 111).

13 Merely transposing the frame of teacher control to worksheets in an individuated curriculum does little, then, to attenuate outcomes which, as Lundgren (1977) describes, are characteristic features of class teaching.

Chapter 7

1 A similar situation is reported by Buswell (1980) though English teaching is said to represent whole class method, rather than the 'mixed' curriculum identified here.

2 In the educationist context, for example, when conversing with other teachers in debate or talking to the researcher.

3 Ball (1981, p. 176) represents the English Department at Beachside as harbingers of this perspective in which 'mixed ability is viewed as an important part of being in a comprehensive school, offering an equality of opportunity to the pupils which was not available under the banding system'.

4 It is extremely difficult to classify the department, in Ball and Lacey's (1980) terms, according to its dominant paradigm. Although the emphasis given by the Head of Department is upon the grammatical, concerns for the sociological and the creative were also shown. This emphasis could, we would suggest, be viewed as a feature and expression of the institutional context and expectations in which the teachers operated, rather than being straightforwardly a reflection of any particular paradigm.

5 The department also contained another two teachers who taught English, but for less than half their timetable.

6 A. Hargreaves (1979) depicts drama (mime) as a curriculum option chosen by teachers for its control potential. This view would not be supported by teachers at Sageton who saw the unpredictability of

outcomes to which this form of activity gave rise, a source of disruption rather than control.

7 For a view on the significance of 'having a laugh', see Woods :1976).

8 'Indulgence', as Woods (1977) argues, is a feature of fraternization.

9 Some pupils, as amply reflected in recent literature, expect teachers to be 'strict' (see Gannaway, 1976; Furlong, 1976).

10 Scholastic Publications (1976–7).

11 For textbooks without supporting worksheets, Ms Pegler used the blackboard to stipulate a series of tasks related to the unaccompanied text.

12 A point also made by Ball (1981, p. 225).

13 See also Ball's (1981) account of History worksheets instruction.

14 Ball (1981), as others in the sociology of education, represents consistently displayed 'difficult' pupil behaviour as synonomously anti-school. This, we suggest, is a misleading and oversimplified view. Such behaviours, in our view, indeed signify opposition to learning experiences made available to such pupils who are, consequently, often anti-learning and anti-teacher. But to make the additional claim that they are anti-school is another matter indeed.

Chapter 8

1 ILEA (1984). *Improving Secondary Schools*.

2 See Davies and Evans (1984).

3 Ibid.

4 See also Edwards and Furlong (1978).

5 As, for example, Ball (1981) does. He presents no data on such pupils which would enable an assessment of the learning problems which they may have experienced.

6 This is an explanation for pupil failure, which has tended to dominate the Sociology of Education perhaps at the expense of a more sophisticated understanding of how children learn.

7 A point made by Bailey and Bridges (1983, p. 47) in critical reference to the DES (1978) report on mixed ability teaching.

8 The importance of this factor in partly determining success was borne out in two first year classes, 1p and 1s. Only 15 pupils had reading ages at or above their chronological age. All 15 achieved 'able' pupil identities as defined in teacher reports, in three or more of the subject areas considered here. Only four other pupils achieved similar 'success'. This factor of course mediates and expresses broader social class differences in pupils.

9 See in particular Ball (1981, ch. 8). He also stresses this point but does not examine in any detail the interactional process by which these outcomes are achieved. Ball's analysis is primarily concerned with the 'innovation process and the implementation of the innovation rather than a study of classroom interaction per se' (p. 279).

Bibliography

Adelman, C. (ed.) (1981). *Uttering, Muttering: Collecting, Using and Reporting Talk for Social and Educational Research*. London, Grant and McIntyre.

Adelman, C. and Walker, R. (1975). Open space – open classroom. *In* A. Harris *et al.* (eds), 1975, pp. 162–70.

Antrobus, A.L. and Moore, S. (1967–73). *Longman's Audio-Visual French Course*. London, Longman.

Apple, M. (1979). *Ideology and Curriculum*. London, Routledge & Kegan Paul.

Apple, M. (1980). Curricular form and the logic of technical control: building the possessive individual. *In* L. Barton *et al.* (eds), 1980, pp. 11–29.

Atkinson, P. and Delamont, S. (1977). Mock-ups and cock-ups: the stage management of guided discovery instruction. *In* P. Woods and M. Hammersley (eds), 1977, pp. 87–109.

Bailey, C. and Bridges, D. (1983). *Mixed Ability Grouping: A Philosophical Perspective*. London, George Allen and Unwin.

Ball, S.J. (1980). Initial encounters in the classroom and the process of establishment. *In* P. Woods (ed.), 1980b, pp. 143–162.

Ball, S.J. (1981). *Beachside Comprehensive: A Case-study of Secondary Schooling*. Cambridge, Cambridge University Press.

Ball, S.J. (1984a). Beachside reconsidered: reflections on a methodological apprenticeship. *In* R.G. Burgess (ed.), 1984, pp. 69–97.

Ball, S.J. (1984b). *Comprehensive Schooling: A Reader*. London, Falmer Press.

Ball, S.J. and Lacey, C. (1980). Subject disciplines as the opportunity for group action: A measured critique of sub-cultures. *In* P. Woods (ed.), 1980a, pp. 149–78.

Barnes, D. (1977). *From Communication to Curriculum*. Harmondsworth, Penguin.

Barton, L. and Meighan, R. (eds) (1978). *Sociological Interpretations of Schooling and Classrooms: A Reappraisal*. Driffield, Nafferton.

Barton, L. and Meighan, R. (eds) (1979). *Schools, Pupils and Deviance*. Driffield, Nafferton.

Barton, L., Meighan, R. and Walker, S. (eds) (1980). *Schooling Ideology and the Curriculum*. London, Falmer Press.

Barton, L. and Walker, S.L. (eds) (1981). *Schools, Teachers and Teaching*. London, Falmer Press.

Bellaby, P. (1977). *The Sociology of Comprehensive Schooling*. London, Methuen.

Bellack, A.A., Kliebard, H.M., Hyman, R.T. and Smith, F.L. (1966). *The Language of the Classroom*. New York, Teachers' College Press.

Berlak, A., Berlak, H., Bagenstos, N. and Mikel, E. (1975). Teaching and learning in English primary schools. *Schools Review* **83** (2), pp. 215–42.

Bernstein, B. (1970). Education cannot compensate for society. *New Society* **26**, 344–7.

Bernstein, B. (1971). On the classification and framing of educational knowledge. *In* M.F.D. Young (ed.), 1971, pp. 47–69.

Bernstein, B. (1977). *Class Codes and Control, Vol. 3: Towards a Theory of Educational Transmission* (2nd edition). London, Routledge & Kegan Paul.

Best, R., Jarvis, C. and Ribbins, P. (eds) (1980). *Perspectives on Pastoral Care*. London, Heinemann Educational.

Bird, C. (1980). Deviant labelling in schools: the pupils' perspective. *In* P. Woods (ed.), 1980b, pp. 94–108.

Birt, D. (1976). All ability History. *Teaching History* **IV**, No. 16, Nov. 1976, pp. 309–25.

Blake, J. and Davis, K. (1964). Norms, values and sanctions. *In* R.E.L. Faris (ed.), 1964, pp. 456–85.

Blackstone, T. and Weinreich-Haste, (1980). Why are there so few women scientists and engineers? *New Society* Feb. 1980, pp. 383–6.

Bloom, B.S. (1971). Learning for mastery. *In* B.S. Bloom *et al.* (eds), 1971, ch. 3.

Bloom, B.S. (1976). *Human Characteristics and Learning*. New York, McGraw-Hill.

Bloom, B.S., Hastings, J.T. and Madaus, G.F. (1971). *Handbook of Formative and Summative Evaluation of Student Learning*. New York, McGraw-Hill.

Bowles, S. and Gintis, H. (1977). Capitalism and education in the United States. *In* M. Young and G. Whitty (eds), 1977, pp. 192–228.

Boyson, R. (1981). The curse of the comprehensive. *Daily Mail* (London), 25 June 1981.

Brickell, H.M. (1971). Two local change strategies. *In* R. Hooper (ed.), 1971, pp. 399–410.

Bricker, D. (1979). Social dilemmas involved in teachers' deviance imputations. *In* L. Barton and R. Meighan (eds), 1979, pp. 153–67.

Buckby, M. (1979). Teaching pupils of lower ability – attitudes in the classroom. *Audio-Visual Language Journal* **17** (2), Summer 1979, pp. 77–81.

Bullock, A. (1975). *A Language for Life*. London, HMSO.

Burgess, R.G. (1980). Some fieldwork problems in teacher-based research. *British Educational Research Journal* **6** (2), pp. 165–73.

Burgess, R.G. (ed.) (1984). *The Research Process in Educational Settings: Ten Case Studies*. London, Falmer Press.

Buswell, C. (1980). Pedagogic change and social change. *British Journal of Sociology of Education* **1** (3), pp. 293–307.

Carroll, J.B. (1962). The prediction of success in intensive foreign language training. *In* R. Glaser (ed.), 1962, pp. 87–136.

Cicourel, A.V. (1964). *Method and Measurement in Sociology*. New York, Free Press.

Corbishley, P. (1977). Research findings on teacher groups in Secondary schools. *In* B. Davies and R. Cave (eds), 1977, pp. 1–17.

Corbishley, P. and Evans, J. (1980). Teachers and pastoral care: An empricial comment. *In* R. Best *et al.* (eds), 1980, pp. 201–25.

Corbishley, P., Evans, J., Kenrick, C. and Davies, B. (1981). Teacher strategies and pupil identities in mixed ability curricula: A note on concepts and some examples from Maths. *In* L. Barton and S. Walker (eds), 1981, pp. 177–95.

Corrigan, P. (1979). *Schooling the Smash Street Kids*. London, Macmillan.

Cox, C.B. and Boyson, R. (eds) (1975). *The Fight for Education: Black Papers 1975*. London, Dent.

Crawford, D.H. (ed.) (1975). *The Fife Mathematics Project: An Experiment in Individualised Learning*. Oxford, Oxford University Press.

Dahllof, U. (1971). *Ability Grouping, Content Validity and Curriculum Process Analysis*. New York, Teachers' College Press.

Dahllof, U. (1973). The curriculum development system in Sweden: some comments of trends and problems. *International Review of Education* **19**, 55–7.

Daunt, P.E. (1975). *Comprehensive Values*. London, Heinemann.

Davies, B. (1982). *Life in Classrooms and Playground*, Routledge and Kegan Paul.

Davies, B. (1977). Meanings and motives in going mixed ability. *In* B. Davies and R.G. Cave (eds), 1977, pp. 18–41.

Davies, B. (1981). Schools as organisations and the organisation of schooling. *Educational Analysis* **3** (1), pp. 47–68.

Davies, B. and Cave, R. (eds) (1977). *Mixed Ability Teaching in the Secondary School*. London, Ward Lock.

Davies, B. and Evans, J. (1984). Mixed ability and the comprehensive school. *In* S.J. Ball (ed.), 1984, pp. 155–77.

Davies, B., Corbishley, P., Evans, J. and Kenrick, C. (1985). Integrating Methodologies: If the Intellectual Relations Don't Get You Then The Social Will, in Burgess R.G. (ed) (1985) *Field Methods In the Study of Education*. London, Falmer, pp. 289–321.

Davies, R.P. (1975). *Mixed Ability Grouping*. London, Maurice Temple Smith.

Dawe, A. (1970). The two sociologists. *British Journal of Sociology* **21** (2), 208–18.

Delamont, S. (1976). *Interaction in the Classroom*. London, Methuen.

Delamont, S. and Hamilton, D. (eds) (1976). Classroom research: A critique and a new approach. *In* M. Stubbs and S. Delamont (eds), 1976, pp. 3–23.

Denscombe, M. (1980a). The work context of teaching: An analytic framework for the study of teachers in the classroom. *British Journal of Sociology of Education* **1** (3), 279–93.

Denscombe, M. (1980b). Pupil strategies in the open classroom. *In* P. Woods (ed.), 1980b, pp. 50–74.

Denscombe, M. (1980c). Keeping 'em quiet: the significance of noise for the practical activity of teaching. *In* P. Woods (ed.), 1980a, 61–84.

Denzin. N.K. (1970). *The Research Act in Sociology*. London, Butterworth.

DES (1977). *Mathematics, Science and Modern Languages in Maintained Schools in England*. London, HMSO.

DES (1978). *Mixed Ability Work in Comprehensive Schools*. HMI Series, Matters for Discussion No. 6. London, HMSO.

Douglas, M. (1966). *Purity and Danger*. London, Routledge & Kegan Paul.

Douglas, M. (1973). *Natural Symbols*. London, Barrie and Jenkins.

Durkheim, E. (1956). *Education and Sociology*. New York, Free Press.

Durkheim, E. (1961). *Moral Education* (ed. E.K. Wilson). New York, Free Press.

Easthope, G., Bell, A. and Wilkes, J. (1975). Bernstein's sociology of the school. *Research Intelligence* **1** (1), pp. 38–48.

Edwards, A.D. (1980). Pattern of power and authority in classroom talk. *In* P. Woods (ed.), 1980a, pp. 237–54.

Edwards, A. and Furlong, V. (1978). *The Language of Teaching*. London, Heinemann.

Eggleston, J. (ed.) (1979). *Teacher Decision-making in the Classroom*. London, Routledge & Kegan Paul.

Elliot, G. (1974). Integrated studies – some problems and possibilities for the geographer. *In* M. Williams (ed.), 1976, pp. 160–6.

Elliot, J. (1976). The problems and dilemmas of mixed-ability teaching and the issue of teacher accountability. *Cambridge Journal of Education* **6** (1/2), pp. 3–14.

Ellis, D.L. and Pearce, M.R. (1976). *Destination France: Survival Language Course*. Harrap Nelson.

Ellis, D.L. and Pearce, M.R. (1975) *French Sign Language* . Harrap.

Esland, G. (1971). Teaching and learning as the organisation of knowledge. *In* M.F.D. Young (ed.), 1971, pp. 70–115.

Esland, G. (1972). Innovation in the school. *Unit 12, Open University Educational Studies, Second Level Course, School and Society*. Milton Keynes, Open University Press.

Evans, J. (1977). An exploration of teachers' perspectives and the process of pupil identity construction in mixed ability teaching: A case study. Unpublished M.A. (Ed.) thesis. London, Institute of Education.

Evans, J. (1982). Teacher strategies and pupil identities in mixed ability curriculum: A case study. Ph.D. thesis. London, Chelsea College.

Evans, J. and Davies, B. (1975). Problems of Change. Teaching and Control in Mixed Ability Curricula: a case study of integrated studies. *In* E.C. Cuff and G.C.F. Payne (eds) (1985). *Crisis in the Curriculum*. Croom Helm, London, pp. 106–137.

Faris, R.E.L. (ed.) (1964). *Handbook of Modern Sociology*. Chicago, Rand McNally.

Ford, J. (1969). *Social Class and the Comprehensive School*. London, Routledge & Kegan Paul.

Fry, E. (1977). Fry's readability graph: classification, validity and extension to level 17. *Journal of Reading* **20**, Dec., 242–52.

Furlong, V.J. (1976). Interaction sets in the classroom: towards a study of pupil knowledge. *In* M. Stubbs and S. Delamont (eds), 1976, pp. 23–44.

Galton, M., Simon, B. and Croll, P. (1980). *Inside the Primary Classroom*. London, Routledge & Kegan Paul.

Gannaway, H. (1976). Making sense of school. *In* M. Stubbs and S. Delamont (eds), 1976, pp. 45–82.

Glaser, B. and Strauss, A. (1968). *The Discovery of Grounded Theory*. London, Weidenfeld.

Glaser, R. (ed.) (1962). *Training Research and Education*. Pittsburgh, University of Pittsburgh Press.

Goffman, E. (1963). *Behaviour in Public Places*. New York, Free Press.

Gouldner, A.W. (1971). *The Coming Crisis in Western Sociology*. London, Heinemann.

Green, A.G. (1977). Structural features of the classroom. *In* P. Woods and M. Hammersley (eds), 1977, pp. 263–71.

Gross, N., Giaquinta, J.A. and Bernstein, M. (1971). *Implementing Organisational Innovations: A Sociological Analysis of Planned Educational Change*. New York, Harper & Row.

Hamilton, D. (1975). Handling innovation in the classroom: two Scottish examples. *In* W.A. Reid and D.F. Walker (eds), 1975, pp. 179–208.

Hamilton, D. (1976). The advent of curriculum integration: paradigm lost or paradigm regained? *In* M. Stubbs and S. Delamont (eds), 1976, pp. 195–213.

Hammersley, M. (1976). The mobilisation of pupil attention. *In* M. Hammersley and P. Woods (eds), 1976, pp. 104–15.

Hammersley, M. (1977). School learning: the cultural resources required by pupils to answer a teacher's question. *In* P. Woods and M. Hammersley (eds), 1977, pp. 57–87.

Hammersley, M. (1980a). Classroom ethnography. *Educational Analysis* **2** (2), 47–74.

Hammersley, M. (1980b). On interactionist empiricism. *In* P. Woods (ed.), 1980b, pp. 198–214.

Hammersley, M. and Hargreaves, A. (1983). *Curriculum Practice*. London, Falmer Press.

Hammersley, M. and Turner, G. (1980). Conformist pupils? *In* P. Woods (ed.), 1980b, pp. 29–50.

Hammersley, M. and Woods, P. (eds) (1976). *The Process of Schooling*. London, Routledge & Kegan Paul.

Hargreaves, A. (1977). Progressivism and pupil autonomy. *Sociological Review* **25** (3), 585–621.

Hargreaves, A. (1978). The significance of classroom coping strategies. *In* L. Barton and R. Meighan (eds), 1978, pp. 73–109.

Hargreaves, A. (1979). Strategies, decision and control: interaction in a middle school classroom. *In* J. Eggleston (ed.), 1979, pp. 134–70.

Hargreaves, A. (1980). Synthesis and the study of strategies: A project for the sociological imagination. *In* P. Woods (ed.), 1980b, pp. 143–62.

Hargreaves, D. (1967). *Social Relations in a Secondary School*, London, Routledge & Kegan Paul.

Hargreaves, D. (1972). *Integrated Relations and Education*. London, Routledge & Kegan Paul.

Hargreaves, D. (1976). Reactions to labelling. *In* M. Hammersley and P. Woods (eds), 1976, pp. 201–7.

Hargreaves, D. (1978). What ever happened to symbolic interactionism? *In* L. Barton and R. Meighan (eds), 1978, pp. 7–23.

Hargreaves, D. (1979). Durkheim, deviance and education. *In* L. Barton and R. Meighan (eds), 1979, pp. 17–31.

Hargreaves, D. (1980). The occupational culture of teachers. *In* P. Woods (ed.), 1980a, pp. 125–49.

Hargreaves, D., Hester, S. and Mellor, F. (1975). *Deviance in the Classroom*. London, Routledge & Kegan Paul.

Harris, A., Lawn, M. and Prescott, W. (eds) (1975). *Curriculum Innovation*. London, Croom Helm.

Hawkins, E. (1979). Why a modern language at all? *Audio-Visual Language Journal* **17** (2), 71–6.

Hawkins, E. and Howson, B. (1974–9). *Le Français Pour Tout le Monde*, Books 1–5. London, Oliver and Boyd.

Hooper, R. (ed.) (1971). *The Curriculum: Context, Design and Development*. London, Oliver and Boyd.

Hoyle, E. (1969). How does the curriculum change? *Journal of Curriculum Studies* **1** (2), pp. 132–41.

Hunter, C. (1979). Control in the comprehensive system. *In* J. Eggleston (ed.), 1979, pp. 118–34.

ILEA Inspectorate (1976). *Mixed Ability Grouping*. London, ILEA.

ILEA (1984). *Improving Secondary Schools*. London, ILEA.

Jackson, P. (1968). *Life in Classrooms*. New York, Holt, Rinehart and Winston.

Jencks, C. (1972). A question of control: A case study of interaction in a junior school. Unpublished M.Sc. (Econ.) thesis. London, Institute of Education.

Keddie, N. (1971). Classroom knowledge. *In* M.F.D. Young (ed.), 1971, pp. 133–61.

Kelly, A.V. (ed.) (1975). *Case Studies in Mixed Ability Teaching*. London, Harper & Row.

Kelly, A.V. (1978). *Mixed Ability Grouping: Theory and Practice*. London, Harper & Row.

King, R. (1979). The search for the 'invisible pedagogy'. *Sociology* **13** (3), 445–74.

Kohl, L. (1970). *The Open Classroom*. London, Methuen.

Kollas, D. (1973). *On Educational Scientific Research*. Pedagogiska Institutionen Lunds, Universitet, Lund.

Labov, W. (1969). *The Logic of Non-standard English*. National Council of Teachers of English, Centre for Applied Linguistics.

Lacey, C. (1970). *Hightown Grammar*. Manchester, Manchester University Press.

Lacey, C. (1976). Problems of sociological fieldwork: A review of the methodology of 'Hightown Grammar'. *In* M. Hammersley and P. Woods (eds), 1976, pp. 55–67.

Leavold, J. (1977). Care, control and the urban school – A study of downtown sanctuary. Unpublished M.A. (Urban Ed.) thesis. London, London University.

Lukes, S. (1974). *Power: A Radical View*. London, Macmillan.

Lundgren, U.P. (1972). *Frame Factors and the Teaching Process*. Stockholm, Almquist and Wiksell.

Lundgren, U.P. (1977). *Model Analysis of Pedagogical Process*. Stockholm, Almquist and Wiksell.

McIntyre, D.I. (1980). Systematic observation of classroom activities. *Educational Analysis* **2** (2), pp. 3–30.

Macpherson, J. (1983). *The Feral Classroom*. Melbourne, Routledge & Kegan Paul.

Mardle, G. and Walker, M. (1980). Strategies and structure: some critical notes on teacher socialisation. *In* P. Woods (ed.), 1980a, pp. 98–125.

Mehan, H. (1979). *Learning Lessons: Social Organisation in the Classroom*. Cambridge, Harvard University Press.

Meyenn, R.J. (1980). School girls' peer groups. *In* P. Woods (ed.), 1980b, pp. 108–43.

Monks, T.G. (1968). *Comprehensive Education in England and Wales*. Slough, NFER.

Monks, T.G. (ed.) (1970). *Comprehensive Education in Action*. Slough, NFER.

Mungham, G. and Pearson, G. (eds) (1976). *Working Class Youth Culture*. London, Routledge & Kegan Paul.

Musgrove, F. (1976). Power and the integrated curriculum. *In* M. Williams (ed.), 1976, pp. 129–38.

Nash, R. (1973). *Classrooms Observed*. London, Routledge & Kegan Paul.

Newbold, D. (1977). *Ability Grouping – The Banbury Enquiry*. Slough, NFER.

Nuffield Combined Science Project (1970). London, Longman.

Pedley, R. (1978). *The Comprehensive School* (3rd Edition). Harmondsworth, Penguin.

Pollard, A. (1979). Negotiating deviance and 'getting done' in a primary school classroom. *In* L. Barton and R. Meighan (eds), 1979, pp. 75–95.

Pollard, A. (1980). Teacher interests and changing situations of survival threat in primary school classrooms. *In* P. Woods (ed.), 1980a, pp. 34–61.

Postlethwaite, K. and Denton, C. (1978). *Streams for the Future? Long-term Effects of Streaming and Non-streaming*. Final Report of the Banbury Enquiry. Banbury, Pubansco Publications.

Pring, R.A. (1975). Bernstein's classification and framing of knowledge. *Scottish Educational Studies* 7 (2), pp. 67–75.

Rampton, A. (1981). *Committee of Enquiry into the Education of Children from Ethnic Minority Groups*. London, HMSO.

Reid, M., Clunies-Ross, L., Goacher, B. and Vile, C. (1981). *Mixed Ability Teaching. Problems and Possibilities*. NFER-Nelson Publishing Company Ltd.

Reid, W.A. and Walker, D.F. (eds) (1975). *Case Studies in Curriculum Change*. London, Routledge & Kegan Paul.

Rex, J. (1961). *Key Problems of Sociological Theory*. London, Routledge & Kegan Paul.

Reynolds, D. (1976a). When pupils and teachers refuse a truce: the secondary school and the creation of delinquency. *In* G. Mungham and G. Pearson (eds), 1976, pp. 124–38.

Reynolds, D. (1976b). The delinquent school. *In* M. Hammersley and P. Woods (eds), 1976, pp. 217–31.

Rubin, D. (1977). Listening: An essential skill. *Audio-Visual Instruction* 22 (8), pp. 31–2.

Rutter, M., Maughan, B., Mortimore, P. and Ouston, J. (1979). *Fifteen Thousand Hours*. London, Open Books.

Sallach, D. (1974). Class domination and ideological hegemony. *Sociological Quarterly* 15, pp. 78–93.

Salmon, P. and Claire, H. (1984). *Classroom Collaboration*. London, Routledge & Kegan Paul.

Sands, M.K. (1979). Mixed ability science teaching: some current practices and problems. *The School Science Review* 60 (213), pp. 616–24.

Sands, M. and Kerry, T. (1982). *Mixed Ability Teaching*. London, Croom Helm.

Schlechty, P.C. (1976). *Teaching and Social Behavior*. Boston, Allyn and Bacon Inc.

Scholastic Publications (1976–7). *Individualised Reading*. Leamington Spa, Scholastic Publications Ltd.

Schonell, F. (1945). *Schonell Graded Word Reading Test 8* (R3 and R4). London, Oliver and Boyd.

Schutz, A. (1967). *The Phenomenology of the Social World* (translated by G. Walsh and F. Lehnert). London, Heinemann Educational.

Sharp, R. and Green, A. (1975). *Education and Social Control*. London, Routledge & Kegan Paul.

Shayer, M. (1978). Nuffield Combined Science: Do the pupils understand it? *School Science Review* **60** (211), pp. 210–24.

Shayer, M. and Adey, P. (1981). *Towards a Science of Science Teaching: Cognitive Development and Curriculum Demand*. London, Heinemann.

Skilbeck, M. (1972). Forms of curriculum integration. *In* M. Williams (ed.), 1976, pp. 124–8.

St. John-Brooks, C. (1983). English: A curriculum for personal development. *In* M. Hammersley and A. Hargreaves (eds), 1983, pp. 37–61.

Stanworth, M. (1981). *Gender and Schooling*. London, Hutchinson in association with the Exploration in Feminism Collective.

Stebbins, R.A. (1975). *Teachers and Meaning*. Leiden, E.J. Brill.

Stebbins, R.A. (1980). The role of humour in teaching. *In* P. Woods (ed.), 1980a, pp. 84–97.

Stephens, M. (1977). Mathematics: medium and message. *Mathematics in Schools* **6** (5), pp. 1–2.

Strivens, J. (1980). Contradictions and change in educational practices. *In* L. Barton *et al.* (eds), 1980, pp. 93–113.

Stubbs, M. and Delamont, S. (eds) (1976). *Explorations in Classroom Observation*. London, Wiley.

Turner, G. (1983). *The Social World of the Comprehensive School: How Pupils Adapt*. London, Croom Helm.

Varnava, G. (1975). *Mixed Ability Teaching in Modern Languages*. Glasgow, Blackie.

Vulliamy, G. (1976). What counts as school music? *In* G. Whitty and M.F.D. Young (eds), 1976, pp. 9–19.

Walker, R. and Adelman, C. (1975). *A Guide to Classroom Observation*. London, Methuen.

Walker, R. and Adelman, C. (1976). Strawberries. *In* M. Stubbs and S. Delamont (eds), 1976, pp. 133–72.

Walker, R. and Goodson, I. (1977). Humour in the classroom. *In* P. Woods and M. Hammersley (eds), 1977, pp. 196–228.

Wallin, E. (1979). Changing the game. *Journal of Curriculum Studies* **11** (2), pp. 183–6.

Warnes, T. (1975). French. *In* R.P. Davies (ed.), 1975, pp. 97–116.

West, G. (1979). Adolescent autonomy, education and pupil deviance. *In* L. Barton and R. Meighan (eds), 1979, pp. 133–53.

Westbury, I. (1973). Conventional classrooms, 'open' classrooms and the technology of teaching. *Journal of Curriculum Studies* **5** (2), pp. 99–121.

Whitty, G. (1976). Studying society: for social change or social control? *In* G. Whitty and M.F.D. Young (eds), 1976, pp. 35–47.

Whitty, G. (1977). Sociology and the problem of radical educational change: notes towards a reconceptualisation of the 'new' sociology of education. *In* M.F.D. Young and G. Whitty (eds), 1977, pp. 26–59.

Whitty, G. and Young, M.F.D. (eds) (1976). *Explorations in the Politics of School Knowledge*. Driffield, Nafferton.

Wiley, D.E. (1978). Conceptual issues in models of school learning. *Curriculum Studies* **10** (3), pp. 215–31.

Williams, A. (1973). Integrated Studies Project. *Forum* **16**, pp. 12–14.

Williams, M. (ed.) (1976). *Geography and the Integrated Curriculum: A Reader*. London, Heinemann Educational.

Willis, P. (1977). *Learning to Labour*. London, Saxon House.

Woods, P. (1977). Teaching for survival. *In* P. Woods and M. Hammersley (eds), 1977, pp. 271–94.

Woods, P. (1979). *The Divided School*. London, Routledge & Kegan Paul.

Woods, P. (ed.) (1980a). *Teacher Strategies: Explorations in the Sociology of the School*. London, Croom Helm.

Woods, P. (ed.) (1980b). *Pupil Strategies: Explorations in the Sociology of the School*. London, Croom Helm.

Woods, P. (1980c). Strategies in teaching and learning. *In* P. Woods (ed.), 1980a, pp. 18–34.

Woods, P. (1980d). The development of pupil strategies. *In* P. Woods (ed.), 1980b, pp. 11–29.

Woods, P. (1981). Understanding through talk. *In* C. Adelman (ed.), 1981, pp. 13–26.

Woods, P. and Hammersley, M. (eds) (1977). *School Experience*. London, Croom Helm.

Wragg, E. (ed.) (1976). *Teaching Mixed-ability Groups*. Newton Abbot, David and Charles.

Wright, E.M.J. and Proctor, V.H. (1961). *Systematic Observations of Verbal Interactions as a Method of Comparing Mathematics Lessons*. St Louis, Department of Mathematics, Washington University, Mimeo.

Wringe, C. (1976). *Developments in Modern Language Teaching*. London, Open Books.

Young, M.F.D. (ed.) (1971). *Knowledge and Control: New Directions for the Sociology of Education*. London, Collier-Macmillan.

Young, M.F.D. and Whitty, G. (eds) (1977). *Society, State and Schooling*. London, Falmer Press.

Index